CHRISTIAN CHURCHES AN
1840–1965: A SOCIAL HISTC
IN CANADA

Religious institutions, values, and identities are fundamental to understanding the lived experiences of Canadians
in the nineteenth and early twentieth century. *Christian
Churches and Their Peoples*, an interdenominational study,
considers how churches influenced the social and cultural
development of Canadian society across regional and linguistic lines.

By shifting their focus beyond the internal dynamics of
institutions, Nancy Christie and Michael Gauvreau address
broad social issues such as the interaction between religion
and changing mores, the key role of laypeople in shaping
churches, and the ways in which First Nations peoples both
appropriated and resisted missionary teachings. With an
important analysis of popular religious ideas and practices,
Christian Churches and Their Peoples demonstrates that the
cultural authority and regulatory practices of religious institutions both affirmed and opposed the personal religious
values of Canadians, ultimately facilitating their elaboration
of personal, ethnic, gender, and national identities.

(Themes in Canadian History)

NANCY CHRISTIE is the Eakin Fellow in the McGill Institute
for the Study of Canada at McGill University.

MICHAEL GAUVREAU is a professor in the Department of History at McMaster University.

THEMES IN CANADIAN HISTORY

Editors: Craig Heron and Colin Coates

NANCY CHRISTIE AND
MICHAEL GAUVREAU

Christian Churches and Their Peoples, 1840–1965: A Social History of Religion in Canada

UNIVERSITY OF TORONTO PRESS
Toronto Buffalo London

© University of Toronto Press Incorporated 2010
Toronto Buffalo London
www.utppublishing.com
Printed in Canada

ISBN 978-0-8020-8949-6 (cloth)
ISBN 978-0-8020-8632-7 (paper)

Printed on acid-free, 100% post-consumer recycled paper with
vegetable-based inks

Library and Archives Canada Cataloguing in Publication

Christie, Nancy, 1958–
    Christian churches and their peoples, 1840–1965 : a social
    history of religion in Canada / Nancy Christie and
    Michael Gauvreau.

    (Themes in Canadian history)
    Includes bibliographical references and index.
    ISBN 978-0-8020-8949-6 (bound) ISBN 978-0-8020-8632-7 (pbk.)

    1. Canada – Church history. 2. Canada – Religious life and
    customs. 3. Canada – Religion. I. Gauvreau, Michael, 1956–
    II. Title. III. Series: Themes in Canadian history

    BR570.C57 2010   277.1   C2010-903924-6

University of Toronto Press acknowledges the financial
assistance to its publishing program of the Canada Council
for the Arts and the Ontario Arts Council.

University of Toronto Press acknowledges the financial
support for its publishing activities of the Government of
Canada through the Canada Book Fund for its publishing
activities.

To Archdeacon Paul Jackson
1938–2006

Contents

Acknowledgments

A work of historical synthesis builds upon the intellectual labours of others, and this one is no exception. Without the sustained energies of a creative group of historians of religion in both English Canada and Quebec, whose work has immeasurably enriched the field over the past two decades, writing this volume would have proved an impossible task. We have relied immensely upon their researches and insights, for which we are profoundly grateful. We also thank our research assistants, David Dowe and Cam Malcolm, who supplied key material on Protestantism. A conversation with Mark Noll was influential in shaping our approach to a historical synthesis of so vast a topic as religion. Ollivier Hubert generously offered his stimulating comments on a number of chapters, while our colleague Kevin Flatt also provided sage advice. Our most immediate debt of thanks is to Craig Heron, series editor for Themes in Canadian Social History, who asked us to undertake the task of writing a resolutely social history of religion. We have been immensely sustained throughout by his enthusiasm, cheerfulness, excellent advice, and sharp eye for a well-turned phrase. Our thanks to Len Husband of University of Toronto Press, who effectively piloted the manuscript through the assessment procedure and ensured that the publication process was a painless one. We are grateful to Kevin Anderson for proofreading the text and preparing the index. We owe a great debt to our dachshunds, Darwin (now sadly departed), Fanny, and Scarlett, who gave us a respite from our work and a more enjoyable venue for discussing Canadian religion on the Bruce Trail. We dedicate this book to the late Paul Jackson, whose constant encouragement and levity during a rather bleak summer were absolutely critical to recovering our momentum.

CHRISTIAN CHURCHES AND THEIR PEOPLES,
1840–1965: A SOCIAL HISTORY OF RELIGION
IN CANADA

Introduction

Until the 1980s, the writing of religious history in Canada was narrow. It concentrated upon the histories of specific denominations, and 'religion' amounted to the pronouncements of the clergy, intellectual developments in theology, and the shaping of organizational structures. In the past two decades there has been an increasing interest in exploring the social dimensions of the Canadian religious environment. This new writing has focused upon the popular response to and participation in churches and their religious associations, the differences in the way various socioeconomic and ethnic groups understood and appropriated religion, and the variables of locality, gender, and age. Generally ignored, however, was the important question of how religion was understood by ordinary people within a particular historical context. Under the influence of the sociology of religion, the new scholarship tended to view religion and the church as largely unchanging and traditional social entities that were either disembodied from or retarded the great dynamic movements of social and cultural change.

This volume begins from the premise that the church as an institutional form was not synonymous with religion as a broader cultural expression. The religious understanding and experience of ordinary people did not necessarily coincide with the prescriptions of the clergy who at various historical junctures defined piety in terms of either attending weekly church services, taking the sacraments, giving systematically to support the church, or regularly attending at communion. Not only did the normative concepts of Christian piety, and the relationship between church and the world, fluctuate vastly over time; but more importantly, much of the way in which a majority of people experienced religion also occurred outside the institutional church. It is this constant tension between the clergy and the laity that forms the central axis of this book. From this perspective, our use of the term 'popular religion' does not mean religious radicalism, but more broadly invites readers to consider it as the beliefs and practices of laypeople, which sometimes stood in opposition to the authority of the clergy and the forms of religion they prescribed, but in other historical contexts more closely adhered to clerical models and the cultural leadership of the various churches. While the institutional churches might alter the way in which they constructed public identities over time, religion itself – that is, the belief in supernatural powers or beings – remained relatively constant between 1840 and the 1970s.

In contrast to notions of 'secularization,' which posit religious institutions and values as expressions of 'tradition' and therefore antithetical to the modern world, we argue that the churches were fundamental to the very process of modernity and that they functioned as one of the most important vehicles by which liberal values were infused into both the public institutions and private lives of ordinary Canadians. Where theories of secularization propose a gradual, ongoing decline of religion over several centuries in the face of processes of industrialization, urbanization, and rationalization, this volume argues that there was no linear decline in religious life in Canada over two centuries, much less a consensus over how religion was defined. What did change was that the way in which the institutional churches intermeshed with the wider society, and this involved a conscious decision on their part to oscillate between more other-worldly and worldly notions of church polity and idealizations of Christian life and living. This was caused not only by the impact of external social forces such as industrialization, urbanization, or modern thought, but also by an inner dynamic in which church leaders sought to alter the role that the churches would play on the terrain of the social. All of this is to argue against the secularization thesis, which has contended that modernization was a linear process in which belief in the supernatural got weaker, the churches were marginalized, and the social authority of religion in the society as a whole was diminished. More recently historians of religion have begun to understand secularization not as social description but as a master narrative, a story that was often used to explain phenomena for which historians did not have sufficient evidence or analytical tools. For example, lacking first-person accounts of what religion meant on a day-to-day basis, historians have taken the clergy's pessimism at face value. Yet clerical discourse itself was shaped by specific historical contexts. In Upper Canada (Ontario), for example, clergy who talked about popular irreligion were in many cases more concerned to recruit more church members in order to found and sustain new congregations. It is true that not everyone attended church, and the census of 1842 shows that not everyone consistently identified with a particular religious tradition, but these sources did not take into account those people who practised their religion privately in the home. Moreover, both Protestant and Roman Catholic clergy at that time often denounced as 'irreligion' forms of popular religious beliefs or practices that diverged from clerical norms. In this case church-going was not related to religious faith but represented one's proclivity for associational life. Regular attendance at church may have been a measure of one's faith, but it might likewise have represented one's sense of public identity and sense of civic involvement, a simple desire for sociability and, in the nineteenth century in particular, a way to display that a person was in good health.

This preoccupation among both the Protestant and Catholic clergy with irreligion reflected a new sensibility among church leaders to connect the wider cultural authority of the church with mass evangelization. In short, the vitality of the church was no longer seen to derive from the support of social elites alone, but, in the era of democratic revolutions on both sides of the Atlantic, it now depended upon making religion accessible to all social classes and cultural groups. The Christian churches constructed a new self-identity as voluntaristic and socially inclusive that dictated the direction of most of the religious projects of the nineteenth and early twentieth centuries. It also stimulated pervasive criticism both within and outside particular denominations that the churches were failing to serve all people from the cradle to the grave. Indeed, the idea that the churches must speak to all people and wholly inform the values of the entire community – an ideal elaborated by the clergy themselves – has been adopted by modern scholars of religion as the authentic standard by which to measure religious decline, without realizing that it was, in fact, a religious paradigm that had been newly articulated by early nineteenth-century clergy.

Major shifts in the social formation of the churches did take place over two centuries, but they occurred in a wave pattern. Some churches sometimes viewed their principal role as fashioning the private identities of their members, but at other times, most notably in the period between 1880 and 1940, the mainstream Protestant and Roman Catholic churches reinvented themselves to erase the distinction between the churches and the world, and they equated their brand of Christianity with the Canadian nation as a whole. Their notion of Christian citizenship was not shared by all religious groups, and even in that period of intense public activity, sectarian forms of religion flourished because they were still attached to an older view of religion as otherworldly in which the world was seen as secular and hostile to the church. If we were to view this process merely from the perspective of the clergy, it might appear that the mainline churches achieved a hegemonic or dominant control over the religious mores of Canadian society. However, once the religious values of ordinary people are also taken into account, a more complex picture emerges which belies any easy or reductionist conclusions regarding either the rise or decline in the influence of religion in the broader society. In fact, there has been a much longer history to the contradiction identified by sociologist Reginald Bibby between what he terms 'exodus' from the churches since 1960 on the one hand, and the 'persistence' of religion on the other. Indeed, this has been the fundamental axis of popular religion in Canada since the 1840s.

We emphasize the substantial resemblances between the various Protestant churches and Roman Catholicism. They experienced remarkably similar permutations in regulatory practices, definitions of Christian piety, relations with aboriginal peoples, and constructions of what constituted formal religion and the way this must ideally interface with broader social identities of age, gender, and class. We concentrate upon the historical experience of the mainstream Protestant and Catholic traditions and give much less space to Judaism and other sectarian Protestant immigrant religious traditions. We are discussing an era in which the experience of the vast majority of Canadians was encompassed by a limited range of dominant Christian groups: Roman Catholic, Anglican, Presbyterian, Methodist, Baptist, and, after 1925, the United Church of Canada, and various small Protestant sects, such as Pentecostalism and the Salvation Army. We present the striking religious pluralism that was so characteristic of the New World social environment and show the contrasts and similarities between the various denominational groups without relinquishing regional and local specificity. We hope the book also provides a benchmark for comparative discussion between the religious historiography of English Canada and Quebec, and that between Canada, the United States, and Western Europe. Canada – both English and French – stands apart from the dominant religious models of both the United States and of Europe, insofar as its religious life was not shaped by either revivalism or by the rise of secularist ideologies; rather, well into the twentieth century, Christianity, both in terms of private and public identities, retained and exercised a social and cultural authority that was unparalleled among industrialized nations.

1

The Religious Cultures of Discipline and Dissidence in Colonial Society

Between 1842 and 1844, the Province of Canada, comprising the present-day provinces of Ontario and Quebec, instituted its first state-managed census. This project of colonial reconstruction and state-building in the wake of the failed Rebellions of 1837–8 organized the population into precise categories of religious adherence, defined by membership in institutional Protestant and Roman Catholic churches. Much to the chagrin of promoters of the Anglican Church, who sought to replicate the British pattern of a single dominant church enjoying a privileged relationship with the state, colonial British North American society manifested an alarming degree of religious pluralism. For example, the religious allegiance of the Upper Canadian population divided neatly into four equally strong religious denominations: Anglicans (22 per cent); Methodists (17 per cent); Presbyterians, divided into Church of Scotland and smaller groups of Seceders (19 per cent); Roman Catholics (13 per cent); and a substantial 17 per cent of the population claiming 'no religion,' meaning they were not members of one of the institutional churches recognized by the census takers. Lower Canada, reflecting its origins as a French and Catholic colony prior to the British Conquest of 1760, was a predominantly Catholic society, with the Roman Catholic Church claiming the adherence of 82 per cent of the population. As in Upper Canada, however, the larger Protestant churches held a substantial proportion of the English-speaking population. This balance of religious competition and pluralism, coupled with the organization of religious allegiance into a small number of larger institutional churches, was replicated in the other colonies of Nova Scotia, New Brunswick, Prince Edward Island, and Newfoundland. This situation marked British North America as different both from Britain and Europe and from the United States, where religious pluralism was more intense and carried the fragmentation of religious identities to a greater extreme. However, this attempt to organize the population into well-defined religious compartments coextensive with large church institutions was undermined by popular religious values and practices. Indeed, between 1840 and 1880, religious identities remained fluid and flexible and the authority of the institutional churches and the state correspondingly weak.

Despite this institutional weakness, it was religion, rather than social and economic structures, that constituted the central dynamic of community formation prior to the 1840s. Both the settlers themselves and the clergy of the various Catholic and Protestant churches who served them believed that the church was the best means to preserve a sense of continuity with their previous experiences. In attempting to erect what one Scottish clergyman in Nova Scotia referred to as a 'Transatlantic Zion,'[1] settlers and their religious leaders insisted that church-building formed the fundamental basis of community life. Public worship in a specifically sacralized space provided a sense of order, psychological ease, and cultural integration. Pauper immigrants from England thought that settlers in the New World sought religion more intensely than in Britain because for them, seeing churches on the frontier landscape held intense symbolic value. The presence of churches telegraphed that the immigrants were, in the words of Elias Elliot, 'among Christian people.'[2] Whether relatively poor settlers endorsed church-building because of cultural convention or by individual choice, they equated collective public worship that the institution provided with feeling settled, comfortable, and at home. It was, for this reason, that settlers and clergy alike preferred many permanent local churches rather than the itinerant preacher, for as Edmund Botterell observed in 1838, the people desired to hear the Lord's word on a daily basis if they could. At the very least, settlers sought the ministrations of a clergyman for important rites of passage such as baptism, marriage, and death. Although it has become a historical truism among historians of Methodism in particular that the system of itinerant preachers was the one best adapted to the frontier conditions of a scattered population, even Nathan Bangs, one of the more celebrated Methodist preachers, commented in 1844 that people so wanted established chapels that they would frequently change their religious affiliation in order to obtain one. Similarly, the Rev. Alexander McLean of St Andrew's New Brunswick told of how people would regularly travel over forty miles to participate in communion services, and when there was no clergyman, homesteaders so craved spiritual sustenance that they would gather in private homes where a prominent layman would read the Scottish form of worship. Indeed, so integral was the church to the very process of getting settled that in all parts of British North America it was the settlers who invited the clergy and only in rare circumstances did the clergy bring settlers to the New World.

Local elites believed that there was a direct connection between public worship and the creation of a collective will or a unified public opinion upon which notions of political power, public order, and social conformity were constructed. The persistent inability to build sufficient churches in a society of poor settlers was therefore deeply distressing. In an era when the churches were so decisively identified with particular ethnic identities, national aspirations, and political allegiances, the competition from various denominations and sects was believed to be destructive of a civic order in which the state was equated with traditional church

establishments, such as the Church of England, the Roman
Catholic Church, and the Church of Scotland. It was from
these quarters that the most frequent complaints about irreligion among ordinary settlers emerged. This discourse
needs to be situated within the context of clerical ambition,
severe financial constraints, and the constant instability created by an environment of tremendous religious pluralism
and competition. In the Niagara area alone there were
Quakers, Shakers, Universalists, Lutherans, Anglicans, Roman Catholics, Methodists, Presbyterians, and Baptists, and
in the Eastern Townships of Lower Canada the state-funded
Anglican and Wesleyan Methodists were constantly under
siege from not only American Congregationalists, but from
a welter of mystical and millenarian sects such as the Millerites and Universalists, groups to whom people turned
during times of economic and political distress during and
after the 1837–8 Rebellions. And even the largest and ostensibly most stable denominations were characterized by ethnic and doctrinal division. Within Anglicanism there were
competing evangelical and high church tendencies; within
Methodism there were divisions, particularly in Upper Canada, between American and British traditions of worship;
Baptists were split along evangelical and Calvinist doctrinal
lines; and the Presbyterians were fractured between the
established Church of Scotland, which affiliated itself with
the British state, and the Free Church, which saw itself as an
expression of Scottish cultural nationalism. Furthermore,
the balance between each of these religious groups varied
greatly both between and within regions.

From the clergy's standpoint, what made matters worse
was that people regularly chose to shift from one religious
group to another either because of a doctrinal disagree-
ment, family pressures, the availability of religious services
that suited their work or family patterns, or simply because
they disliked the particular clergyman! In this intensely pluralistic religious frontier, the discourse of irreligion was simply a rhetorical trope laden with class and gender overtones

that accused ordinary settlers of not adhering exclusively to one particular religious orthodoxy under firm clerical control. At one level this narrative of religious declension was a way to critique popular religious practices. Clergymen were particularly intolerant of individual choice especially by women. In 1865 Sarah Smith was dismissed from First Baptist Church in Montreal because she flouted the authority of the minister by holding to what he called erroneous and unscriptural doctrines. In truth, she only wished to join the Methodist Church. Claiming that the settlers were simply spiritually ignorant was simply a means of critiquing the religious group which most threatened you in your particular locale. For example, Rev. Alexander Ross, a Church of Scotland clergyman, castigated the Baptists for having a leader who supposedly preached that the Bible was dangerous. What he really feared was that the Baptists along the Talbot Road in Upper Canada were extremely effective in proselytizing and drawing off Scottish settlers to their form of Calvinist worship thus depleting Ross's own congregation of the much-needed funds to pay his salary. Methodist missionaries from Britain were particularly exercised about the religious deficiencies of those whom they labelled 'Americans' largely because they refused to conform to the more hierarchical Wesleyan Methodist pattern of worship and church governance. And Anglicans' charges that Methodists were disorderly did not mean that Anglicans were orderly and Methodists wildly enthusiastic; rather they were criticizing Methodists for undermining the Anglican principle of a unified national church establishment.

The language of order and disorder was a rhetorical device to undermine people who preferred a culture of voluntarism (where people chose and financed their own churches) and freedom of religious expression. Clergymen most frequently complained about religious decline in letters to ecclesiastical superiors from whom they were soliciting additional financial support. By constructing a vision of an irreligious populace, ambitious clergyman could all the better claim that they had been the means of salvation for the souls of immigrant backsliders. Ministers employed by the Upper Canada Bible Society consistently drew attention to the prevalence of illiteracy and spiritual ignorance to underscore the progress which they were making in saving the frontier for Protestantism. In this context, the rhetoric of irreligion was directed at Roman Catholicism in the backwoods of Canada. Given the strong political and denominational biases which the discourse of irreligion represented, one must take with a grain of salt observations such as that made by the Presbyterian clergyman-weaver Mr Donaldson that the Methodists did not keep the Sabbath or practise family worship in their homes. The culture of European settlement in the New World was a not a religious tabula rasa that was radically transformed by the arrival of heroic clergymen.[3] Following the lead of historians of Canada's First Nations who have so ably deconstructed clerical propaganda, historians of European settlement must likewise pay due attention to popular religious agency as a valid form of religious expression which was instrumental in constructing both the marginal and mainstream forms of Christianity even if it did not wholly conform to notions of religious orthodoxy outlined by clerical elites.

In Britain prospective emigrants would already have experienced a fair degree of religious choice. Since the late eighteenth century the Anglican Church in England and the Church of Scotland had been slowly losing their pre-eminent position as the national churches as dissenting evangelical denominations became more influential and numerous. The new settlements in the Maritimes and the Canadas were characterized by yet higher degrees of religious pluralism such that ordinary immigrants like David Gibson, a Scottish crofter, were faced with a bewildering array of choices that led to a dissolving of fixed religious identity. What clergymen perceived as loss of faith was seen by the immigrants themselves as a period of deep spiritual reflection wherein they seriously considered their choice of spiritual homes. Gibson admitted that he had become a backslider – not one of the unfaithful – but that he kept family worship while he was considering whether to become a Presbyterian, Congregationalist, Lutheran, Baptist, or Methodist. Meanwhile, Gibson continued 'reading the Bible fearfully that I may know my duty to my God and to my fellow men hoping that in due time my knowledge will be more perfect, in things which belong to eternity.'[4] Gibson would have been numbered among those in the 1842 census who declared no religious preference or creed.

It was commonplace for parishioners (and even clergymen) to change religious affiliation several times during their life course. J.I. Little has minutely detailed the religious itinerary of the Eastern Townships peddler Ralph Merry, who first attended the Baptist church near his home, but upon his conversion experience, broke with that denomination because he could not accept the Calvinist doctrine of election. Turning first to the Methodist Protestants in the 1830s, Merry was successively attracted by the premillenarian doctrines of Millerism in the mid-1840s and the Adventists, who succeeded the Millerites in the late 1840s, all the while continuing to attend Methodist and Baptist quarterly meetings. However, what was more important to Merry's religious life was not the corporate rituals and disciplines of these religious groups, but the personal religious rituals that he practised, notably hymn singing, daily Bible reading, and early-modern quasi-magical practices like bibliomancy, the random selection of biblical verses to provide divine sanction for his daily decisions. Mary Bradley from New Brunswick tried to join several religious groups before settling on the Methodists. Joshua Barnes was born an Anglican, but, after immigrating he and his sister broke with the family's religious tradition and became Methodists, but eventually Barnes joined the Free Will Baptists. While rival clergymen might castigate the Methodists as a sly, sneaking sect, ordinary people saw the world in terms of a broader evangelical culture whereby they might easily move from evangelical Anglicanism, to Methodism, or to the Baptist and Congregational churches.[5]

Ordinary people clearly displayed a high degree of religious knowledge and as a result claimed their own religious expertise, believing that they and not the clergyman determined what was doctrinally correct or orthodox. From the perspective of the clergymen, however, this environment of religious experimentation and popular agency created an organizational nightmare. Intense religious pluralism compelled many denominations to alter their styles of worship or modes of disciplining their recalcitrant members. In large part, religious pluralism conferred a higher degree of sacredness upon the private home than would have prevailed in Europe. Because of the proliferation of religious groups not every group in each location was able to support a regular minister. Many, therefore, had to hold 'public' worship in private homes. Indeed, because of the multiplicity of religious backgrounds among immigrants, traditional pastoral strategies of uniform religious instruction had to be revised, and, as in the case of Rev. Monson in Dartmouth, Nova Scotia, this involved a greater degree of personal evangelism and catechizing in individual homes. Indeed, one of the most important innovations was the importance of home visiting in several denominations, a duty much commented upon, especially by Anglican clergy, who vociferously resisted this New World practice. Thomas Radcliffe spoke of how Anglican clergyman were also forced into having to go on circuit like the maligned Methodists, where they were often burdened with baptizing numerous children and churching several mothers at once. Like the Catholic Church in Lower Canada, which was forced to soften its rigid regulations regarding intermarriage with Protestants, some Anglican clergy had to rid their marriage service of the words 'to obey' in response to the objections of American-born women. Likewise, William Bell, a Presbyterian clergyman from the Ottawa valley, made arduous journeys to marry couples (many of whom could not pay for the service) during the winter months, the preferred marriage season among Scottish farmers, for fear that if he refused he would lose prospective church members. Moreover, because of the effectiveness of short and simple Methodist sermons, Anglicans had to streamline their long liturgy and repetitious invocations of the Lord's Prayer. Many clergy had to reluctantly defer to popular demand by changing the timing of public worship to enable their members to attend services at a rival church, or in some instances they had to suspend services altogether when a Methodist revival was nearby because their congregation would attend en masse out of sheer curiosity. The most problematical effect of pluralism was that an already inadequate supply of money in a generally impoverished society was further carved up by the proliferation of several competing religious bodies, with the further detriment that ministers were often inadequately paid and thereby further forced under the control of their congregations.

Perhaps the greatest impact that the combination of religious pluralism and the inadequate funding of church institutions had was that it forged greater religious cooperation and unity than otherwise would have prevailed. It was not unusual in the early period of settlement for congregations to meet either in private homes, schoolhouses, taverns, or courthouses, or for different religious groups to fund and share a common meeting house. In Ancaster, outside Hamilton, all the churches shared one union church, while in Hamilton proper the first Lutheran service was held in 1854 in the schoolroom of the Congregational church, which like many pragmatic churches would have rented out space for other religious groups. However, the cooperative spirit induced by lack of financial resources was a fairly superficial one that often degenerated into greater tension and competition. On one particular Sunday the Catholics taunted the Presbyterians with whom they shared a building in London, Upper Canada, by extending their mass for the entire Sabbath and preventing the Presbyterians from holding public worship.

Indeed, an ostensible ecumenism among Protestants was

simply the fruit of a profound anti-Catholicism. It was the pervasive fear of the 'strong seas of French Catholicism' in Montreal that drove St James Methodist Church towards a greater degree of cooperation with other evangelical denominations especially around the cause of evangelizing French Canadians and establishing day schools for Protestant children. Indeed, one of the best known interdenominational associations, the Upper Canada Bible Society, sold Bibles at cut-rate prices to the supposedly illiterate and unchurched settlers to forestall the expansion of Roman Catholic missions. More tellingly, the Society was really the voice of mainstream Protestantism, defined by Methodism, Presbyterianism, and Anglicanism, insofar as it erected the Bible as the only standard of religious truth. In so doing it hoped to clamp down on the circulation of tracts by religious fringe groups such as the Universalists, Millerites, and Mormons, despite its posture of religious cooperation. At the local denominational level, however, religious cooperation was a necessity for community endeavours, such as Sunday schools, temperance societies, charitable work, and tract societies. These organizations have been seen as instruments of social control, clerical authority, or the initiative of wealthy laymen; they expressed what was in fact the reality of popular religious practice, namely the high degree of religious fluidity within a wider evangelical culture.

Given the weak institutional network of churches, informal family worship was also common. Indeed, if one owned the requisite religious objects such as the Bible, the Book of Common Prayer, or the catechism of one's denomination, one could closely replicate the ritual of public worship in the home. Yet these practices continued even after a local church had been built. Many families and their members did not regularly attend church service. For example, Henry H. Ardagh, a young lawyer and nephew of Rev. Samuel Ardagh, the evangelical Anglican clergyman at Shanty Bay, Upper Canada, recorded in his journal the many occasions when he did not go to church either because of inclement weather or because other family members were in attendance to represent the family as a whole. Far from being a lukewarm Christian, Ardagh preferred to form a tie with the local congregation by teaching Sunday school. For the Ardagh family in general, public worship was an occasion for sociability and intellectual stimulation. Anna Ardagh, the clergyman's daughter, displayed her most regular church attendance when she was courting her prospective husband. Like many other Christian families the Ardaghs believed that the centre of spiritual growth occurred within the family circle, either during family prayers twice daily or through personal reading and reflection during what was called 'closet' prayer.

Although there are examples of laity using the private reading of spiritual books at home as a means to flout clerical authority, as did a few particularly pugnacious elders at Dundee Zion Presbyterian Church (St Andrew's, Lower Canada), clergymen from all denominations strongly encouraged the practice of family worship largely because they saw the family as a 'public' entity that functioned in symbiosis with the institutional church, forming mutually reinforcing systems of public order and discipline. In Methodism this merging of the public and private spheres of religious experience was illustrated by the fact that prayer and class meetings often met in private homes well into the late nineteenth century, and this custom was revived in urban centres through cottage prayer meetings, especially in working-class neighbourhoods. For this reason, in the Methodist Church family worship was one of the tests of membership, and while the Presbyterian Church never made it a condition of church membership, it, like the Anglican Church, strongly endorsed family worship and upheld in particular the authority of the father, which was assumed to flow from the clergymen downward.

Historians have contended that, because of consistently higher levels of female church membership in all Christian denominations, women not only were more pious than men but also determined the religious identity of the family. However, Jack Little and Ollivier Hubert have shown that both Anglicanism and Roman Catholicism did not uphold a notion of Christian motherhood or a notion of separate spheres where women acquired authority in the family through the moral education of the children. In Catholicism the clergy astutely cultivated the notion that the priest was the father of the parish, and in Protestantism a similar patriarchal model pertained to the figure of God as the father of the fatherless and husband of the widow, a common invocation upon the death of the male head of the family. The male heads of households were believed to be but surrogates of the male clergyman, and indeed they shared the same sense of religious authority. When a Presbyterian father from Toronto discovered that his daughter had given birth to an illegitimate child he suspended her from communion, a function generally exercised by the ministers or church elders. Religious authority, therefore, was conceived as distinctly male. Indeed, the notion of male citizenship and voting rights within the various churches flowed directly from their pre-eminent role as religious educators and leaders of family worship. While mothers may have taught the rudiments of catechism to very young children, the obligation of examining and tutoring them in sound religious doctrines regularly fell to the father.

In many denominations, most notably among the Methodists and Quakers, it was common practice for men and women to sit as individuals on opposite sides of the church. From the 1840s onward, however, parishioners wanted to rent a family pew, where their family's spiritual identity could be represented as a whole. In this respect Protestant practice began to mirror that of Catholicism, where, as Ollivier Hubert has demonstrated, individuals were classed according to their place within the family. Thus the family as a whole constituted the basic social unit and the status of one's family within the church hierarchy depended solely upon the father's position in society. There was, however, some scope for individualism, for the sacraments of confession and communion were taken separately. Similarly, within Protestantism, church membership was an individual choice. Indeed, as Hannah Lane has shown, a large number of Methodist families in St Stephen, New Brunswick, were religiously divided.[6] This tendency towards greater individualism was fraught with family tension. Witness the fate of Sister Buchanan of St George Baptist Church in Peterborough, who was charged with being a church 'transgressor' for having missed three covenant or church discipline meetings because her husband, who belonged to another church, refused to drive her.

Family tribalism was nonetheless at work in determining religious choices. Wives were particularly instrumental in shaping the level of church affiliation of their husbands. Moreover, individuals were tried separately for moral delinquency in Presbyterian and Baptist church courts, but in some churches there is also striking evidence that the family as represented by the father continued to be seen as the primary religious unit. In the Baptist Church of Paris, Upper Canada, Brother Anscombe was dismissed from membership because of the licentious behaviour of his daughter; and in 1858 Jane Brown, who was merely an occasional adherent, was disciplined by the Kirk Session of her Presbyterian church by virtue of her mother's status as a full church member. By the mid-nineteenth century the notion that family prayer upheld the sacred authority of the male head of household was slowly giving way to a greater evocation of Christian motherhood. As a consequence, clergymen became wary of private religion when it had the potential to enhance female authority in the domestic realm and by extension the public sacred space of the church proper. Until the popularity of mass Sunday schooling among Protestants and mass indoctrination of catechism in Catholic schools in the late nineteenth century, clergymen could not entirely relinquish the family as a nursery of piety.

Throughout the nineteenth century, clergymen consistently sought ways to diminish such popular religious practices for fear that they might lessen the desire to attend public worship and thus diminish the authority of the church as a visible symbol of religious and civic order. While at the level of popular religion ordinary parishioners shared overlapping religious views and practices such that they found it easy to move between denominations and intermarry, this popular ecumenism was not a feature of the discourse surrounding the relationship between the churches and the colonial state. Indeed, the most decisive conflicts between various religious groups hinged upon their views of the relationship between the church and state. It is possible to see colonial society divided into two dichotomous worlds, that of order represented by the Anglican Church and experience represented by Methodism, which in turn expressed a conflict between Tory and Reform political perspectives, if one approaches the problem of church and state from the perspective of religious leaders, the Anglican Bishop John Strachan and the Methodist champion Egerton Ryerson.[7] However, if one broadens the framework to include the intense religious pluralism of colonial society, a much more variegated picture emerges.

Firstly, it was the Roman Catholic Church that had the closest involvement with the political order, for since the establishment of New France the parish was the basic unit of civil and local government. Under British rule the powers of the parish priest were further enhanced insofar as he functioned as the intermediary between the government and the populace. To this end priests were directed to collect information for government authorities, and the pulpit was further politicized as priests were required to communicate all government decrees to their parishioners. A similar expectation prevailed in Upper Canada among government officials who assumed that the church was an extension of state power and the duty of its clergy was to teach the laws and loyalty to the British crown. This ideal of a confessional state whereby one's religious allegiance was the primary determinant of political citizenship could hold true only if one church held a monopoly in the society, as the Church of England did in Britain. In Upper Canada, the Church of England had a privileged position through land grants from the Crown to support its clergy, the Clergy Reserves, which comprised one-seventh of the land in each township. In other colonies, Anglicans benefited from direct government subsidies to clerical salaries and the building of churches and schools, as well as educational provisions conferring Anglican pre-eminence in college education. Prior to 1831 in Upper Canada, the Church of England also possessed the quasi-exclusive right to perform marriages. In the New World environment of religious pluralism, other churches held quite different views of their connection with the state. The Anglicans had to compete with a well-entrenched Roman Catholicism in Lower Canada and with a British rival establishment, the Church of Scotland, which also argued that it had a special relationship with the government. Furthermore, the whole idea of the connection between church and state was adamantly rejected by numerous dissenting groups, which clung to an intense other-worldliness in which the purity of their churches was registered by the degree to which they were removed from the purview of the state and politics.

The Rebellions of 1837–8 formed a critical watershed in these debates because they exposed the depth of the fault line that separated Tories and Radicals. Many churches lost members who disagreed with their clergy's politics. In Lower Canada, because the parish was both a religious entity and an arm of the state the radical Patriot attack on the colonial connection with Britain became a contestation over the *civil* authority of the clergy. Patriots and clerics throughout the 1830s violently disputed control of church vestries and parish schools, but Catholicism itself as a spiritual system was not under attack. Every Catholic priest in Lower Canada but one was loyal to the British crown. In Upper Canada the Anglicans, the Church of Scotland, and most Methodist clergy remained loyal to the colonial government. But the political views of Baptists could get them arrested. In 1838 in Pickering the minister George Barclay was accused of being 'a vile old preaching traitor' on the grounds of his Baptist faith alone. The republican constitution drawn up by the radical leader William Lyon Mackenzie had as its first article the eradication of all church establishments, thus separating church and state. It was not surprising that his followers locked a particular Tory Anglican minister, Rev. V.P. Meyerhoffer, out of his Markham church as an act of political protest. There is much evidence to suggest that there was a close affinity between religious dissent and radical politics. The leading Methodist congregation in Toronto, Metropolitan Methodist, was the headquarters for a number of artisan rebels who were church members. Upper Canadian Methodism therafter split into British Wesleyans and reformist Canadian Methodists. In the 1836 election just prior to the rebellions British Methodists voted Tory and those with fewer British ties voted Reform.[8] The real division between religious groups was not order and evangelicalism but partisans of church establishment, who saw the connection of the churches as pillars of the civic order, and voluntaryists, who defined the church as a spiritual society removed from worldly concerns.

In the Maritimes where there were no clergy reserves and no rebellions, Methodists had generally upheld the notion of an Anglican ascendancy, but in the 1840s they began to disengage themselves from the Anglican orbit, challenging Anglican dominance and engaging directly in political affairs. By the 1850s they were creating an alternative engagement between the church and the state in the form of a public evangelicalism that sponsored such moral reform issues as temperance, non-sectarian schooling, and Sabbath regulation. The 1857 election constituted the high-water mark of this movement when the 'Smashers' party (pro-prohibition) was backed by 70 per cent of Methodists and most other evangelical denominations. By contrast, in Upper

Canada, the colonial and British governments attempted to reform the Clergy Reserves by giving the clergy of other denominations access to their revenues. However, with the political conflicts of the late 1840s and early 1850s, and the rise of a new political party led by the evangelical Free Church Presbyterian George Brown, specifically dedicated to their abolition, moderate and conservative politicians, and most church leaders, acquiesced in a settlement that divested the Anglican Church of the Clergy Reserve lands and removed the issue from the political sphere. After this, religious denominations no longer identified with particular political parties as they had during the Rebellions and its immediate aftermath. As a result, other than the movement by Egerton Ryerson for state education, no evangelical reform politics emerged until much later in the century.

Although the concept of other-worldliness was usually associated with smaller sectarian groups of Protestants, the notion that the church no longer was part of the civil structure even influenced the Roman Catholic Church. Particularly after 1840, Roman Catholicism was strongly affected by ultramontanism, a movement characterized by greater uniformity and regularity in the education and conduct of the parish clergy and an intense, highly public and demonstrative devotional culture. Laypeople were encouraged to participate more frequently in the key sacraments of confession and communion and to enlist in forms of church-sponsored associational life dedicated to temperance, moral improvement, charity, mutual benefit, and the assertion of ethnic identity. Finally, ultramontanism enthusiastically insisted upon the supremacy of the Pope and the clerical hierarchy, even in civil matters. In Quebec, ultramontanism was often coupled with conservative politics and involved frequent clerical pronouncements against liberal causes such as state-controlled public education. Historians have frequently presumed that this movement's equation of Catholicism and nationalism led to a closer alignment with the state. However, Christine Hudon has recently shown that in fact ultramontanism, out of its desire to enhance the authority of the local priest, placed a greater emphasis upon the church as a spiritual community removed from the control of the state after the 1840s.

Under the conditions of intense religious pluralism what was considered in the Old World to be a profession that conferred elite status upon the clergy was, in the New World, a most unenviable career which more often than not disappointed those ambitious young men anxious for upward mobility. Some of the luckier clergymen, such as Rev. William Bell, who was funded by the British government to serve in the military settlement of Perth, was paid the large sum of £200, and was granted a town lot, in addition to a large farm. Bell, an artisan with strong radical political convictions, believed that in assuming such a prestigious post he had become the leading figure in the settlement. His expectations were dashed, however, when he found himself having to doff his hat to the local Tory magistrates and half-pay officers who continually attempted to thwart his authority within his own religious domain. His critique of manly leisure activities such as drinking, card playing, and horse racing had distinct class overtones, and in his advocacy of temperance associations and mechanics institutes he became a spokesman for an emerging culture of middling social status. During the eighteenth century in New France, most of the clergy were from France and of elite birth, but by the 1840s Catholic priests were drawn from similar socio-economic positions to Bell's: two-thirds were sons of farmers and one in six sons of artisans, while few were drawn from the ranks of the professions. Like their parishioners, Methodist clergymen came from artisanal, farming, and small business backgrounds.

Anglican clergy who were funded by the Society for the Propagation of the Gospel were drawn from a higher social status and for that reason they were the most vociferous complainers about their falling class position in the New World, even though they were guaranteed £150 per year until 1835. Thereafter, their plight was especially acute because the tradition of being paid by an overseas missionary society created the unenviable situation that Anglican congregations had never developed a custom of voluntary support for their minister. By the 1850s a survey of Anglican parishes in Lower Canada highlighted the persistent financial penury of the ministers, who saw it as their right to be paid at least £150 or $600 per year. What Anglican missionaries feared was that their poverty confined them to a rank substantially below that of gentlemen. Despite the Methodist efforts to 'cultivate the manners of a Christian gentleman'[9] among their clergy, even the best paid only earned £60 per year and had to pay for their houses, which were usually furnished in the most spartan manner. Besides the care of their children, for which they received an additional allowance of $5 per child, their biggest expense was the provisioning of their horse while on circuit. By contrast, the most stable incomes were enjoyed by Catholic priests in Lower Canada, as three-quarters of them earned $600 per year through a mandatory tithe, whereby 1/26 of the cereal crops and peas would be turned over to the local parish church. Like Protestant ministers, priests were paid largely in kind prior to the 1850s, but outside the older parishes priests could not legally collect the tithe. Like their Protestant counterparts they therefore had to rely upon a combination of pew rents, voluntary subscriptions, and casual dues for performing baptisms, marriages, and funerals, which could, in some cases, become quite lucrative. For example, the cure of Drummondville, Marjorique Marchand, earned a stellar income of $1645, which made him a wealthy man in a predominantly working-class town.

Such extra income varied greatly by locality and by the particular wealth of congregations, so many Methodist ministers supplemented their incomes by selling tracts or Bibles. Almost every clergyman, irrespective of denomination, also had to earn money from farming on top of onerous clerical duties. In denominations such as the Baptist and Presbyterian churches, where one's congregation could dispense with your services, owning a farm was a liability. If forced to move, a minister would have difficulty selling his farm at a profit and thus had to accede to the demands of their parishioners with the consequent further loss of authority and social distance from them. One Church of Scotland minister was incensed to learn that his congregation believed that the clergyman did not work as hard as labouring men and so should not be paid as well. However, the clergy were not entirely powerless because they were able to play upon the deep desire of people for a settled clergyman. In Quebec, Catholic bishops often simply withdrew a priest if the congregation was reluctant to pay the tithe.

Some clergymen were particularly inept. Mr Salmon, the Anglican curate from Hamilton, was allegedly incapable of even *reading* the prayers. Others were actually resistant to the needs of their parishioners. Some objected to visiting the sick and dying and insisted that certain rites, such as infant baptism, be carried out during public worship and not in private homes. Ministers sought out every method to ease their workload. The heroic efforts that Methodist circuit riders undertook to expand their society's membership are well documented, but even Congregationalist Lewis Sobin, who had a settled church, recounted that he travelled 800 miles through the Eastern Townships and preached 190 times. Father Charles Bellemare, who served a parish north of Trois-Rivières, not only conducted services in his own parish, but travelled hundreds of miles every winter to preach to the forest workers. Even when ill, Drummondville's priest Father Marchand had to receive fifty to sixty callers at his house and hear confessions for two hours. His regular schedule included settling local disputes, hearing confessions, listening to complaints about the tithe, and sorting out marital conflicts, in addition to performing his appointed rituals during public worship. By the 1870s, when numbers of parish clergy grew substantially, most Catholic priests were able to shift the most disagreeable tasks, such as visiting the sick and catechizing young children, to their assistant priests. Most priests also wanted convents built in their parish for the nuns, who would provide an obedient source of female labour. Despite the apparently democratic nature of Methodist theology, leaders of the denomination decided where and how long a minister would serve and they also dictated whether they could marry. Moreover, because the Methodist societies depended upon uncertain financial support, winning the approbation of their flock was especially important. According to *The Christian Guardian* in 1843, a Methodist minister must patiently endure those who arrived late, were noisy, or slept during the sermon. He was even told not to chastise noisy boys in the gallery and even to allow dogs in the church. This is a far cry from the Catholic, Presbyterian, and Baptist clergy, who felt no constraint about inveighing against infrequent attendance, refusal to pay pew rents, immoral behaviour in the community, and disturbances at religious services.

From the perspective of the paying parishioners, it followed that clergymen could be likewise scrutinized by the people. Within the Presbyterian and Baptist traditions the notion of the covenant, whereby all church members oversaw and punished one another's lapses in behaviour, extended to the clergyman himself. A newer kind of contractual relationship within the parish church was emerging whereby parishioners who paid believed they had an independent right to question the behaviour and doctrinal perspectives of the clergy. In 1824 the Church of Scotland minister Rev. McLaurin of Williamstown, Upper Canada, was censured in a petition signed by ninety-four parishioners not only for defrauding them of church funds but for what they considered the more serious charge of inattendance to duties. Elders were also prey to communal vigilance as they were most commonly drawn from the wealthiest quarters of the community. The sacred contract of the covenant thus provided more marginal members of society, the working classes and women, the ability to publicly regulate the behaviour of their betters. The largely working-class congregation at St Gabriel's Presbyterian Church in Montreal was able to control and bring to heel a minister they disliked by accusing the Rev. Henry Esson of frequenting a house of ill-repute and holding a full church disciplinary hearing with testimonies from prostitutes who were able to invert the power structure of their society by describing in lurid detail the sexual improprieties of one of the most important leaders of Presbyterianism of his day.

Formally, Catholic priests only answered to the Bishop, but community gossip powerfully served to control their actions.[10] Those who criticized the priest were not anticlerical, for their monitoring of the priests' behaviour functioned within a mutually understood system of expectations governing clerical conduct. The ideal priest was supposed to be obedient, tactful, temperate, sexually pure, and of course, pious. During the nineteenth century, despite increasing clericalization of Quebec society, parish scrutiny expanded as the parish became more elaborate and parishioners were better acquainted with Roman Catholic doctrines regarding morality. The expanding network of lay associations with their heavy emphasis upon clean living and devotional intensity also created a sense of independence, which in practice could often place the laity on a more equal footing with the parish priest. For example, a storeowner in the Gaspé announced to the community that he thought that the local lay confraternities – especially the St Patrick Society – were doing more to promote piety in the village than the parish church and its priest. Although a main source of the priest's power was in the confessional, the increasingly spiritually aware parishioners adeptly used Catholic doctrine in their letters of protest to the Bishop in order to have ineffective priests removed. The most scandalous case of sexual delinquency by a priest was that of Father Alfred Vigeant, who was accused of bestiality and so was sent to Ontario, then to the United States, and finally to Mexico. For the most part priests were transferred not for sexual impropriety or for intemperance but for failing to perform religious rites properly and for failing to build consensus in their parish. However, this being said, sexual misconduct was sufficiently prevalent that Bishop Bourget insisted on placing grilles in the confessional ostensibly because female penitents had complained about unwanted sexual advances in that sacred but intimate space.

There were clergy like the Rev. Charles Cotton, an Anglican minister in the Eastern Townships, who did little to live up to even the lowest standards of his profession because he failed to visit the sick, did not attend funerals, refused to baptize outside the Church of England, and left his congregation bereft of services during winter because he could not provide a stove to heat the church. Yet there were also charismatic and energetic clergymen of extreme piety and commitment. Whether a particular denomination might flourish within a community often depended upon the personality of the minister. Prior to 1850, there was no massive expansion in church adherence or membership. Steady growth in church membership remained elusive, and in church surveys and the decennial census church members were recounted as people left and returned to a particular denomination throughout their life course. After a career of constant toil, sacrifice of private life, lack of sociability, and financial uncertainty, most ministers would have experienced little job satisfaction. After giving 190 sermons and traveling eight hundred miles, Rev. Lewis Sobin added only five new members to his Congregational church. Protestant ministers at least had the comfort of a wife and family, but Catholic priests had no intimate confidants in whom they could trust, for the ideal of clerical conduct within Catholicism involved the rejection of worldly society. Until the emergence of superannuation funding in the late nineteenth century, clergymen had to serve until ill health or death prevented them from doing so. Christine Hudon has estimated that prior to 1880, 60 per cent of priests died while still ministering to their parish. And during that tenure of office many clergymen would have experienced lapses in spiritual growth similar to those of their parishioners. Because clergymen occupied a rarefied spiritual space in which they mediated between God's demands and human conduct, their existence was encumbered by feelings of intense unworthiness, depression, and morbid introspection. All clergy would have understood the sense of deficiency that prompted the Baptist minister Joseph Clutton to exclaim: 'O miracle of grace that such a poor polluted worm as I am should be able to preach the blessed gospel so that the Lord's people should be comforted.'[11]

Clergy from all denominations believed that 'manly independence as ministers'[12] depended upon better remuneration, and it is not surprising that a large part of the clergyman's office was directed towards raising money. With the general expansion of wealth throughout the nineteenth century this obsession with church finance became more acute as the adornment of expensive church buildings became the means to affirm the public visibility of religion. In industrializing cities like Montreal, by 1860 church expenditures had risen above $2000 per year at the Anglican Christ Church Cathedral and included the minister's salary, the organist's stipend, a substantial poor fund, contributions to the Ladies' Benevolent Society, pew openers, the organ blower, the church cleaner, advertisements in newspapers, and church maintenance. Working-class churches in urban centres were often the hardest to maintain financially despite a large membership base because each parishioner was able to give less. With an annual expenditure of over $6000 and only 11 per cent of their congregation drawn from the business and professional classes, St James Methodist continued the tradition of the class meeting much longer and created a panoply of voluntary associations which included several women's societies, youth groups, and Sunday schools so that each age group within the family and not just its household head would be exhorted to give. Even in less ostentatious rural churches clergymen constantly set about to devise strategies for raising money, most of which went to paying their own salaries. These included local subscriptions from members and from the community at large, special revival meetings, taxes on heads of households, weekly collections, collections at communion, special charity services, and, above all, pew rents. In Protestant denominations these paid the minister's salary and in the Catholic Church were the basic income of the parish vestry. From the pulpit, the clergy constantly pressured their hearers into financially supporting the church and most held a contractual view that if they were providing a spiritual service it was part of one's religious duty to pay for it. Here was the economy of salvation at its most basic. An Anglican clergyman from Mascouche, Quebec, Rev. O'Grady believed that paying for one's pew gave one a personal stake in the church community and hence encouraged regular attendance, which in turn encouraged more commitment and higher levels of giving.

Pew owning was clearly important to people, but not merely for reasons of class status. It is true that owning a pew conferred a particular status on its owner, but more often than not it was a visible symbol of family piety, in a religious culture where the central social divide was frequently viewed as not between rich and poor but between the saved and the sinner. In particular pew owning was a largely male preserve and served to uphold the authority of the male patriarch. Hence one of Curé Marchand's working-class male parishioners fought tooth and nail to keep his customary pew, stating 'I will have my pew.' That pew renting was viewed as a fundamental expression of male religious citizenship is well illustrated by the fate of Mrs Hill. Once her abusive husband died the church vestrymen swept in and pressured her to relinquish her pew on the grounds that, without a male head of household, she no longer constituted a family. It was not merely a means for the upper middle classes to affirm their control of the church, for pew renting appealed to people of all socio-economic backgrounds and largely working-class churches did not wish to dispense with the pew rental system. Because one paid for a pew it conferred a sense of entitlement upon laity, who often used this system of property as a power base to contest or thwart the aims of the clergy.[13]

Some of these struggles had class overtones, as in the case of the St Stephen, New Brunswick, Baptist Church, where the deacon who controlled the majority of the pews voted to withhold the salary of the minister when the latter delivered a sermon criticizing the custom of local employers in the lumber industry paying their workers in kind rather than in cash. On other occasions, class relations were not in evidence; rather, doctrinal issues came to the fore such as occurred at St James the Apostle in Montreal, where a protest by evangelicals against a ritualist clergyman was effected by parish members and outsiders who bought up many family pews and converted them to individual sittings, thus increasing their voting weight in the vestry elections and ridding themselves of an unpopular minister. Clergymen clashed with parishioners, who frequently refused to pay their annual pew rental, and imposed draconian measures. They might deny membership, church ordinances, and sacraments, including baptizing children, and refuse to provide letters of testimonial for those moving to another community. Sometimes refusal to pay was on political grounds such as in the case of a radical Presbyterian farmer near Perth who withheld his pew rent for ten years because he equated it with a tax or tithe.

The best seats were not necessarily occupied by the wealthy and the fewer free seats by the poor and marginal. Historians of early modern religion have empirically demonstrated how society's class hierarchy was replicated within the pattern of church seating. Many churches simply charged flat rates for pews with higher rates for church members and lower ones for adherents. At St Andrew's Presbyterian church at Lachine, Quebec, division was not between members and hearers, but between families and those who were unmarried. There is no correlation between socio-economic status and levels of payment (although it should be said that the Hudson's Bay Company owned two pews for which it paid the handsome sum of $20.00); indeed, one seems to have paid a flat rate per person, and so people with larger families paid more. That the space within the church no longer served as a class identifier is one of the benchmarks in the transition to modernity. Clergymen often advocated free seating in the expectation that this would draw higher attendance, especially from the poorer segments of the community, but lower rents did not mean higher working-class membership.

Thus, while the language of the market economy infused the language of Protestantism, such as 'profiting' from prayer and reading the scriptures, describing death as 'paying a debt to one's Maker,' keeping a close 'accounting' of one's failings, and the temporal prosperity which some expected to flow from attentive prayer and performance of religious exercises, there were still overtones of an older moral economy of mutual obligation in which the most important measure of status was piety. Thus, the Baptist minister Joseph Clutton could remark in 1874 that he had buried Mrs Martha Nickel, 'a Baptist for many years – much respected though poor.' Her reputation was based on her constant commitment to the church rather than merely her socio-economic level.

Protestant churches, whether in rural, small-town, or urban areas, rarely reflected a homogeneous class composition. Religious involvement, be it on the basis of full membership, regular adherence, occasional attendance and use of sacraments, pew renting, or complete disconnection from the institution, was not a function of an individual's or family's class position. In her study of industrializing Montreal Jane Greenlaw has shown that Protestant denominations were dominated by the working classes including artisans and other workers. Only the Congregational church had a definitively middle-class cast to it; by contrast, the Presbyterian

Church contained the most impoverished parishioners. St James Methodist could best be described as a working-class institution with 41.7 per cent skilled workers and 47 per cent other workers, with only 11.3 per cent of members from the dominant classes, namely professional and large commercial interests. Even in urban areas, where one might expect to uncover a greater degree of economic stratification and class alienation, churches were highly mixed in terms of social composition. A similar class profile characterized urban Roman Catholicism. In her study of urban Montreal parish life, Lucia Ferretti has concluded that skilled workers were the most active members in the church, a finding substantiated by Brian Clarke for Catholics in Toronto, where he has estimated that upward of three-quarters of officeholders in parish voluntary associations were working-class men and women. In Erskine Presbyterian Church in Montreal the overwhelming majority of officeholders were working-class. Even churches that have been presumed to be bastions of the elite, such as the Anglican Church, were composed largely of middling sorts, namely common farmers, small tradesmen, and artisans.

To be sure, there were sufficiently poor people, like Mr Galbraith of St John's Presbyterian, in both Protestant and Catholic churches who did not attend service because of the want of proper clothing to account for the existence of numerous church-based charities whose central purpose was to sew clothing to foster church attendance among the poorest in the community. Evidence from across church denominations in various industrial and non-industrial communities clearly demonstrates that while financial contributions to the church may have constituted a greater burden for working-class families, they were not averse to contributing. Despite the willingness of working-class people to pay for their spiritual comfort, by the end of the nineteenth century, most urban churches in industrial centres such as Hamilton, Ontario, had instituted free seating combined with the anonymous envelope system, largely in deference to the needs of working-class families in a period of falling standards of living. For example, Gould Street Presbyterian Church in Toronto had no problem in 'getting heads of families in less affluent circumstances' to pay pew rents; rather, it was those unmarried and youthful hearers in the 'single-sittings'[14] who regularly defaulted on payments. Thus the level of religious commitment rather than class was the primary determinant of church involvement. The building of massive Gothic churches and the expansion of voluntary societies, all of which demanded a financial contribution, cannot be read as markers that churches had become inexorably middle-class by the 1870s; rather, even the most elaborate urban churches were still largely built by the modest contributions of many people.

Nineteenth-century Protestantism in Canada was strongly influenced by the evangelical movement, which exerted a powerful impact on culture and society in English-speaking societies on both sides of the Atlantic. Evangelicalism stressed the primacy of the individual religious experience, especially repentance for sin and a definite experiential moment of personal conversion, over older communitarian religious polities and rituals. In particular, evangelicals strongly emphasized the primacy of the Bible over creeds and confessions, while firmly insisting upon the capacity of human reason to understand God's will and purposes. Evangelical believers were also expected to lead lives of dedicated religious activism in missionary and moral causes. Although American religious culture strongly felt the impress of evangelicalism in the years between 1780 and 1840, which spawned a welter of new Protestant sects and religious movements, its effect on Canadian Protestantism was more tempered and diffuse. First, its impact on the churches was uneven, strongest in Methodism, a direct offshoot of the eighteenth-century evangelical tide, and among Baptists. Anglicans and Presbyterians certainly experienced evangelical currents, but in these churches, the individualism so associated with the evangelical movement

was constrained and channelled by older corporate structures and practices, and often, as in the case of Anglicanism, aroused partisan opposition from adherents of older
tendencies. In these churches, whose origins were prior
to the eighteenth century, the culture of personal Bible
reading was always conducted with reference to early modern denominational markers such as the Anglican Book of
Common Prayer, or the Westminster Confession and Shorter Catechism in the case of Presbyterians. The existence
of disciplinary machinery like church courts among Presbyterians and Baptists, and the class meeting and Book of
Discipline among Methodists, also limited the scope of religious individualism, and the common practice of parents
and ministers communicating religious knowledge by rote
learning tended to limit the scope for individual religious
expression. Second, because of the stronger presence of
religious establishments, whose values drew in even groups
like the Methodists, the Canadian religious environment
was less hospitable to the exceptional, charismatic individuals and extraordinary movements that made the American
Republic a freewheeling marketplace of new religious ideologies. Only by the 1880s, when the institutional churches
evolved new strategies premised on the culture and values
of individualism, did evangelicalism secure wider purchase
within Canadian Protestantism.

Historians have often pointed to a deep gulf between
the rational, ordered religion of the Anglicans and the
enthusiastic, emotional religion of the heart that characterized Methodism.[15] Yet, if one examines the actual content
of church sermons and rituals, there was actually little to
distinguish between various denominations. Typically, in
Upper Canada, both within Anglicanism and within dissenting religions, the sermon was scrupulously rationalistic and
focused upon issues of church doctrine and intellectual
scriptural knowledge. Historians have been attracted to the
analysis of mass revivals – episodic upsurges of more devout
piety and greater attention to religious practice, which they

generally equate with evangelical forms of Protestantism and view as caused by intense, often emotional moments of individual spiritual experience. Their analysis has been particularly influenced by the highly charged testimonies that have been preserved from these sporadic but flamboyant manifestations of piety. But revivals did not comprise the main current within Methodism or other Protestant evangelical groups in any specific period. There is little evidence to indicate what proportion of Methodists (or non-Methodists) actually participated in revivals, but we do know that the numbers of converts were much smaller than those claimed in the often exaggerated accounts of revivals where thousands were supposedly in attendance. In addition, it is clear that revivals may have appealed mostly to American settlers and that for the most part the emotional language that suffused their accounts can be better understood as a form of advertising rather than actual social description. Special revival missions became a feature of ultramontane Catholicism after 1850 with a similar aim of bringing about conversion among special groups such as youth and working-class people. To a greater degree than within Protestantism these large Catholic meetings were closely linked to temperance crusades largely because men were their central target group.

These spiritual events may have been stimulated by the economic and political instability of the late 1830s, and at times revivals were special events designed to replace adherents lost through transiency or to lure backsliders back into the fold. For this reason they flourished more in the 1860s and 1870s, when social mobility increased, a view which challenges the belief current among historians that revivals were important prior to 1840 but that they declined throughout the nineteenth century due to the increasing respectability or middle-class nature of congregational life. However, revivals were never a dominant feature of Canadian Methodism and were highly local in character. Thus, it is important to focus upon the internal dynamics of congregations rather than broader economic or social conditions to explain their rise and fall. In fact, a revival might refer to a mass meeting but it could just as easily denote a slight rise in the spiritual temperature of a class or prayer meeting. The large-scale outdoor camp or revival meeting was less common than the protracted meeting, usually held in the winter months in a local church. It often was not created by the clergyman but was the result of a spontaneous and often slight increase in conversions, which then formed the occasion for holding further meetings. How a typical in-church revival unfolded is best illustrated by Rev. Joseph Clutton's account in his Baptist church. What was termed a revival began with a slight upsurge in piety at a well-attended prayer meeting which had been touched off by the great commotion surrounding a debate about Darwin's theories of evolution. It was not conducted by the minister but by the laity, who then invited local Baptist preachers to intensify the atmosphere through salvationist preaching. What was described as 'an extensive awakening among the people' in fact only lasted one month and amounted to thirty converts, most of whom were young people. In this instance the revival was simply part and parcel of the ordinary ritual progress whereby the children of members made a transition from Sunday school to full adult membership symbolized by baptism.

However one might view the relative importance of revivalism, it is clear that by the 1840s because of the influence of British religious customs – the result of high immigration after 1815 –theory and doctrinal issues in religion dominated over experience and spontaneity. The majority of the clergy within Methodism and Presbyterianism were trained within the Enlightenment tradition of balancing piety and intellect. Although many ministers reflected upon the need for a more simple and plain style of preaching compared with that practised in Britain, this did not mean that sermons were simply emotional and empty of theological content. By 1843 Methodist ministers were being told that preaching must expound scriptural passages with familiar illustrations because the people wanted to follow along with their Bibles open on their laps before them. Ordinary Methodists were more doctrinally sophisticated than their competitors were prepared to acknowledge. Thus the supposedly rationalistic Presbyterian minister William Bell was truly unnerved when a Methodist class leader showed up to hear his sermon for the express purpose of publicly challenging him on the question of perfection! So much for our image of the merely enthusiastic and sentimental Methodist creed. The notion that true Methodism was wholly encompassed by the emotional and experiential was a construction of many clergymen who, in the wake of theological disputes over evolution in the 1870s, wished to excise doctrine from the Methodist tradition for fear that the science of theology might only lead to doubt. In practice doctrinal sermons predominated over salvation preaching even within Methodist circles, where salvation sermons remained irrefutably scriptural in emphasis. It was the spontaneous group participation in prayers and hymns that created the atmosphere of emotional intensity that often produced conversions. More significantly, according to the Methodist organ *The Christian Guardian*, conversions occurred most frequently when the clergyman visited in private homes rather than through the stimulus of either public worship or the mass revival.

What most distinguished the various denominations were their particular church rituals. In the Anglican Church the Book of Common Prayer united the clergyman with his audience. By contrast, the religious culture of Presbyterianism was highly oral in nature: a great emphasis was placed upon hearing the word of God through the sermon, while the communion, which involved a three-day period of sermons and prayer, was deemed of much greater importance than regular church attendance, at least until the late nineteenth century, when financial demands dictated that weekly worship become the norm. In Methodism the oral culture of the sermon was important, but of greater substance was attendance at ordinances, which included the weekly class meeting, the New Year's watchnight service, and the 'love feast,' a small intimate gathering of members which took place before the quarterly meetings for confession and spiritual nurture and which culminated with a sharing of bread and water as an expression of mutual fellowship. Ritual was the key element in all religions, and it was the participation in the repetitive practices of particular forms of worship that lent a sense of 'comfort,' a word in common use in this period to denote a sense of belonging and fellowship with a particular church. As in Protestantism, weekly attendance was of much less importance than performance of Easter duty of confession and communion within Catholicism. For Catholics as for Protestants, religious duties were not terribly onerous prior to the late nineteenth century, at which time various denominations abandoned older concepts of religiosity, which might include a combination of personal religious knowledge, proper conduct, baptizing and marrying within the church, with an annual pattern of taking the sacraments. By the 1880s, largely driven by financial considerations, all denominations made weekly attendance and the weekly offering the primary benchmark of religiosity. By the turn of the century, weekly attendance had so definitively become the criterion of being a good Christian that thereafter clergy (and historians) concluded that if people fell short of this high standard of religious involvement the society was in the process of secularizing. Because of the new importance placed upon weekly devotions, even within Catholicism the sermon took on new importance. In previous decades, the clergyman's authority rested upon his command of the ritual performance of mass;[16] by the later nineteenth century his authority derived from his expert knowledge of theology and doctrine. A similar process had occurred within various Protestant denominations, for between 1840 and 1870 the Methodists, Presbyterians, and Baptists had all built a network of church colleges that accelerated the professionalization of the clergy. The result was to create a greater intellectual and social distance between the congregation and its minister, who could by virtue of his education and salary now claim middle-class status. The demands of religious practice were fairly light between 1840 and 1880. In Methodism persistent non-attendance did not result in dismissal from the society, and the Presbyterian and Baptist disciplinary courts were most interested in reintegrating transgressors into the community after confession of sins rather than expelling them. However within both Protestantism and Catholicism a theology of fear, founded upon the image of a punishing God, formed the central pillar of religion. This pessimistic and rigourist cultural sensibility directly connected this period with early modern cultures. Although Presbyterian ministers believed that Methodists were too modern in placing too much emphasis upon the free will of humans, all religious groups in this period left very little room for human agency because they saw God as providential, as a directly intervening force both in nature and in human relations. It was not uncommon for Presbyterian and Methodist churches to hold days of fasting and thanksgiving either to ward off natural disasters or to celebrate the community's deliverance from God's wrath, a practice generally associated with pre-modern societies. For the clergy, the central purpose of religion was to foster submission to the will of God, and the most efficacious means of doing so was through human affliction. Themes of sickness and death thus loomed large in sermons, family letters, and prayers. Indeed, Isaac Watts's *Death and Heaven* (then in its sixteenth edition) was one of the most popular tracts of the day. Because death was believed to be one of the strongest ways to arouse people to an earnest profession of religious belief, funeral sermons were always attended in great numbers and featured more prominently in the New World than in Europe. And in order to instil religious feelings in the young, children in both Protestantism and Catholicism were commonly taken to funerals, even if they rarely attended church. In fact, in Catholic children's catechisms an important place was reserved for the discussion of death. Catechisms stressed that God was a severe judge, and, not until the introduction of a new catechism in 1888 did the once-frequent references to Satan largely disappeared. The church gave greater credence to the idea of individual agency in achieving salvation. In various Protestant faiths many people sought conversion and church membership as a result of the death of a close family member. So all-consuming was the emphasis upon hell and a vengeful God in various religions in this period that it is not surprising that great numbers of people flocked to the Universalists for they propounded a joyful heaven for the saved and the unsaved alike. Although by the 1870s the harsher sermons on death and damnation began to give way to a more positive theology of Christian love and redemption, the religion of sin and fear persisted at a popular level. In Protestantism this took the form of admonitory letters to younger family members describing in excruciating detail the marks of a 'good' Christian death or the keeping of a personal journal to record deaths. In Catholicism this popular religious preoccupation with death accounted for the continued expansion of confraternities such as the Bonne Mort [Good Death] and explains the ability of poor Catholics to endure the regimentation of old age homes that they chose to enter to ensure spiritual care in their dying moments.[17] Just as in Protestantism, Catholic preaching that had dwelt upon sin, death, and hell began by the 1860s to be balanced by a greater insistence upon what Christine Hudon has called the sentimental religion of the heart, whereby salvation was made easier by the practice of frequent communion and less inquisitorial forms of confession.

The high level of religious pluralism in early Canada meant that people had more opportunity to make individual religious choices. However, once a person decided on a particular denomination that suited their religious needs, individual self-expression was extremely limited. In certain sacred contexts, most notably prayer meetings, individuals – and this included women – were expected to pray spontaneously and exhort one another. However, in all other domains of religious life the particular rituals of each denomination were designed to curtail individualism and to promote conformity within each church. Personal religious expression was considered dangerous for all religious groups, from the highly institutionalized churches such as Roman Catholicism, to religious societies such as the Methodists, which have been conventionally seen as forums for greater personal religious expression, to the legalistic Presbyterian Church. All denominations continued to embrace pre-modern values that emphasized coercive systems of social order that were expressed through church ritual. When an individual had disgraced the cause by behaving contrary to church ordinances, they were thus termed to be walking in a 'disorderly' fashion. The Wesleyan Methodists insisted that once one became a committed member of the church it was imperative that individualism be subsumed to the corporate imperative that all must 'walk by the same rule and mind.'[18]

Thus, beneath the emergent modern notions that one could voluntarily belong to a church persisted strongly legalistic institutional structures that aimed solely at pressuring parishioners to an exact obedience of the rules and regulations. While Methodism may have expounded the ideal of a personal experience of God's grace, it was nevertheless a highly structured system of rules called the Methodist Discipline. The Discipline demanded public worship, family worship, daily reading of the scriptures, fasting, attendance at quarterly communion, and most importantly participation in the weekly class meeting. To remain a Methodist in good standing you had to be free of debt, give to charity, help one another in business, and marry within the faith. Each of these tests of membership was not always enforced, but the Discipline was a systematized structure of moral control exercised through persuasion in the more convivial atmosphere of the local class meeting. There you were expected to recount your spiritual progress, and if this was inadequate you were admonished and encouraged to greater effort. If this regulation through conversation failed, you were turned over to the church court to be disciplined and perhaps expelled. For the most part, this more modern concept of control through an internalized self-scrutiny functioned well because we have only sporadic instances, such as that of James Paterson, an abusive husband from St James Methodist in Montreal, who was expelled because he failed to reform himself. In addition, class leaders were constantly monitored for doctrinal purity at monthly leaders' meetings.

This kind of self-examination appears more modern and less punitive in its ideas of control, especially when it is compared with the Baptist and Presbyterian churches' use of older legalistic structures of church courts to discipline members. In those courts, women were regularly reproved for sexual delinquency, though the most common sexual misdemeanour was pre-marital sex among couples who voluntarily brought their sins before the church elders because they wished to reintegrate themselves into the congregation and assure that their children would be baptized.[19] Adulterous women often had to make a public confession before the congregation for several Sundays while being chastised by the minister. Far more often, men were the delinquents, charged with drunkenness, failure to attend communion, being disputatious with the minister, and dishonest business practices. Clearly, the commitment to becoming a church member was a very serious step, and in doing so the member signalled that he would not only scrutinize the behaviour of other members but that he was willing to be watched over in turn because he believed that individual sins were also the collective sins of the whole congregation. In this way, the ritual of the disciplinary court represented a public cleansing and communal reconciliation. The Methodist class meeting, the Baptist and Presbyterian courts, and the Catholic confessional all served to cement group identity because it distinguished between the sinners and the redeemed, the truly pious and the lukewarm, and in coercing the recalcitrant these rituals of discipline created a uniformity of mind and behaviour. Ironically it was the church with the closest relationship to the state, the Church of England, that possessed the weakest disciplinary apparatus and relied almost exclusively upon the appeal of the liturgy to maintain group coherence.

Of course, not every church member was willing to meekly submit to church regulations. Some church rituals that elevated church unity, such as the four-day Presbyterian communion where the tables were fenced to keep out non-members, were generally well attended. Most Presbyterians also piously accepted the decisions of the church courts because they wished to maintain the purity of their church community. Similarly, popular adherence to the Catholic Church's requirement of yearly confession was near universal in the nineteenth century, although prior to 1870 there were significant lapses in the obligatory practice of communion. Yet a substantial minority of dissidents contested church regulations. Most commonly, individuals refused to obey the rules, but in extreme situations there could be collective resistance. A wealthy group of New Brunswick Methodists, for example, objected to the strictness of the Discipline and completely disrupted the congregation. Most of those who resisted were men. Women were more likely to subvert the legal machinery through a pretence of cooperation. Protestant clergy and Catholic priests constructed a discourse of female moral superiority that made women the pivotal figures in religious education because they, and not fathers, could be relied upon to promote spiritual conformity. Young, unmarried men were particularly intent on resisting the church's intrusion into domains which infringed upon their notions of masculinity that included male social rituals of drinking, dancing, and horseracing. Men came into particular conflict with the church authorities over the issue of Sabbath breaking because this was seen to impinge upon their ability to making a living. Most significantly of all, men adamantly rejected any attempt to regulate family relations that trenched directly on patriarchal power. One Presbyterian in Almonte, Upper Canada, hotly declared that whether he had abused his wife was no business of the church court. As men got more disaffected women came to dominate the covenant meetings, thus turning them into female power bases. The structure of church discipline was thus eroded. To have these key regulatory bodies in female hands was seen by many clergymen as imperilling the public authority of the church as a whole.

When recalcitrant church members either refused to pay for their pews, sought to evade disciplinary hearings, or continued to flout church authority, clergymen usually effectively turned the tables on these dissidents by using the threat of denying religious sacraments. If Catholic parishioners disputed the parish priest's authority by refusing to partake of the sacraments, the bishop would bully them into submission by simply removing the local priest. But as the century progressed church leaders began to use educative rather than punitive means to ensure conformity so that the authority of the institution would not be compromised through unseemly wrangling. When Rev. William Bell, a Presbyterian minister, refused to baptize children because he thought the parents irreligious, they simply found another clergyman. Of course, the most popular means of showing one's disapproval with either a clergyman or a particular church polity was simply to shift one's denominational allegiance. Another option was to remain an adherent and not seek full church membership, thus avoiding the regulatory apparatus of the congregation. Among Methodists of St Stephen, New Brunswick, there were four or five times more hearers than members. In Halifax, Nova Scotia, in the Church of Scotland, the ratio was one member to ten adherents. The majority of church members were women, who joined at various points in the life course. In St

Stephen, New Brunswick, roughly two-thirds of evangelical church members were women: 69 per cent of Congregationalists, 68 per cent of Methodists, and 63 per cent of Presbyterians. There was, however, greater gender parity among married men and women. For both sexes the highest level of religious commitment was reserved for adulthood. The available evidence suggests that religion did not constitute a fixed or primary identity in the nineteenth century because the dominant practice of changing churches several times during the life-course meant that denominationalism was not growing in this period. If most people did not have a particular denominational loyalty, they did, however, hold an identity as part of a broader evangelicalism that grouped Anglicans, Methodists, Congregationalists, Presbyterians, and Baptists.

The lowest level of church membership was among unmarried men. Many did not want to give up many of the rituals of male conviviality such as drinking. They were not irreligious; rather they considered membership to be a very serious step. Their transiency could deter them, or they might prefer to visit many churches to meet and court young women. For working-class men who were saving to get married, church membership was costly. Some also had to work on Sundays. Because most denominations had circuits, a clergyman might be in your vicinity on a weekday when the majority of men would not be available to hear his sermon. It should be noted, however, that women with young children were also less likely to be church members.

Generally speaking, the male life course was not favourable to a fixed religious identity. Indeed, multiple church affiliations often better served the status needs of men especially those who used the church to build business networks. Simply because men did not become church members did not mean that they were not active in church life. For example, in Shefford in the Eastern Townships the prayer meetings ceased for want of numbers when the militia was called up during the Rebellions. Male church involvement often took the form of pew renting, leading a Sunday school class, or becoming church stewards, none of which necessitated full church membership. Stated another way, because women were not allowed to be office holders nor, with rare exceptions, did they pay for the pews when married, church membership was a crucial marker of religious commitment that men could display in other ways.

Many historians have assumed that female church membership demonstrated greater female piety and that they sought church participation because civic political participation was closed to them. However, church office holding was likewise closed to them and their rate of participation in church voluntary associations was never sufficiently strong to indicate that women joined in order to fulfil a proto-feminist desire for leadership. Women would have perceived the public institutional church as a largely male space whose regulatory structures were controlled either by male laymen or, as the nineteenth century progressed, by male clergy. Because closet or private prayer was one of the few spiritual venues where women were in control, personal spiritual reflection assumed the predominant role in women's religious lives. In religious matters women were modern individualists insofar as personal spiritual reflection occupied a greater role in their lives, whereas men retained a stronger allegiance to traditional corporate forms of religious expression centred on the leadership roles both in conducting household prayer and in managing the public institution of the church.

People who chose an institutional affiliation nonetheless continued to fashion their own religious identities. They decided how often they attended church, parents determined when they would baptize their children, and in Catholicism parents or midwives would perform their own sprinkling in the absence of the priest. The power of the priest was only effective because the faithful were willing to submit to it. Within Protestantism, people who had no church affiliation still held sufficient religious beliefs to demand the consolation of the minister for rites of passage, most notably baptism and death. The persistence of popular religion reveals a terrain of blending and negotiation that occurred when clergy had to defer to popular desires. The local priest in St Hyacinthe tolerated the customary New Year's charity festival in which parishioners paraded through town with a beef heart on a pole, even distributing apples and candies to the children, but he also attempted to reinvent this custom as a Catholic event by handing out holy pictures. In the Ottawa Valley the Presbyterian Minister William Bell was less successful in managing the Highlanders' continued belief in ghosts, goblins, and other superstitions. Bell also sought to stamp out the charivari, as did the Catholic church hierarchy in Lower Canada, but Bell was more tolerant because these popular protests against irregular marriages conformed to Bell's anti-Catholic biases and because they reaffirmed his desire to reform popular morality. So when an aged former priest married his servant, Bell welcomed the charivari not only because it raised $40.00 for the building of a local church, but because when the groom later died of the effects of alcohol Bell was able to use the story as temperance propaganda. Popular mores were not simply squelched by the clergy. Despite his antipathy to superstition Father Marchand of Drummondville as late as 1883 agreed to lift the spell on a farmer's cows.

Throughout the nineteenth century Protestantism and Catholicism evolved from a more rigourist and coercive style of religion to a more optimistic, inclusive, and appealing faith, in many respects, as a response to popular mores. The Catholic Church placed many restrictions on marriage, which included marrying a Protestant, marrying without witnesses, marrying cousins within the fourth degree, or marrying people in common-law relationships. Prior to 1850 all requests for dispensations for marriage had to be referred to the bishop, but as a result of pressure from parishioners who asserted their right to the sacrament, only in severe cases of public sin, such as bestiality, unmarried

couples openly living together, or renting a house to prostitutes, most people were permitted by the parish priest to
marry whom they wished. For similar reasons, by the end
of the nineteenth century many types of misbehaviour that
might have resulted in a public shaming were now dealt
with in private conversation with the minister. By the 1870s
the Methodist class meeting had mutated into a painless
prayer meeting where individuals were no longer called to
account but where the class leader simply gave a sermon,
said prayers, and sang hymns. And because so many Methodist families were religiously mixed, the closed love feast
was, by mid-century, opened up to non-members and non-
Methodists in order to salve public demands. Movements
towards greater distance between clergy and congregation
represented by the wearing of a decorative gown were stu-
diously resisted by St James Methodist in Montreal; and in
deference to occupational and family commitments many
churches followed the lead of First United Presbyterian in
Galt, which in 1883 altered the customary ritual of the four-
day communion because of time constraints imposed by
industrial life.

In contrast to previous decades, clergymen generally
squelched any commingling of solemnity and festivity in
religious rituals by the end of the century. In Cape Breton,
for example, the Presbyterian communion festival, which
had functioned both as a religious and recreational event
for various age groups, was reformed by the clergy in the
1870s into a tightly controlled and orderly event because
young people had come to usurp the occasion for court-
ship, displays of current fashion, drinking, and carousing.
After 1870, as parishioners became better socialized into
religious orthodoxy and an acceptance of clerical authority, clergymen began to draw a sharper distinction between
normative religious practices and popular religiosity, which
was now discarded as irreligious, unrespectable, and disorderly. Ministers generally tolerated the fact that the evening
service was a youth service in which the upper gallery would

be the site for hand holding and whispering. After 1870, youth culture was channelled into the formal structures of youth societies, which were controlled by the clergy. Similarly spontaneous public declarations of one's spiritual state from the pews was not seen as unusual, but by the turn of the century Metropolitan Methodist Church in Toronto saw this behaviour as indecorous, despite the fact that this downtown church continued to sponsor mass urban revivals.

Clergymen also established unity in their congregation by introducing a kinder, gentler religious experience. Armed with an optimistic message of salvation, church leaders were better able to socialize future church members, especially as Sunday schools began to proliferate by the late nineteenth century. That became a key moment in the transition from regulation by coercion to regulation by education. Gone were the images of Satan, death, and damnation; in their stead appeared richly illustrated picture books with joyful stories of redemption through Christ's love, which, by contrast with traditional doctrinal sermons, appealed directly to the emotions. There emerged within Catholicism a similar pattern. After 1850 the older rigourism was replaced by Liguorianism, a less pessimistic view of human sinfulness, which emphasized frequent communion for the purpose of spiritual solace rather than denial of absolution. With this turn to ultramontanism there was a transition from the control through a forbidding, distant ritual reserved for a devout elect to religious hegemony achieved through the more welcoming aspect of ceremony and theatre, where churches were ornately decorated with statuary and masses enriched with instrumental and choral music.

The rise of lay associational life was a further manifestation of this transition to a more inclusive and inviting religious sensibility. Church associations were not simply impositions of middle-class culture. Their central purpose, both within Catholicism and Protestantism, was to reinforce the pastoral position of the clergy and to create new ties between them and their congregations. These associations were meant to entice more laity into the church, but they remained under the control of the clergyman. What distinguished the Catholic and Protestant traditions prior to 1870 was that the Catholic Church under ultramontanism was relatively rich in associational life, whereas most Protestant denominations rejected the notion of associations, including temperance societies, because they remained wedded to the idea of the church as an other-worldly institution untouched by secular concerns. As late as 1876, Metropolitan Methodist Church in Toronto argued that the temperance movement might prevent the spread of 'personal religion.' Moreover, control of drinking was much contested within Methodism, and it was on this issue that a schism occurred in the Wesley Methodist congregation in St Stephen, New Brunswick, in 1844. *The Christian Guardian* stated in 1844 that it supported temperance meetings but that a purely religious meeting would better serve the purpose of conversion. A temperance meeting might conflict with the class meeting, especially when it was an already difficult task to get men to become church members. Wesleyan Methodists in the Eastern Townships stayed well clear of the temperance movement for fear of alienating wealthy members. On the other hand, the Baptists were more willing to create temperance societies within their churches to get men to go to church, and they believed that the taking of the pledge would ease men towards the recognition of other sins and greater religiosity. While the Methodists and Presbyterians forged links with the temperance movement, they were reluctant to create their own temperance societies within the church until later in the century, even though the Presbyterians and Baptists disciplined church members on an individual basis for public drunkenness.

By contrast with the continued other-wordliness of Protestant denominations, Catholicism embarked, in the words of René Hardy, on a 'conquest of civil society.' Catholic churches both in Quebec and English Canada had created a vast network of associations and recreational organizations, asylums, hospitals, and educational institutions. Most lay voluntary associations and confraternities were created between 1870 and 1885, with an average of 7.5 of these organizations per parish by the end of the nineteenth century. During the 1840s and 1850s there was an explosion of temperance societies, and, like other confraternities, they were viewed as a means to teach doctrine and to proselytize, especially among men, the Irish, and the working classes. Temperance sermons formed a staple of Catholic preaching and served as the centrepiece of the popular revival mission. Nearly every parish had temperance societies with extremely high levels of adherence (87 per cent) in the 1850s. They declined slightly in the 1870s either because the clergy had resigned themselves to a certain level of intemperance or because drinking was under control. Many older confraternities were also resurrected and embellished. In the 1830s the Society for the Propagation of the Faith and the Association of Holy Childhood, both of which were directed to women, raised funds for charity and foreign missions (prior to the 1870s the only ongoing female associations in Protestant churches fulfilled a similar charitable function). The most popular associations were those that made minimal demands on their members: for this reason the Confraternity of the Scapular was very successful because the only requirement was the wearing of a ribbon around the devotee's neck, and the St Vincent de Paul, which demanded a regimen of personal devotion as well as visiting the poor, faltered. In part, the rapid expansion of lay associations indicated a profound devotional revolution among the Catholic laity, but people joined both for sociability and spiritual reasons. In the parish of St- Pierre-Apôtre, one in seven male household heads, half of them working-class, joined the Men's Congregation because it provided death benefits. Whatever the reason, clergymen welcomed and promoted these organizations because they were effective strategies in fostering greater church attendance and activism. Some organizations such as Le Cercle

Saint Pierre, which provided a room for billiards, cards, newspapers, and smoking for male youth, were less effective. Only higher-status men could afford the prohibitive membership dues at $2 per annum. Apart from the Men's Congregation, these organizations were generally supported by the wealthier members of the parish and thus may have contributed to class divisions. Impoverished Catholics turned to charitable institutions because they could not afford the dues for associations with death benefits.

Sloppier record keeping often masked the fact that local Protestant congregations also provided for the poor with regular charity sermons, ladies' visiting societies, such as the Dorcas Society, which also sewed clothing for the poor, maintained poor funds, and held fund-raising parties at the houses of needy families. Ministers frequently referred the needy to secular relief societies and promoted the creation of day schools for the poor. The outdoor relief provided was not markedly inferior to that given by secular institutions, and was given to people in their homes which prevented them from being stigmatized in institutional care. Some churches had a system of regular relief, especially for women. Even though the Dorcas Society from St James Methodist in Montreal gave in kind rather than in cash, they fed and clothed between forty-five and fifty-two people a year in the 1870s. Although the women visited families to determine need, these visits were not intrusive inquiries into their moral behaviour, for the criterion for receiving aid was dependent upon one's level of religious commitment. Presbyterians and Methodists required membership or regular attendance to get charity. Anglicans, however, assumed that all citizens were part of the national church and therefore were entitled to relief. Within Protestantism, charity was thus one of the most effective mechanisms for bolstering church membership among the working classes. A similar notion of charity prevailed within Catholicism, for the St Vincent de Paul Society accepted the notion that poverty was a constant feature of earthly society. The basis for giving rested upon the recipient's piety or upon the need to save children for the church. The St Vincent de Paul male visitors were therefore most concerned about the family's religious practice and encouraged attendance at Catholic schools and participation in devotional societies. More significantly, the St Vincent de Paul believed that the poor saved the rich by enhancing the piety of the giver. Just as in Protestantism, if you had no church citizenship you were not entitled to help. An active leader in the Montreal St Vincent de Paul Society, George Clerk, was not sentimental about the poor and categorically denied a helpless Widow Beers of Griffintown any aid when she could not produce her daughter's baptismal certificate or give evidence that her dead husband had converted to Catholicism.

By the 1870s, then, as a result of strategies of clerical control, be they through the persuasion of the sermon, the educational venues of the prayer meeting and the Sunday school, the sociability of the voluntary association, the inducements of charity, or through the more coercive mechanisms of discipline and confession, members of all denominations showed much greater allegiance to institutional religion. In short, a greater proportion of the population attended church even if they did not conform to all religious norms. While there might have been more movement between churches, and individuals within families were more inclined to go their own ways religiously, what one encountered inside the church was a far more ordered environment than that found in 1840 because of the shift in power from the laity to the clergy. Greater uniformity also produced new forms of resistance, but most church members ultimately chose to conform to the moral precepts of the church, even if they did backslide or at first resist. As more churches were constructed and more clergymen recruited, they could more easily offer multiple services on the Sabbath in addition to several weeknight prayer meetings targeted for men, women, and youth. Larger numbers of people went to church. In his study of St John, New

Brunswick, T.W. Acheson has estimated that church attendance grew more rapidly than the population of the city, reaching 66 per cent of the permanent residents of the city by 1846. This compares very favourably with rates of church attendance in British and European industrial cities. In Quebec the spectacular recruitment of priests during the nineteenth century along with the creation of smaller dioceses and parishes meant that clerical oversight, as well as clerical ministrations, were far more available in 1880 than in 1840. By 1890 in most parishes only 1 per cent of Catholics did not perform their Easter duties compared with 25 per cent in the 1840s and 1850s. In addition, a greater proportion of the population was attending communion at the end of the century largely because it was promoted as a nourishment of the soul and not as a reward for enduring the rigours of confession.

Between 1840 and 1870 the church became a formidable institution of social discipline because it had the capacity to adapt to popular expectations and to change the content of the religious message to accommodate elements of modernity. Although pockets of resistance remained, most notably the freedom to change churches, the cultural venues for popular expression had been greatly reduced: female preachers and class leaders were extinct; by 1878 the Methodist General Conference eradicated personal speaking in the class meeting; the demise of the church courts meant that an individual could no longer give testimony; the eradication of public penance closed off symbolic avenues of community control and spiritual reintegration; spontaneous prayer was regarded as outmoded; popular religious customs were either reformed or eradicated; and lay associational life came under the control of an increasingly professionalized clergy. Religion, both Catholic and Protestant, took on the overtones of a clerical hegemony by the 1870s. This hegemony was effective because it was not simply imposed on but depended upon the consent of the parishioners, who still exerted some control over the clergyman by choosing to give or not. Despite the varieties of religious choice and practice in the pluralistic religious environment of early Canada, the power of the institutional church rested upon the fact that the majority of ordinary people shared a belief in a providential God, a conviction which transcended class and ethnic divisions. Many believers remained unchurched in 1840 largely because of the absence of permanent churches and clergy. Despite clerical rhetoric that persistently lamented widespread irreligion, between 1840 and 1870 the presence of the institutional church with its various rituals for conformity became far more effective at organizing and overseeing the religious lives of Canadians as rates of attendance increased. While the religious horizons of ordinary people remained bounded by the limits of their local congregation throughout this period, hints of a more profound change were beginning to ripple through Protestant denominations, which began to stress 'the supreme importance of personal religion.'[20] In short, Protestant churches were specifically instructed to evangelize 'strangers,' and clergymen who did not gain 'marked spiritual results'[21] – those who did not produce large numbers of converts – were demoted or dismissed. This signalled the churches' transformation from being closed, other-wordly communities severed from the wider society and dependent upon a core of local families, to more open and anonymous institutions that set about, in the late nineteenth century, to evangelize Canadian society.

2

Machinery of Salvation:
The Making of a Civic Christianity

Arriving in Toronto in 1906, a young Methodist working-class lad named Frank Roberts encountered a religious landscape radically altered from that known by the majority of church adherents of the previous generation. Since the late 1880s, the urban churches had taken over the cultural and social leadership within each of the Christian denominations, both Protestant and Catholic, even though the majority of Canadians still lived in small towns or rural settings. Because churches in large urban centres such as Montreal, Toronto, Hamilton, and Winnipeg were now determining both the shape and tone of religious life, a strikingly different set of priorities was established. For example, there was greater attention paid to evangelism because of the new focus upon outreach to the unchurched, a strategy that was premised upon the notion that the churches had a much greater role to play in constructing the wider civic culture. This marked a rejection of the other-worldliness that was so characteristic of religious practices in pre-industrial society. After the 1880s, the changed industrial and urban character of Canadian society demanded new strategies, and the principal target group of the new evangelism of the late Victorian era was that represented by Frank Roberts, a young, unmarried male immigrant who had arrived in Canada without his family and who was, as a result, believed by church authorities to be all the more vulnerable to the anonymity and temptations of urban life. Fearing that city life was the crucible of secularism, clergymen set about creating a host of new church associations that would distinctly entice young men into the church. Then, they hoped, men and women would marry within a particular denomination and they and their offspring would become dependable financial contributors to the church. The new evangelism, characteristic of the mainline Protestant churches, was a direct response to the new urban reality and tried to expand the cross-class complexion of the institutional church while at the same time focusing upon specific age and gender groups.

The rising power of the urban clergyman did not go uncontested. Indeed, the period between 1880 and 1910 was one of the most conflictual periods in Canadian religious history. Not only did tensions develop between socio-economic groups, but new priorities produced gender antagonisms, intense theological disputes, rural-urban conflicts, and sectarian splintering. More significantly, the old concept of the unchurched that might be applied to anyone irrespective of class, social status, or gender was replaced by new notions of respectability, which gave an ethnic and racial complexion to the meaning of the term 'the unchurched.' By explicitly equating Christianity with Canadianness, it constructed a category of the 'other' that rendered an individual an outsider both to the church and to the nation as a whole.

At the end of the nineteenth century the idea of church adherence was recast to place less emphasis upon regular participation in church rites and greater weight upon participation in a wide range of associational forms of church organization. In addition, not only did being religious include participation in the church proper, but the individual's moral conduct in the whole of society was also deemed to be a measure of whether one was a good Christian or not. A previous generation of churchgoers would have defined religiosity more narrowly in terms of participation in church rituals or in terms of familial prayers and devotions.

By the late nineteenth century, a new group of clergymen no longer saw a division between the church and the world, or between the sacred and the secular, for in their view the whole of society was deemed to be Christian or potentially Christian. This new idea of a Christian public sphere involved the creation of religious discourses, practices, and organizations that looked to 'saving the social' by moving outside individual church congregations to bring sinners to repentence. Because the Protestant mainline churches, as well as the Roman Catholic Church, began to subscribe to this notion of a Christian public during the three decades after 1880, clergymen became much more willing to participate in civic life. There was also much more interdenominational activity at this time. By contrast with preindustrial societies where the authority of the clergy rested upon their mastery of theological knowledge and their control of church ritual and discipline, the young clergymen who came to prominence in the late nineteenth century who wished to promote the church as the leader of modernity in Canadian society believed that they derived their power from the degree to which they could speak on behalf of a larger Christian public. This in turn involved a confident belief that both clergy and laity could participate in the broader society without endangering faith or personal morality. Rather than 'secularization,' notions of Christian belief had infiltrated the pathways of urban culture.

The engagment of the churches with the social was not a narrowly political one even though it involved the creation of Christian subject-citizens; rather, it involved the churches speaking on behalf of the public good on a wide range of questions. Modernist clergymen effectively reinterpreted the idea of the civic sphere in such a way as to create a notion of Christian citizenship that rendered the state subordinate to the churches. In effect, Protestant clergymen were engaged in a project similar to that of the Catholic ultramontane clergy earlier in the nineteenth century who envisioned the churches as superior to the state because they were responsible for creating public morality. This new formulation of 'Christian citizenship' had the effect of relegating the unchurched or non-Christian religious groups to the margins of Canadian society by virtue of their ethnicity or class position using the new categories of the 'loafer' (young men who were not yet church members), the 'pauper' (who must be morally regulated rather than given material aid as in the past), and the 'foreigner' (who had to be christianized according to Anglo-Saxon norms before they could be deemed Canadian citizens). There was also a new construction of femaleness as otherness. Since the integration of the church with the public realm, with its language of intellectual piety, was emphatically linked to the campaign to get men into the church, it was contrasted with the heartfelt religion of a bygone era, which became increasingly equated with the sentimental spirituality of women. Henceforth, maleness was identified with social Christianity, progress, and modernity; femaleness with tradition, emotion, and private religion. In this regard, clergymen became the leading voices of the notion of separate spheres for men and women.

This metamorphosis of the mainline churches away from an inward-looking other-worldliness generated considerable popular and clerical resistance to its implementation. Historians have sometimes bought into the critique developed by the defenders of an earlier 'mythical' period of evangelicalism, such as the American revivalist Dwight Moody, who saw a modern liberal Protestantism as secular and merely masquerading as religion. The proliferation of holiness groups, the noisy advent of the Salvation Army, and the spread of Pentecostalism were less a reaction against middle-class control of mainline churches than a dissent from the new social evangelism. Indeed, the continued debate within the Methodist, Presbyterian, and Baptist churches often adopted the language of a critique of materialism and consumerism. Many historians have seen this as evidence of an emerging middle-class hegemony, but in actual fact it involved a more fundamental contest over the degree to which the institutional church would either be other-worldly or embrace the broader society. Rather than a class critique, this was a battle over the cultural space which the church would occupy in industrial society. Would the definition of the church be restricted to church adherents and church members of a particular congregation or would it denote all members of society who could be potentially evangelized? Where younger clergyman argued that all aspects of life should be informed by religion, many defenders of tradition worried that they could no longer see the dividing line between the world and the church that had once been such a fundamental part of Protestant identity. By the late nineteenth century the voice of the traditionalists had weakened, either because the disgruntled had left to join a new religious sect or because the newer church members were being socialized into the new concept of the Protestant public.

The scope of evangelism was thus broadened in the late nineteenth century from awakening the spirituality of backsliders within a given congregation to bringing 'strangers' or the unchurched into houses of worship. And although mass revivals may have waned, evangelism actually expanded because it occurred through a variety of new church organizations principally aimed at welcoming people who had never been spiritually catechized or socialized within the home. Every Protestant denomination established urban missions, usually as an offshoot of a particular downtown church, to target the upwardly mobile members of the working classes who were perceived to be the unchurched. Every clergymen was exhorted to develop evangelistic programs that included the creation of urban missions, cottage prayer meetings, young people's societies, bible classes, Sunday schools for all age groups, mother's meetings, and temperance societies, all of which were geared to bringing about both a conversion experience and a commitment to church membership. In addition, the modes and manifestations of spirituality were becoming more tightly regulated so that in 1893 the Methodist Committee on Evangelists and Evangelism could authoritatively declaim against 'physical manifestations not calculated to commend our common Christianity,' and included in these proscriptions any ecstatic emotionalism or immoderate public display. This was, of course, calculated to recommend religion to the 'hearts and consciences of men.'[1]

During this period each denomination participated in a process of radically altering their church rituals, regulations, and practices in an effort to make their churches more socially inclusive. As a consequence of making their church more amenable to the mobile urban population, the Methodist Church had pressed in 1878 for the loosening of attendance at class meetings as a requirement of Methodist membership on the basis of ensuring greater inclusiveness. The class meeting declined first in large urban communities like Hamilton, where a groundswell of working-class immigration meant that by 1907 a mere 15 per cent of church members were enrolled in class meetings and only half of these actually attended. New churches such as Barton Street Methodist never implemented class meetings for fear that they would alienate the previously unchurched because of their rigid monitoring of individual moral conduct. In 1910 the Methodists quietly removed moral strictures against drinking, dancing, and cardplaying, in favour of a new stress upon the 'educated Christian conscience' as a guide to morality rather than an external conformity to rule. By the early twentieth century Methodist leaders, who assumed a wholly literate reading public, preferred to rely upon the less invasive educative method of regulation through a flood of printed matter from the Methodist presses. The older, more rigid forms of control were, however, reserved for the truly 'deviant,' and thus institutions with intensive moral scrutiny were devised for unwed mothers, the intemperate, and the criminal.

Presbyterian church courts were similarly in decline by

the 1890s, and the practice of personal catechizing of families by ministers and elders was eradicated. Although the pastoral visiting of families continued, elders were explicitly ordered to refrain from any inquisitorial or confessional methods of evangelizing. The Catholic Church also rid itself of the last vestiges of rigourism by instituting the practice of daily communion, which was now used as an inclusive method for transforming the masses into good Christians rather than as an instrument to separate the institutional church from a populace the clergy deemed innately sinful. In turn, once communion was made more inviting for the parishioner, the local priest was less likely to make the experience of confession too exacting or punitive. In both Catholicism and Protestantism the older emphasis upon references to death and damnation as methods for conversion were abandoned in favour of a more positive approach to sermonizing which preserved the recognition of sin but propounded a more optimistic message of salvation through Christ's love. Indeed, the very notion of what constituted a 'conversion' experience was altered during this period, again to focus upon making the church a more inviting place for those outsiders to religion. As Newfoundland Methodist clergyman R. Edis Fairbairn explained, many people committed to a life of Christian service had refused to become church members because they thought the requirements for a decisive conversion set such a high standard they could never live up to it. In a society characterized by increased geographical and social mobility and a greater proliferation of leisure and associational opportunties beyond the church, making religion more accessible was an obvious priority. Within Catholicism, both in Quebec and English Canada, the new priority was in constructing a more humane religion; thus organizations such as the Apostleship of Prayer (Sacred Heart), which stressed the humanity of Christ rather than divine punishment, grew by leaps and bounds and, by 1896, included one-quarter of the entire archdiocese of Toronto within its membership.

With the widespread creation of settled churches, itinerant preaching circuits and mass revivals were no longer
necessary and had given way to an emphasis upon ordinary
means of grace through the sermon and the taking of the
sacraments. In turn, the supposed demise of 'spontaneous
enthusiasm,' which has been often cited as the emascula-
tion of Methodist tradition, represented a shift in power
from the American-dominated Episcopal Methodists, who
promoted mass revivals, to control of the denomination by
Wesleyan Methodists, who had always been exponents of a
more ordered and temperate piety. Thus the conflict was
not simply one between traditionalists and modernists, but
marked a continuation of conflicts which had always riddled Methodism, and it was only at this juncture that opponents of change constructed a mythical version of old-time
religion characterized by emotionalism, spontaneity, anti-
intellectualism, and localism. However, the fact that the
Methodist Church decided to send out publications to the
aged, invalids, mothers at home with young children, men
who had to work on Sundays, the indifferent, and the poor,
rather than insist that they come to Sunday service, was a
recogntion that within a large metropolitan centre such
as Toronto there was a complex mixture of cultural traditions, socio-economic gradations, and family contexts that
demanded new approaches. These alterations in church
practices were not wholly the creation of liberal Protestantism, for even fundamentalist Christians like the Baptist T.T.
Shields, who began his ministry in Hamilton, saw the virtue
of adopting modern advertising techniques – he sent out
over one thousand circulars each Friday evening to his predominantly working-class parish – even though he resisted
using church entertainments to raise money. Like all urban
clergymen, he accepted the logic of inclusiveness, which necessitated an expansive evangelism dedicated to converting
the previously unchurched masses.

Urban congregations led the way in introducing innovations to the style and content of religious practices. For

example, one of the largest downtown Presbyterian churches in Toronto, Gould Street Presbyterian, was inspired by J.J. Kelso, best known as a leading child welfare reformer, to make the church more attractive to the mobile, urban population, especially unmarried working-class men. The church therefore introduced an active Men's Brotherhood featuring invited lecturers who spoke on social topics, a revised Wednesday evening prayer meeting to interest young folk, more gospel singing, and a special bible class for both children and adults that encouraged parents without servants to come to church. Many clergymen, both conservative and liberal, perceived the city as the catalyst for the growing social and ethnic divisions that they believed were corrosive of spirituality and of their civic project to redeem the nation. Ministers who received urban postings in the late nineteenth century, many of whom had been raised in rural areas and small towns, saw around them merely moral degradation, unassimilated immigrants, the expansion of leisure, and the erosion of family life, which, from the perspective of the church, was so integral to the preservation of the moral order. The Presbyterian Church was particularly exercised by the notion the the urban setting was a 'battleground of civilization and religion'[2] where the forces of irreligion, atheism, and 'Jesuitism' lurked to undermine the 'natural' expansion of Protestantism. Presbyterians borrowed the discourse of the irreligious city from their Scottish predecessors and were particularly influenced by the city mission work of Thomas Chalmers in the 1820s. The religious conservatives denounced urban blight out of a desire to preserve an imagined rural utopia, while the liberals saw an opportunity for renewal and a rationalization for introducing the revisions that they were promoting in terms of the broader social role of the churches. In Quebec, conservative elements within the Catholic Church went so far as to identify Catholicism as a wholly rural phenomenon and equated country life with the essence of the French-Canadian nation itself.

Clergymen from the Methodist, Presbyterian, and Catholic churches increasingly identified poverty and moral decay with specific ethnic and class elements. Prior to the 1870s, Irish Catholics had been the targets of a virulent (and frequently violent) anti-Catholicism in which Catholic-Protestant tensions were played out in street parades, which sometimes degenerated into brawls between the Orange and the Green in cities such as Saint John, New Brunswick, in 1849. In Montreal, parading was generally peaceful, as the Catholic clergy of that city exerted effective control over nationalist societies. In marked contrast, Toronto's Irish Catholic clergy were, until the 1880s, frequently unable to bring secular Irish republican nationalist societies to heel, largely because the latter offered a more attractive venue for male conviviality than did voluntary associations sponsored by the church. However, by the 1890s, with the upward mobility of Irish Catholics, especially in Ontario, and the integration of English-speaking Catholics into the political state, Protestant-Catholic violence was on the wane. It was replaced by new forms of public anti-Catholicism, such as the Equal Rights Association and the Protestant Protective Association, which articulated a discourse that seamlessly equated Protestantism, the English language, and a comprehensive Anglo-Canadian identity that stood in opposition to 'French' ultramontanism, which Protestant champions believed dominated Quebec and threatened, by conspiratorial means, to seize control of the national government. Catholic-Protestant conflict shifted from the streets to political struggles to control public institutions such as the school system. This new Protestant nationalism called forth a response by English-Canadian Catholic leaders, whose quest for public authority sought to demonstrate that Catholic citizenship was equally committed to the English language and an overarching sense of Canadian nationality. In Toronto after 1910, the established Catholic population, the majority of whom were descendants of Irish immigrants but who now identified with the new Canadian

nation and were experiencing upward mobility, recreated
the pejorative attitudes that had been directed towards their
forefathers by claiming that three-quarters of the waifs and
delinquent children served by Catholic charities, like the St
Vincent de Paul Society, were 'foreign' Catholics. In a similar manner, the Methodist Church cast the working classes
as the agents of dechristianization. As early as 1878 E.H. Dewart, editor of the *Christian Guardian* and a self-proclaimed
conservative, castigated the working classes for their indifference to the teachings of the church and desparingly
observed that workers were 'too low down in the pit to be
reached by the rope let down by the churches.'[3] In many
cases, this construction of working-class irreligiosity arose
more out of a fear of the rise of working-class participation
in labour organizations such as the Knights of Labour than
as a true reflection of working-class religious behaviour.

Before we accept Dewart's ruminations about working-
class irreligion it must be remembered that he was a longtime advocate of tailoring the church's message to the
middle classes. Like many urban ministers, Dewart feared
that congregations composed entirely of working-class people would be unprepared to construct the large, gothic
stone churches which had become so popular and which
were so crucial to Methodism's new self-identity as a national denomination. In addition, his portrait of the Methodist church as a class-specific institution alienating to the
working classes was a way for him to critique modern innovations, such as the introduction of social evangelism
within the church, which he believed was compromising
old-time Methodism with its emphasis on other-worldiness
and emotional piety. For those who championed the building of impressive church buildings as a means to make visible the power of the sacred in modern society, wealth and
refinement were connected to a higher type of piety. There
remained a large number of clergymen, like Alexander
Sutherland, the Secretary of Missions for the Methodist
Church, who adhered to the older view that poverty fos-

tered piety; for this reason they, like the Salvation Army, a movement created by advocates of old-style Methodism, critiqued industrialization because it created greater wealth and materialism that were thought to be so destructive of spiritual self-reflection. This group within Methodism was not as dismissive as Dewart was about the possibilities for working-class piety, but at the same time, they feared, as did S.D. Chown, a progressive minister at Carlton Street Church in downtown Toronto, that if the Methodist Church remained unreformed it would lose the labouring and poorer classes, who would be seduced by the temptations of urban culture or the radicalism of labour unions. The remedy for the supposed slippage in working-class church attendance in Chown's view was to create a host of church-run associations which could compete with secular voluntary organizations and to revise old-style evangelism in the direction of the social redemption of the city. While his concept of social redemption included a host of reforms in the areas of politics, housing, industrial relations, and temperance, he nevertheless believed, as old-time Methodists did, that poverty and social problems were the result of human sin and could only be reformed through the personal conversion of the masses.

The notion that the mainline Protestant churches, especially Methodism, had become middle-class institutions and were losing the allegiance of the urban masses was a construct of urban clergymen in this period of rapid industrialization and urbanization. Too many historians have agreed with them. Massive new stone churches actually had socially mixed congregations, and workers often contributed to their construction. Small-town churches may have been more dominated by the middle classes and thus alienated some working-class people from mainline Christianity, particularly where industrial conflict was already in existence. In bigger cities such as Montreal, the large number of churches meant that working-class people could exercise greater choice, and, indeed, they had a greater potential for worshipping in predominantly working-class congregations. With a church firmly under working-class management, social relations were much less conflictual. Interestingly, on the Canadian prairies, where there was relatively greater social homogeneity than in the cities, church commitment was so low that many churches failed to survive even during a period of massive immigration. Pointing to the spatial dispersal of population upon the prairies, George Emery has pointed to explanations for low church affiliation beyond class identity.

The story is actually one of increasing church attendance across all socio-economic groups and, in particular, a distinct rise in working-class participation in church life within the mainstream denominations. The period actually saw not secularization but a sacralization of urban space. In a period of increasing urbanization between 1882 and 1896, two church surveys by the *Toronto Globe* showed no decline in church attendance. In 1896 46 per cent of all Torontonians were in church on any given Sunday, a statistic which bears a close resemblance to the rate of church membership of Methodists for small-town New Brunswick in the early nineteenth century. However, if one disaggregates the Toronto figures for 1896 by denomination, 75 per cent of Methodists, 66 per cent of Presbyterians, and 31 per cent of Anglicans were attending morning and evening services on Sunday. Church affiliation was clearly on the rise, especially in the city; in the 1840s, whereas two-thirds of St John, New Brunswick, Methodists attended church, three-quarters of all Toronto Methodists were doing so by 1896. More tellingly, the 1901 national census revealed that only 0.5 per cent of the Canadian population did not identify with any religious organization! While the vast majority of Canadians identified with a church or religious group and most attended religious services, there was a gap between these figures and the continuing low levels of church membership in most denominations, which continued to hover around 20 per cent.

By the 1880s the leadership in the Methodist and Presbyterian churches was dominated by those ministers with a
decidedly urban sensibility. It is no accident, then, that the
arrival of this new leadership on the scene was accompa-
nied by a formidable centralization and bureaucratization
of both these denominations. Rather than a symptom of
spiritual weakening, this process of church consolidation
can be read as a symbol of the successful campaign of the
churches to bring a larger proportion of the population
under pastoral care. Those living through these immense
changes to the organization of religion saw it as a sign of advance and believed that only by reforming the church and
bringing it into line with modern culture would the church
survive as a dominant institution on the Canadian cultural
landscape. In the heyday of nationalist movements across
Canada, it was not unusual that the mainline Protestant
denominations would likewise aspire to be transcontinental
entities, but as the state expanded its frontier of white settlement westward onto the prairies, the church served as
one of the principal vanguard institutions that accelerated
this process of white domination; however, it was also constrained at the level of local church growth by the increased
centralization of all the financial and planning apparatus of
both the Presbyterian and Methodist churches in Toronto.
Certainly the pre-eminence of both Ontario and its capital
Toronto were reaffirmed within the realm of religion. Indeed, the waning financial power of Montreal was symbolized by the fact that the Presbyeterian church headquarters
was moved to Toronto in 1876, coinciding with the union
of the various Presbyterian bodies. The Methodist Church
followed suit in 1884, when the Primitive Methodists, the
Bible Christians, the New Connexion, the Methodist Epis-
copals, and the Wesleyans combined to form the single
largest Protestant denomination in Canada, though one
decisively ruled by Ontario. Moreover, Victoria College, the
first Methodist university, with a long association with the
small town of Cobourg, Ontario, moved to a downtown To-

ronto campus and thus affirmed the rise to prominence of a cadre of clergymen-professors, such as Samuel Nelles and Nathanael Burwash, dedicated to fostering a clericalization of their denomination around the idea of an intellectualized Christianity.

The increased centralization and formalization of mainline Protestantism included such vast organizational machinery as a central financial department, a national missionary board, a board of publications, a board of education that standardized Sunday school and youth work, and, by the early twentieth century, a board of evangelism and social service. Nonetheless, an intense sense of localism persisted, in particular among working-class urban congregations that exhibited high levels of self-determination. These became sites of resistance against innovation from the centre. Thus, alongside class and gender fissuring during the late Victorian era, conflict was just as fierce along the rural-urban, central, and local geographical fault lines. Indeed, much of the defence of old-time religion was just as much a contest over urban and rural power bases as it was a debate between conservative and liberal theological perspectives on the role that conversion, emotional piety, and revivalism would play in the life of the denomination.

The Methodists' and Presbyterians' move to consolidate (and, indeed, to seek union with the Anglican Church as well) flowed from a fear that Roman Catholicism, which had the largest church in Canada, would crush Protestantism with its weight of numbers. Just as compelling was finance. As we saw, clergymen, whose salaries depended upon the number of financially solvent church members, were most conscious of money matters and devoted a good deal of their time to this aspect of their profession. In small-town churches, tried and true systems of fund-raising such as pew rents and class meetings were retained, but in both the new and old urban churches, especially those that had recently constructed megalithic Gothic structures, the burden of church debt was often overwhelming, thus inducing the creation of new methods for solvency. Abolishing pew rents in favour of the more anonymous envelope system, whereby a family would commit to a certain weekly contribution, may have been a way to reduce class distinction and social hierarchy in a more democratic age, but the new system undercut the power of well-established local families to challenge the minister in the realm of doctrine. Pew rents had generally disappeared by the late nineteenth century in most urban churches and a few decades later in rural congregations. In many churches such as Knox Presbyterian in Hamilton, the envelope system actually produced less revenue because recalcitrant parshioners used the privacy of the new system of giving as means to shirk their obligations. Champions of the envelope system therefore had to look to older methods of fund-raising, such as weekly dues collected from class meetings and new fees from each of the specialized church associations, Sunday schools for all age cohorts, young people's societies, and so on. St James Methodist Church in Montreal epitomized the classic dilemma of a church plagued by debt. Although a very old and well-established congregation, its wealthy cadre of members were not reliable contributors. As a downtown church, St James sustained both a mission church in Griffintown and extensive charities while having to pay its increasingly professionalized ministerial staff, who demanded upwards of $2,700 for the first minister alone; and most downtown churches had at least one assistant pastor. The Epworth League for Methodist young people was created as a formidable fund-raising body and a group that could visit the sick and lead prayer meetings and thus save a church the cost of an assistant minister.

The proliferation of new church associations after 1880 was less reflective of increasing middle-class cultural dominance within Protestantism than a direct response to the greater financial demands upon each congregation. Even churches with a predominantly working-class constitutency, such as Hamilton's Barton Street Methodist, had a vibrant array of church organizations to attract new church members. Despite their working-class status, they gave liberally to their church, which they viewed as a fundamental element of their working-class identity. Giving in this instance was seen as a further expression of working-class control of their church edifice and not the emulation of middle-class values. Some of the wealthiest congregations, like Central Presbyterian in Hamilton, were in fact the most hidebound and consistently refused to embrace modern organizational structures. Even the most traditional churches, including those in rural areas, began to discover that congregations that relied solely on Sunday worship failed to attract new members, especially when, in a more mobile society, the family no longer functioned as the principal agency of Christian social reproduction.

Financial contribution was seen as a visible sign of one's salvation. When clergymen inveighed against materialism, they were not impugning the accumulation of wealth; they were criticizing those church members who used their earnings for secular concerns rather than for the enhancement of the sacred. With a heightened sense of competitiveness with secular organizations and with other religious denominations, many clergymen spoke of the need for an aggressive evangelism and used every opportunity in their clubs and publications to remind young and old alike of the interconnectedness of spiritual perfection and systematic giving. Indeed, the growing perception that relentless demands for financial support were diluting the spiritual purity of traditional Methodism drove many into the arms of the Salvation Army, the holiness movements, and Pentecostalism. Rev. W.H. Withrow, a leading figure in Methodism's educational enterprise, maintained that the key to Methodism's success lay in its ability to mould itself to various social conditions, 'to the cultured and wealthy city congregation, to the frontier hamlet, to the fishing village, the mining camp, the Indian mission, or the squalid purlieus of poverty.'[4] All mainstream Christian churches did find a way to both preserve and enhance the cross-class character of religious participation despite the massive urbanization and transformations and growing class antagonisms within the industrial workplace. Many historians have assumed a direct transposition of workplace values into the realm of spiritual life and have therefore concluded that it was 'natural' that a growing polarization between the classes defined the Victorian church. The unstated premise of this historiography is that religion and the working class are mutually hostile entities. It is automatically assumed that industrialization eradicated 'traditional' social mores and that in the mature state of industrialism the typical working-class response to religion was one of disconnection or alienation. In many respects, the centralized churches of the industrial age were much more responsive to the needs of the people than were their localized, frontier predecessors, largely because there was a greater recognition that workers, once they began to assert their collective interests, constituted a legitimate and enduring element of modern society.

Rather than seeing religion and the working class as mutually hostile, we suggest that church adherence may not have been simply a function of social class and that working-class people may have seen religious organizations as a counterbalance to the conflictual world of workplace politics. Certainly, for middle-class families religion could be a means to affirm their own understanding of their lived experience, but not by excluding the working classes. Methodism is often presented as a form of class control in which values such as frugality, temperance, self-control, and a commitment to upward social mobility, which together make up a sense of respectability, were imposed upon working-class people. Working-class people may not have wholly shared the values of the middle classes, but they did not dispute the notion of respectability itself. Thus the middle and working classes shared a sense of respectability which hinged upon certain notions of moral behaviour. Frederick Brigden, a skilled printer and engraver, believed that evangelical culture was integral to his everyday life experience and that there was just as natural a fit between his Protestantism and his self-identity as there was for an upwardly mobile, skilled artisan. The two-class model, which has often formed the theoretical basis of discussions about urban religion, needs much refinement. Although the workers who were regular church members may have chafed under middle-class leadership, they nevertheless continued to participate in all the religious ordinances of the church, apparently for reasons of spiritual solace, which may have been completely unconnected with either their level of wealth or their consciousness of class.

In fact, the vast majority of church adherents in late Victorian Toronto were either workers or members of the lower middle class, like small shopkeepers and clerks, and only 10 per cent of the church-going population were from the upper middle class, represented by manufacturers and professionals. Indeed, Frank Roberts, the young British working-class immigrant whom we met at the beginning of this chapter, first attended Sherbourne Street Methodist upon his arrival in Toronto because he was attracted by the forceful preaching of Rev. George Jackson, a fellow British immigrant who also ran a popular social for young people after the Sunday evening service, which appealed to Roberts's need for sociability and sense of belonging in the absence of his family. Eventually, Roberts shifted his allegiance to Metropolitan Methodist, with short interludes at various Presbyterian, Anglican, and even, on one occasion, St Michael's Roman Catholic Cathedral, where a pretty girl took him one Christmas. It is clear that Roberts's pattern of church affiliation was directly motivated by his desire to meet and court young women. There was a high correlation between the greater availability of churches and levels of church attendance, thus explaining the much higher levels of working-class church involvement in large urban centres like Hamilton, Montreal, and Toronto. With its characteristic proliferation and plurality of religious denominations, each with a wide range of religious services and organizations, the city effectively catered to the needs of various socio-economic groups, and in each neighbourhood there was a greater tendency for congregations to becoming homogeneous in terms of class. This, in a number of instances, led directly to greater independence for working-class people, especially those who saw themselves as upwardly mobile and expressed this in a firm desire to manage and control their own religious lives within the structure of the mainstream church.

Although many of the churches which ultimately became working-class began as missions created and funded by middle-class churches – such as St Luke's Anglican and Barton Street Methodist in Hamilton, Inspector Street Mission and Point St Charles Congregational in Montreal – their working-class membership quickly raised the funds to transform them into regular self-governing congregations. Thereafter, each place of worship became a distinct niche within the urban landscape for the assertion of working-class self-identity. In all of the above examples, despite the vicissitudes of working-class existence, the cyclical pattern of the industrial economy, and the high levels of geographical mobility, these congregations all evolved a highly articulated and active organizational life, one that created what was, in effect, a parallel universe catering to working-class educational, recreational, and employment needs. Barton Street Methodist, for example, contained a full panoply of Sunday schools for all age groups, young people's clubs, Bible classes, sports facilities such as a gymnasium and ice-skating rink, and an employment bureau where the minister, Rev. H.L. Livingston, adeptly used his contacts with the managers of industrial firms like Westinghouse to provide young immigrant British men with that essential passport to Canadian society, a paying job. In addition, these working-class congregations found the wherewithal to build large and expensive places of worship, housing upwards of several hundred people. For people whose economic status was often extremely precarious, the decision to make regular financial contributions that were necessary to the functioning of such large congregations clearly meant that organized religion was sufficiently important to them that they would divert a considerable portion of their personal incomes to sustaining the visible presence of the sacred in industrial society. Certainly there were the loafers, the irreligious, and those who did not attend church either because they lacked suitable clothing, had work patterns that conflicted with church services, or were burdened with child care and domestic responsibilities, but this does not detract from the overwhelming evidence that working-class people, as did those further up the socio-economic ladder, saw religion as crucial to their lives.

The most conspicuous transformation in the late Victorian churches lay not in their changing class composition but in the way in which the age structure was dramatically altered from a pattern of undifferentiated familial congregational worship to a more individualistic style of church adherence characterized by age-specific forms of religiosity. In the 1880s both the Protestant denominations and the Catholic Church recognized that familial socialization had never been an optimum method of producing committed Christians who in the Catholic tradition would regularly take the sacraments or in the Protestant churches become regular church members. Catholics proceeded to anchor religious socialization almost entirely within the state-funded school system. This process almost entirely displaced the family – most notably women, who hitherto were the principal educators of very young children. Within Protestantism, the Sunday school had existed since the early nineteenth century, but most of these were union Sunday schools, in which several denominations collaborated to educate children and adults in the basic tenets of Christianity and therefore did not socialize them into denominational loyalty. The large, newly built urban congregations, with their large burden of debt, worried that the next generation of

Methodists or Presbyterians might not become adequately socialized into their particular denominational cultures. So the greater integration of the Sunday school into the church apparatus was also a distinctly urban phenomenon. Most new rural churches on the prairies did not possess Sunday schools. Even in older settled areas in Ontario classes might only be held in the spring and summer months. The Sunday school also became popular because its annual procession of dutiful children of all ages was one of the best public advertisements for the benefits of Christianity. Perhaps to compete with ultramontane Catholicism's gaudy public events, such as the parade honouring Corpus Christi, all the Montreal Protestant churches gathered together on New Year's Day thousands of scholars who processed through the city with banners and flags upon which were written object lessons on missions for the deaf, blind, French, aboriginals, and Chinese. In return, the scholars received handouts of candy and in the churches collected approximately $5000. So popular had the idea of the Sunday school become by the late nineteenth century that even small and tradition-bound religious sects like the Quakers and the Disciples of Christ had adopted it to bring unchurched families into contact with religion. The Sunday school was created not as an exercise in social control but in order to better establish denominational boundaries, and in fact its greatest successes were with working-class families. The most popular organization in Barton Street Methodist in Hamilton, whose composition was 83 per cent working-class, was the Sunday school, which had more children enrolled than church members. Through systematic giving the Sunday school raised over $1500 annually and represented the whole life course with 400 infants in the cradle roll and 370 in adult classes.

By the 1880s, then, the Sunday school had become the centrepiece of the evangelical project of creating new converts. In 1862 only 3 per cent of Methodist members were converted through the Sunday school; this had risen to 19 per cent by 1894, and by the first decade of the twentieth century fully 60 per cent of all children had been socialized within the Sunday school system. By 1910 the Sunday school had become a complex, well-calibrated machine: each age group, beginning with the cradle roll for babies, had its own series of lessons, which were imbued with a very positive message of Christian love, and through each age transition a new publication was made available. *The Sunbeam* was geared for the youngest readers; *Pleasant Hours*, the best-selling Methodist magazine, to older children; and *Home and School* was aimed at older adolescents with its special emphasis upon temperance and missionary work. Like their Catholic counterparts, the separate schools, the Protestant Sunday schools emphasized denominational loyalty, the spiritual benefits of systematic giving, the evils of drink, and the training of young people to take civic leadership roles in both the nation and the British Empire. By the late nineteenth century the training of Sunday school teachers had become standardized and professionalized, and the Christian message contained within the teaching had shifted from rote learning to an emphasis upon storytelling. The stories presented a more humanized and accessible Christ, who was portrayed as the children's friend, where previous generations of schoolchildren would have been treated to moral admonitions on the theme of imminent death and God's punishment for sin.

The Sunday school was explicitly designed to circumvent the family, which was no longer seen to be the crucible for Christian nurture and conversion. Similar to Catholicism, the impact of the rise in importance of the Sunday school within the church apparatus was to reduce the independent control of the family in how they religiously socialized their children and to dramatically enhance the power of the clergy in shaping the religious values of the rising generation. A by-product of this transformation was an assault on the status of mothers within the family, who had hitherto been viewed as the primary moral guardians of both the family and by extension the society at large. This was an unprecedented institutional intervention into the conceptualization and organization of the family hierarchy, for while religiously inspired philanthropic bodies such as the St Vincent de Paul Society within Catholicism or the various Protestant Ladies' Homes for orphans and the elderly had sought to control the families of the poor, the regulatory strategy adopted by the Sunday school was far more pervasive because its goal was to encompass all families irrespective of wealth. Many traditionalists such as the Presbyterian Rev. D.H. MacVicar articulated a dissenting discourse which exalted the family circle as the religious and moral centre of the church and nation. The traditional notion that there was a natural hierarchy in which religious influence flowed from God, to the clergymen, to the head of household, and finally to children was disrupted in this period by the creation first of Sunday schools and second of youth societies, which asserted that the most important religious relationships were the horizontal ones between individuals within specific age groups. In this respect, the mainline Christian churches, far from being defenders of conservative values, were in fact among the principal subverters of family authority prior to the emergence of the cultural revolution of the 1960s and the expansion of the welfare state.

The central concern of both the Sunday school promoters and those who advocated the creation of bodies such as the Epworth League within Methodism, the Brotherhoods in the Presbyterian Church, and the Baptist Young People's Union was how to produce committed and dues-paying church members at an even earlier age. In the 1880s, clergymen frowned on the extremely popular Christian Endeavour Society and the YMCA, both of which likewise encouraged the participation of youth in church life because they were interdenominational organizations that did not foster loyalty to a particular church. The Catholic Church had a long tradition of associational life, but devotional societies such as St Vincent de Paul that were aimed primarily at men had been singularly unsuccessful in enrolling large numbers of young men. Ethnic societies such as the Ancient Order of Hibernians, not directly under the control of the clergy, were more popular in enlisting male support and were therefore viewed with scepticism by church authorities. It was only after the beginning of the twentieth century that male devotional societies such as the Holy Name Society, which was dedicated to organizing the recreational life of Catholic boys and encouraging men to visit the sick and impoverished, became a significant feature of the church; in some Toronto parishes it was so popular that 50 per cent of men were involved with the society's work of constructing the ideal of Catholic citizenship.

The Protestant interdenominational Young Men's Christian Association (YMCA) was not alone in attracting youth; dynamic youth organizations within individual Protestant denominations performed a similar function. The YMCA was nonetheless a formidable rival for while one out of every seventeen Canadian boys belonged to it at the time of the First World War, less than one-third ever became actual church members. While these institutions taught moral precepts, particularly to underprivileged youth, they were dominated by a non-doctrinal muscular Christianity that emphasized physical action and the development of the body at the expense of the kind of spiritual introspection so essential to a conversion experience.

Like the YMCAs, the Methodist Epworth Leagues were intended to integrate youth into the church polity. Evening prayer meetings that were previously open to all ages were transformed into age-specific League meetings devoted to missionary, temperance, and literary themes with one evening a month set aside specifically for youth sociability. In many respects the Epworth League in tandem with the Sunday school replaced the class meeting as the central soul-saving mechanism within Methodism. At the Epworth prayer meeting young people were no longer scrutinized by the elders but by their peers. There was a great deal of resistance to the introduction of the Epworth League because, quite rightly, its opponents recognized that it undermined the centrality of the class meeting, which was so evocative of the uniqueness of Methodism's religious experience. At the zenith of the Epworth League's popularity in 1906 there occurred a mass resignation of class leaders at Sherbourne Street Methodist, one of the first congregations to experiment with the youth after-service social under Rev. George Jackson. Furthermore, many of the League's opponents (and most present-day historians) saw it as destructive of evangelism. Although it is true that the League may have interfered with the working of the class meeting, it was part of a general campaign, which included the Sunday school, to transform the conversion experience from a primarily adult experience to one for children and youth. There had always existed several competing approaches to spiritual awakening beyond periodic revival campaigns. In the early nineteenth century Methodism possessed the class meeting, local protracted meetings, the Quarterly meeting, as well as private visiting and personal contact between family and friends, all of which were seen as sites for conversion. By the late nineteenth century these sites had been expanded further to include the Sunday school, the Epworth League, and the Junior Epworth League, but what was new was that these focused primarily upon the youngest age cohort within the church. Evangelicalism had not declined; rather, the sacred venues where conversion could occur had multiplied and had become more structured around age cohorts than around the traditional notion of the intermingling of age groups in the class meeting or Sunday worship. Episodic mass revivals continued to occur, for example those of the Crossley and Hunter evangelistic team, which visited Toronto in 1893. In terms of raising the public profile of religion within the city as a whole, revivals were immensely successful; however, as a record of the subsequent church affiliation of the converts indicates, few ended up joining Metropolitan Methodist, which had sponsored the revival, and indeed, those who were listed in connection with the church had already been committed themselves prior to the revival.

The idea that true 'manhood' rested upon loyalty to a particular denomination and that this loyalty manifested itself in church membership and systematic giving was a theme returned to again and again in Epworth League publications. Therefore, the overriding preoccupation of the new cadre of clerical and lay leaders who promoted youth organizations within Methodism and Presbyterianism was how to counteract the feminization of the church, where membership and the class and prayer meetings seemed dominated by women. For example, in Methodism class meetings were 80 per cent female in the 1870s and 68 per cent of church members were women. In London, Ontario, in 1913 two-thirds of those attending morning service were women, as were just over half of those at evening service. More disturbing, one of the most powerful women's organizations, the Ladies' Aid, came into continual conflict with the minister because they did not believe that their spectacular fund-raising successes should merely serve the agenda of the clergy and in many cases preferred allocating their funds to overseas missions. As a means to counteract the power of laywomen within the Methodist Church, the Epworth League was introduced with the specific aim of encouraging young men to become lay activists within the congregation and to identify personally with their minister. By the 1890s local men's meetings had become the creatures of the clergy. Their emphasis upon assisting the minister in his pastoral duties in visiting the sick, helping the poor, and supplying the financial backing and personnel for mission work was but a skilful ploy to push women out of those spheres in which they had been so powerful. For all the rhetoric that exalted pious women as the mainstay of religion, there was a groundswell of opposition to the power of women within the Protestant denominations. As Rev. W.H. Hincks stated in 1900: 'The mother alone cannot bring her boy to a virility, as masculinity, a manhood of Christian life and thought unless she has her husband by her side.'[5] Just as women's activity in the public sphere was expanding during this period – insofar as they were instrumental in founding a string of settlement houses, redemptive homes for prostitutes and unmarried mothers, and orphans' asylums – strategies were being developed within the church proper to relegate women to the margins and place them under the firm control of the male clergy. And while both men and women joined the Epworth Leagues, the discourse of the organization was wholly tailored to men, and indeed the emphasis that it placed upon intellectual piety and the evangelism of social action was a none-too-veiled critique of the heartfelt religion of women. Henceforth women were identified with the outmoded old-time Methodism of emotion and inward-looking spirituality and men were seen as the worldly ambassadors of modernity and progressive forces within religion.

In the late nineteenth century the churches became one of the leading institutions in shaping notions of masculinity and femininity. But this gender polarity was not divided between the private family and the public sphere, for in these decades youth organizations constantly insisted that men had the key domestic role as religious educators for their boys. The rhetoric about the waning influence of the family was in fact a critique of the female-dominated family. Moreover, it was a critique of men who had become too engrossed in notions of selfhood, which focused merely upon individual self-improvement and personal choice. To this end, the Epworth League became a central mechanism for securing men for the church by ensuring that they meet, court, and marry women all within a particular denomination. Recognizing that unmarried men were the least likely to either attend church or become church members, the Epworth Leagues were fashioned into organizations adapted to patterns of heterosexual sociability that now exemplified urban youth. The key to counteracting the clergyman's nightmare of the rising tide of mixed marriages was the weeknight and Sunday evening service youth social, where the friendships of both men and women were deployed to attract mobile immigrant youth such as Frank Roberts into the precincts of the church. When we first met Frank Roberts, upwardly mobile clerk and son of an English Methodist minister, he was visiting various churches on Sunday but was just as easily seduced into the male camaraderie of the pool hall, tempted by prostitutes, and given to spending much of his time unproductively wandering the streets of Toronto in idle conversation with acquaintances. Prompted by a young woman to join the Epworth League, Roberts quickly became socialized into a culture of active Christianity, which then led him to becoming a church member through the church choir, where male and female friends were eventually instrumental in converting him. Having absorbed the ideal of Christian manliness articulated in the various youth societies within Methodism, Roberts began to apply himself to his studies, eschewed theatre-going, the pool hall, smoking, and drinking, and we last see him spending his evenings in morally uplifting leisure activities, singing hymns around the piano with the new male and female boarders at his new Christian abode. In Roberts's case the new Methodist youth organizations offered an effective substitute family of peer associations which counteracted the anomie of city life and functioned as critical mechanisms for the new 'masculine' evangelism.

Earlier in the nineteenth century a minister had to prepare his Sunday sermon, participate in weekday prayer meetings, visit the sick, attend to the pastoral care of his congregation, and give due attention to the financial health of the local church. By the late nineteenth century the local clergyman was responsible for overseeing a now complex bureaucracy and coordinating a great number of lay activists. He participated at an array of board meetings, special services, and social fund-raisers. And, in this new age of expertise, he had to acquire a high standard of education, with a mastery of not only theological principles but also the historical and linguistic bases of the Bible in order to better respond to queries and doubts from an increasingly well-educated laity. Faced with the new urban reality of competing secular societies and entertainments, the ideal clergyman had sufficiently honed rhetorical skills to attract a crowd and to comment authoritatively upon both the secular and religious events of the day.

The Methodist Church in 1883 had instituted a standard that compelled all new ministers to attend college for a minimum of two years, and by the end of the century, a clergyman who had ambitions of promotion had to have an undergraduate degree prior to entering the ministry. The older career path by which an inspired and enthusiastic Christian convert could become a class leader, lay preacher, and, after a short reading course, a probationer was gradually discarded; however, in 1900 only 50 per cent of the Methodist clergy had college training. Older apprenticeship patterns persisted in newly settled areas where clergy were in short supply, such as on the prairies, where it was still possible for an uneducated immigrant lad, like Albert Aldridge, to be hired by James Woodsworth, the superintendent of missions, as a Methodist preacher while working as an unskilled labourer on the Canadian Pacific Railway. However, Aldridge eventually had to acquire a college degree if he wished to keep his job. With their long-standing traditions of having a learned clergy, the Presbyterian and Anglican churches were less affected by the increasing literary requirement of the profession, but Methodists and Baptists (who had the Woodstock Literary Institute and by 1887 McMaster University) experienced a radical cultural divide within their denominations over the issue of an educated clergy. Greater professionalization of the clergy did not, however, automatically translate into a middle-class clergy, for there were many ministers within Methodism such as the unskilled worker Albert Aldridge, A.E. Smith, the son of a janitor, and Rev. Oliver Darwin, a blacksmith from Yorkshire; but the intention behind the new educational standards was to enhance the status of the profession and thereby make the church more publicly authoritative. This new emphasis on intellectual culture within Methodism meant that Victoria College came under considerable criticism from rural parishes, and, indeed, by the 1920s the clergy had become a largely urban class, as few recruits were drawn from rural areas. This was in contrast with Quebec Catholicism, where both the church hierarchy and parish priests continued to be staffed by sons of farmers.

In recently created missions such as those in western Canada, the church was not an attractive career because of the poverty of congregations. However, even a prominent urban Presbyterian minister like Rev. Dr John Proudfoot of London, Ontario, discovered to his chagrin that his immense scholarly attainments and his high public profile as secretary of the denomination's home mission work did not protect him from the kind of lay control which so dominated church life earlier in the century. His London congregation tired of his neglect because he spent much of his week teaching at Knox College in Toronto and specifically resented his unwillingness to take an active part in initiating new youth associations. In 1889 they fired him. Ministers were still accountable to their congregations, although not to the extent as in previous decades when the clergyman was a direct financial client of their pew holders. In response, clergymen sponsored new organizations, like the Epworth League, over which they had ultimate control. Nevertheless, in urban areas, where some clergymen were being paid upwards of $2,500 a year and where sermons were regularly reported in the secular press, the intellectual attainments of the clergy were particularly scrutinized. Thus clergymen faced even greater pressures to assume the mantle of intellectual leadership within the society at large.

Within Catholicism priests fared better than their Protestant counterparts because their authority resided in control of the sacramental mysteries of ritual in which the priest was the ambassador of God, in his office uniting heaven and earth. In his role he could exact performances of submission, as did Father Charles Bellemare in 1891, when he forced a young man to finally pay his tithe. The fact that by the 1870s Quebec priests typically had attended the expanded network of *collèges classiques* with a further stint at the seminary for specific theological training widened the gap between the cultural attainments of the clergy and their people. In English Canada the cultural rift between clergy and people was further accentuated by the Canadianization of what had been prior to the 1890s a largely Irish church. After that point, English-speaking Catholics in Toronto began to submerge ties to Ireland and embraced many of the values of Canadian society. However, with the arrival of large numbers of European immigrants in this period, together with the growing awareness of the unprecedented rate of intermarriage between Catholics and Protestants, church leaders wished to bring the archdiocese into more rigid conformity with canon law, especially under Archbishop Dennis O'Connor, who sought to retrench Catholicism along more Roman lines. The Irish-Canadian element in the church responded with vigour to what they thought of as an assault upon their power within the diocese.

This group was most vociferous in seeking to Canadianize and anglicize those continental European immigrants from Italy, Poland, and Ukraine who by 1921 made up 20 per cent of Catholics in the Toronto archdiocese. Frustrated with the reluctance of adult immigrants to become assimilated and to join Canadian-style church associations or attend mass regularly, priests deemed them irreligious. The Protestant churches had a similar attitude to immigrants; and despite the fact that many downtown Toronto churches provided special outreach for immigrants with mother's meetings, English classes, reading rooms, and gymnasia, these failed to lead to sucessful evangelism. As Enrico Cumbo has argued, the Toronto Catholic archdiocese made little attempt to accommodate Italian Catholic sensibilities and only took action because of Protestant competition for Italian souls. For example, the first Italian parish was built in 1908 just two years after a second Methodist Italian mission was launched. Hamilton, with an equally large population of Italian male workers, had an Italian priest by 1908 and built a parish church only in 1912. Because the Canadian Catholic clergy viewed Italian men in particular as mere peasants and pagans, relations between the church and the immigrant Catholic community remained extremely strained until the 1940s. The clergy failed to understand that Italians were not irreligious but merely had a different pattern of devotion from the western European norm. Italian men did not see themselves as any less faithful for failing to attend mass, which they generally saw as the duty of women, and they continued to see the church as the locus of important rituals, especially those centred around the village patron saint. With the increase of familial immigration following the First World War women began to participate more fully in New World church practices, but they attended mass and other church sacraments not merely to conform to priestly construction of religiosity but also to further their own style of religious practice – attending church to light candles for the dead and obtain holy water for their own family shrines, which they continued to view as more central to their faith than the formal religion of the parish church. Similar conflicts befell the Ukrainian community in western Canada, but there relations were exacerbated by the fact that the Canadian Catholic Church did not allow the Eastern rite traditions. Ukrainian Catholicism was based upon a ritual with considerable ceremonial and linguistic differences from the Latin rite that gave a semblance of unity to western, central, and southern European Catholics; most notably, Ukrainian Catholic priests were allowed to marry. The resistance of Canadian Catholic authorities ensured that in the first two decades of the twentieth century, Ukrainian Catholics were not able to recruit priests from their homeland. Like the Italians, the Ukrainians resisted attempts by the Catholic Church to Latinize their religious culture. Protestant churches, especially the Presbyterians, thus had a significant opportunity to make inroads among them. For example the Presbyterians funded an Independent Greek Church in 1903 and provided training for Ukrainian clergy at Manitoba College. However, these efforts led not to assimilation but to the further promotion of ethnic particularism and nationalism.

Unlike Catholicism where the authority of the priest was considered by and large sacrosanct, that of the newly professionalized Protestant ministry was open to question because it rested upon the terrain of biblical interpretation. By the late nineteenth century, this involved the relationship between Christianity and the Darwinian doctrine of evolution. Most Methodist and Presbyterian clergymen would have agreed with Nathanael Burwash's contention that both the Bible and nature were the creation of 'one perfect God.' Protestant clergymen by and large were quite open to the idea of evolution because its emphasis on progress and improvement converged with the optimistic evangelicalism to which they subscribed.[6] A much greater threat to both belief and the traditional authority of the minister were the new German methods of analyzing the Bible that gave priority to rational intelligence over the experience of faith. Between 1850 and 1880 both the Methodist and Presbyterian churches had developed an accommodation between the view that the Bible was the inspired word of God and the idea set forth by biblical criticism – the historical study of the Bible – that scripture was open to human interpretation. Conservatives preferred the subordination of reason to biblical revelation and sought to limit the application of biblical criticism. To avoid an irrevocable split, Methodist leaders like Samuel Nelles and Nathanael Burwash of Victoria College agreed to confine the historical and critical study of the Bible to college classrooms so that these new ideas would not destabilize the church by making their way into the pulpit and introduced them surreptitiously into the new Epworth League, where adolescent boys would become conversant in the new historical study of the Bible. For the most part, the accommodation between modernizers and conservatives held until the first decade of the twentieth century. From the perspective of the people in the pews, most sermons remained traditional in their format and doctrinal in emphasis, apart from the few special sermons or lectures that stressed social reform issues. The minister of Knox Presbyterian Church in Hamilton was typical of most clergymen of the day. Rev. Mungo Fraser was a modernist, insofar as he abolished pew rents and established male youth groups to study the new notions of biblical criticism, but his sermons were derived directly from biblical verses and it was only on 'extraordinary occasions that he referred in the pulpit to current events or local topics.'[7]

By 1905 Rev. William Hincks observed that there had been a decline in the belief in the supernatural, which he attributed to biblical criticism, the theory of evolution, and the emphasis in the church upon social righteousness at the expense of soul saving. This, generally speaking, was the perspective of the conservative elements within Methodism who believed that the learned discourse of the modernists was eroding the uniqueness of Methodism, notably its emphasis on emotive, soul-saving evangelical sermons. Although Methodism had never been a religion merely of emotion or feeling, but had always balanced rational inquiry with the moving of the spirit, in this period a conservative backlash against those who had made an accommodation with modern thought – biblical criticism and Darwinistic evolutionary ideas – reinvented Methodism tradition as exclusively the domain of the heart and emotions: emotional conversionism was now promulgated as the classical manifestation of Methodist piety. By 1909, one year before the General Conference officially endorsed the teaching of biblical criticism in the various church colleges (Victoria College in Toronto, Mount Allison in New Brunswick, Wesleyan College in Montreal, and Wesley College in

Winnipeg), conservatives within the church had become better organized and resisted further incursions of intellectual Christianity. They worried that the centrality of college learning for clergymen had removed them from the realm of popular religion and that the new theology was placing less emphasis on sin and that this would ultimately weaken evangelistic impulse. The heavy use of church publications rather than the oral culture of the Sunday sermon and the weekday participatory prayer meeting was also criticized as appealing too narrowly to the urban middle classes.

There was some validity to the conservative complaint that this intellectualized piety, aimed at attracting men into the church, was driving away those who valued the more traditional, simple message of salvation, and forcing many into the arms of new sectarian forms of Protestantism such as the various holiness movements and the Salvation Army. Centred on the doctrine of 'entire sanctification,' holiness was a tendency that affected a number of Protestant denominations in the late nineteenth century but caused particular difficulties for Methodism. In contrast to mainstream Methodists, who viewed sanctification as the result of a long process of prayer, religious commitment, and moral living *after* the experience of conversion, holiness preachers insisted that converts could instantaneously achieve a state of perfection. By the late 1880s, fissures appeared in the Methodist Church centred around the figure of Rev. Ralph Horner, whose forceful preaching garnered him the high-profile position of conference evangelist, but whose adoption of holiness teachings and his critique of the 'materialism' of the denomination aroused the suspicion of Methodist leaders. It has been argued that the Salvation Army had significant proportions of working-class men and women who saw it as a site for launching a critique of the materialism of the mainstream churches. It is open to question whether this amounted to an oppositional working-class consciousness or merely represented a reaction against modernity, a view shared by a range of socio-economic groups within Protestantism, who merely preferred a more enthusiastic and less formalized style of religious practice. The creation of the Salvation Army and of various holiness and Pentecostal movements was similar to the schisms within Methodism of earlier decades, and their social profile of skilled workers and small farmers generally reflected the social composition of Methodism itself. Those who joined these new movements desired above all else to rediscover the purer, more evangelical religion which had characterized old-time Methodism and were in search of a smaller, more localized religious community that had not become enmeshed in worldly considerations of financial encumbrances, church building, and clerical professionalization. Similarly, the branch of the holiness movement led by Ralph Horner, an ex-Methodist evangelist, drew all its members from farms and small towns, like the Salvation Army drawing upon the lower middling and artisanal groups for its strength. Holiness adhered to many of the conventions of the old-style Methodist discipline, namely the wearing of plain dress, a simple evangelistic message, and a commitment to other-worldliness, and thus became a defence of the pre-industrial island community and a countercultural alternative to the compromise with modernity in the urban church. Above all, holiness movements, in extolling the benefits of experiential religion over the intellectualized piety of the mainstream denominations, offered a critique of the new professional ethos of the clergy. What all these evangelical sects had in common was a reliance upon lay preachers, both male and female, who had no formal education and relied exclusively upon their personal religious experience to claim authority to speak and lead a congregation.

Aimee Semple McPherson, the celebrated Pentecostal revivalist, exemplified this diffuse culture of popular evangelicalism whereby one could shift freely between denominational identities. In becoming attracted to the Salvation Army in her small-town setting of Ingersoll, Ontario,

McPherson, whose parents were farmers, was less interested
in either the class complexion of this sect or its raucous style
of street preaching, than in its standard Wesleyan emphasis
on sin, the new birth, and Christian perfection. Women
were particularly drawn to the Salvation Army because it offered significant opportunities for preaching and religious
leadership that was denied them in the mainline denominations, which were increasingly catering their intellectualized religious message to a male audience. Moreover, the
Army's emphasis upon popular hymns and gospel music
appealed greatly to single young people, especially those
in rural areas and small towns, where mainline churches
lacked the density of organizational life characteristic of
downtown congregations, which were better able to attract
mobile youth like Frank Roberts. That those who joined
the Salvation Army were protesting against the perceived
loss of zeal within Methodism and against the increased
financial machinery of the modern church is illustrated by
the Rev. P.W. Philpott. Known as the 'blacksmith preacher,'
Philpott attained high rank within the Salvation Army but
resigned in 1892 to found the independent Christian Workers Church because the Army was too given, in his view,
to ecclesiastical control, which, in turn, diminished the
local self-government of both the preacher and his largely
working-class congregation. Philpott defined his movement
as one of the common people, whose religion of salvation
placed a priority upon the unadulterated Bible, which individuals could interpret for themselves and was not reducible
to a socio-economic critique of capitalism even though he
believed that his simple gospel message would speak to the
'worker that need not be ashamed.'[8] Like the mainstream
churches that arose in working-class neighbourhoods, Philpott's worker's church and the Salvation Army created an
other-worldly sphere far removed from the slipstream of
capitalism, in which ordinary people could exert control
over their spiritual lives even while they remained subordi-
nated by capitalist domination outside them.

No irrevocable gulf occurred in the late nineteenth century between the consolidated mainline Protestant denominations and a number of popular religious movements that critiqued their materialism and formalism. The sporadic mass revival campaigns that punctuated religious life, both in urban and rural areas, constituted an enormous public outreach program to the unchurched, especially young men with no apparent religious affiliation. With their modern advertising techniques and parades with banners such as those featured in Dr Ruben Torrey's 1906 campaign in Toronto and Calgary which read 'Get Right with God,' urban mass revivals drew public attention to the presence of religion in Canadian society, as all the revivals were extensively reported in the secular newspapers. During the 1885 visit of the American evangelist Dwight Moody to Toronto it was estimated that 25,000 people or half the city came out to hear his message of personal conversion. Yet, as in the past, these revival events mostly awakened backsliders who were already interested in religion. Revivals were nonetheless instrumental in extending the moral reform agenda of the churches: as a result of the Crossley and Hunter revival in Souris, Manitoba, it was said that 60 per cent of the bar trade dried up. In part, official church support for such mass events represented a compromise with the more conservative defenders of the old-style evangelism and were tolerated because they were thought to appeal more strongly to working-class men and youth largely because many of the campaigns highlighted moral causes such as temperance. For example, in the 1893 revival in Thorold, Ontario, led by the popular team of Crossley and Hunter, two-thirds of the male converts were working-class, but most of these did not join churches following their conversion. Indeed, from the evidence of both local working-class churches such as Barton Street Methodist in Hamilton and the working-class neighbourhoods of north-end Winnipeg, the simple truths of sin and salvation that characterized traditional evangelism seemed to resonate with ordinary people, who were likewise attracted by the fact that revivals often did not expect monetary contributions.

Mainline church leaders, such as Samuel Nelles, were generally wary of mass revivalism because they stood outside the culture of clerical professionalization and control that they were so assiduously attempting to foster. Nelles contrasted 'sensible religion' of the ordinary means of grace in the weekly services to that unrestrained emotionalism and unscriptural preaching of the mass meeting, a view which merely reflected the fact that two-thirds of all Methodists were Wesleyans, who had always censured the emotionalism exemplified by American revivalism. More troublingly, not only did the revivals' emphasis upon the unmediated encounter between the individual and God deprive the local clergy of their role in bringing about salvation, but the non-denominational character of these mass revivals was viewed by the clergy as a means to undermine denominational loyalty. Since the main underlying purpose of evangelical outreach was to create committed and stable church members, the Methodist and Presbyterian churches preferred to rely on in-house evangelism, most of which occurred within the Sunday school and the various youth organizations.

Mainstream churches were much more committed to the city mission work in the slums of large metropolitan centres such as Montreal, Toronto, and Winnipeg because their emphasis on the religious education of children often led to the creation of new congregations. Influenced by movements among both the Presbyterian and Methodist denominations in Glasgow and London to regenerate the slum populations, these city missions were specifically aimed at working-class and immigrant families; through their child-care programs, mothers' meetings, summer camp work, and medical services they attempted to instruct the unredeemed 'offscourings of society' in the cultural values of the respectable middle and working classes. What is novel is that the late nineteenth-century urban missions formulated a new attitude to the poor and contributed to diffusing a new view of poverty in the wider Canadian society. In the early nineteenth century, church charity did not attach a moral stigma to the poor, as those relieved were, in most cases, church members who already had standing in the local community. By the 1880s, however, the urban missions specifically aimed their charity at the unchurched and were responsible for making the general public aware of a growing differentiation between 'poverty,' which was viewed as an attribute of the respectable, church-going working classes, and 'pauperism,' a moral failure ascribed to immigrants and those poor who remained outside the churches and therefore lacked the values of thrift, punctuality, and hygiene. Urban mission workers constructed the 'paupers' as objects of an intrusive moral scrutiny and regulation. Although these new notions of respectability were crucial to establishing an overt distinction between middle- and working-class people, they were also critical to reinforcing divisions within the working class itself. The poor were not mere passive objects of these middle-class control strategies, however, for working-class and immigrant families utilized the social services such as daycare programs for their own ends but consistently refused to become religious converts.

In part this was because the Canadianization and conversion efforts of urban missionaries were often at cross-purposes: at the All People's Mission in downtown Winnipeg, making Methodists was a low priority compared with the assimilationist agenda of remaking Polish immigrants into good Canadians. J.S. Woodsworth, a prominent Methodist clergyman and social activist, who headed the Mission, was much more interested in the assimilationist purposes of using social services to teach 'the Gospel of Canadian citizenship,' while some of his associates – including the deaconesses, women who had a professional training in evangelism and social assistance, and the student mission workers – were far more committed to a traditional evangelistic message, which sought to 'preach salvation' in order to convert the 'foreigners.' Just as with the Italians in

Toronto, the east European immigrants of Winnipeg had a strong sense of their own religious faith, and the only lasting converts to the All People's Mission occurred among British immigrants, many of whom had already been Methodists back home. At Montreal's All People's Mission, there was outright hostility to their combined assimilationist and conversionist agenda. Idealistic accounts by progressive ministers like J.A. Macdonald, the editor of the *Globe*, portrayed the settlement house and city mission as emblematic of social harmony and class reconciliation, when in fact these institutions were outposts of aggressive evangelism for both spiritual and national conversion. Typical of the integrationist impulse behind this view of Christian citizenship was the extremely popular novel *The Foreigner*, written in 1909 by the Presbyterian minister C.W. Gordon (under the pen name Ralph Connor). This novel told the story of how a Russian immigrant, Kalman Kalmar, one of the so-called 'undigested foreign mass,' was successfully converted by a medical missionary and thus absorbed into the body politic. Christianization was thus the principal means of Canadianization.

Although little studied by historians, the medical missions became one of the central mechanisms of hospital building on the prairies. Like other missions, these were usually headed and staffed by women and were frequently more effective in integrating immigrant and aboriginal peoples into a connection with the church. Indeed, the prominence of women within the whole structure of mission work meant that they were the primary agents of social discipline in this period. Where the minister sought to redeem through the spoken or written word within the church proper, missionary women relied on more intrusive disciplinary methods. Where in a previous generation such strict regulatory approaches would have been normative for all church members, now they were reserved for the marginal and the morally deviant in society. Fallen women and prostitutes were confined in redemptive homes, the intemperate in asylums; paupers were visited in their homes, immigrants were regulated within the mission, and aboriginal children were incarcerated in residential schools. Although the urban space provided greater levels of choice and voluntarism for the respectable members of the working and middle classes, redemption was a far less voluntary act for those considered marginal by reasons of ethnicity, economic behaviour, or moral failure. As the moral guardians of the home, activist religious women – and by association the church – were able to assert an expertise in the treatment of moral deliquency and social problems that conferred greater claims for religion in the sphere of the 'social' public.

Those clergymen and laypeople who espoused the new evangelism or 'social' Christianity believed that the road to salvation did not merely end in a conversion experience but involved a life of Christian service. This appealed to those like the reformer and Presbyterian activist Agnes Maule Machar, who in her dislike for the elitism of theological debate sought out a form of religion that was experiential and nondogmatic. For this reason she not only liked the evangelical truths of the Salvation Army, but she also became one of the principal female architects of a new outlook in religion which connected evangelism, social reform, and national progress. This equation, however, was accomplished earliest in large cities. For example, at the third-largest Presbyterian church in Canada, Knox Church of Hamilton, an old-style evangelical preacher was replaced in 1903 by Rev. E.A. Henry, who was interested in issues of temperance, Sunday observance, and methods to promote industrial peace. Imbued with the tenets of the new social evangelism, Henry believed that he had the authority to pronounce on current topics: 'My aim is to make the pulpit in touch with every department of a man's life. The pulpit should be in line with the times. I believe in practical, progressive, aggressive religion ... Anything that is of concern to the people, should also be a concern to the church. I never smoked, neither danced. These matters may be left to a person's own conscience.'9 In eschewing the moral strictures of an earlier piety, this Presbyterian clergyman hoped to fashion a more up-to-date kind of religion that emphasized social topics in an intellectual rather than merely heartfelt way in order to make the churches more appealing to men. In constructing a new notion of Christian citizenship in which the churches were considered the keystone of national righteousness and progress, evangelism was no longer simply the individual's route to heaven, but the masculine terrain of civic redemption.

Social Christianity conferred religious meaning on movements of social and political reform but it did so without stripping evangelicalism of its central emphasis upon individual sin and salvation. Far from being an expression of the breakdown of evangelical identity among Methodists and Presbyterians in the face of new industrial and social challenges, the new social evangelism was an optimistic and self-conscious critique of industrial society and replaced the amoral individualistic liberalism of Thomas Malthus, Herbert Spencer, and John Stuart Mill with the social ethics of Jesus. The Catholic Church espoused a similar view, when in 1913 Archbishop Neil McNeil of Toronto articulated a Christian sociology: 'There is now running a strong reaction against industrial individualism. Not liberty, but co-operation is the watchword of today. Poverty has to be studied in its causes as well as in its effect. Today Christian charity grapples with the economic and social ills that underlie poverty, and is, therefore, largely social in its operations.'10 This did not mean that the redemption of the social was prior to the salvation of the individual. In the United States, such a social gospel did exist, but in Canada there was perhaps only a handful of real social gospellers, such as Salem Bland, a professor of New Testament at Wesley College, Winnipeg, and J.S. Woodsworth, who left the ministry in 1913 to head the Canadian Welfare Council and who truly believed that the reform of the social must precede individual conversion. The vast majority of Methodist and Presbyterian clergymen would have adhered to the view enunciated by G.M. Grant in the 1880s that the only true social reconstruction lay not in the application of human sciences to the problems of industrialization but in a revival of religion; by this he meant the conversion of individuals. In the view of E.H. Dewart, longtime editor of *The Christian Guardian*, saving the city or the nation began with the spiritual reformation of the individual and all institutional power in the civic realm had its source in the power of individual morality. 'The churches,' concluded Dewart, 'as the organ of that power, have much more to do with the reformation of society than has science or legislation.'[11] The solution for the collapse of social harmony occasioned by the conflict of capital and labour was to be found not in secular trade unionism but in the recognition of a sense of universal brotherhood that was informed by the social ethics brought about by establishing the Kingdom of God on earth, which in the final analysis could only be accomplished by the salvation agency of the churches.

Many modernists in the mainline Protestant denominations remained wedded to the efficacy of individual redemption as the basis of social reform and laced their recommendations with the rhetoric of personal moralism. Some ministers, like the Methodist Rev. C.S. Eby, leaned further towards a form of Christian socialism and campaigned for shorter working hours, trade unionism, and the right to strike. In Toronto Archbishop Lynch went so far as to endorse the Knights of Labour in the 1880s. His Quebec counterparts condemned such radical movements of working-class consciousness and sought in light of papal teachings, such as the 1891 encyclical *Rerum Novarum*, to sponsor Catholic trade unions that would compel labour leaders to accommodate their platform to Catholic doctrines. Most ministers did not call for any decisive structural challenge to capitalism and merely relied upon rather anodyne prescriptions for social change based upon Christian social ethics.

As inoffensive as the concept of the Kingdom of God on earth might appear to present-day eyes, it created considerable furore within the Methodist and Presbyterian churches, where the advocates of social Christianity remained the minority until 1910. Conservatives within Protestantism regarded it as a wholesale negation of one of the 'unique' characteristics of Methodism, namely, conversion; the introduction of social reform topics into the rituals of Protestant worship must have driven many into the arms of the Salvation Army. Indeed, it appears from local studies that the emotional orthodox religion was deemed sufficient for working-class people and that social Christianity exerted a much greater appeal to middle-class congregations. It must have come as a shock to those habituated to the simple gospel message to be told that social service work was as important as inward-looking piety as the means of religious revival and prompted many to conclude that Christian social service was placing 'the brotherhood of man' ahead of the personal contact of the soul with the 'fatherhood of God.'

In fact, social evangelism spread more easily through organizations such as those devoted to youth, which had a much lower profile within the denomination. The Epworth League in particular became the central vehicle by which the newer notions of social Christianity entered the Methodist church. Its organ, *The Canadian Epworth Era*, consistently declaimed against a self-absorbed and meditative form of piety and espoused a practical Christianity which would penetrate into the marketplace and the state. Otherworldliness was constructed as a merely female trait, while Christian social reform was deemed the purview of men. Reorienting the church into the wider civic sphere was intended to draw young men into more active Christian work. The purpose of evangelism was to train young people not simply to reflect upon their inner spiritual lives but to consider the outer life of the community: Christian charity was intended to help the poor and to teach courage, self-respect, self-reliance, and independence in the young male benefactors. Although the League was composed of both men and women, soon after its inception it took a turn towards a distinctly male-oriented concept of Christian service. This involved the reinterpretation of practical church work to include broader notions of public service that encompassed an interest in 'righteous government' and 'righteousness in the nation.' By 1911 the Epworth League possessed its own Department of Citizenship, which taught young men a new conception of the interconnection between the sacred and the secular and a new relationship of the individual to civic organizations and the state, which expressed a progressive new liberalism and a critique of laissez-faire political economy, the competitiveness of the marketplace, and the inequities of modern industrialization. Ultimately, however, the central message was more orthodox in its concern to shore up the family, the stability of the state, and the integrity of commerce, all of which depended upon the spiritual vitality of the church. At its heart, social Christianity, with its emphasis on the authority of the church to speak on questions within the wider public spheres, was part of a broader attempt to masculinize the church and construct a practical, aggressive, and virile form of religion.

3

'Their Advance in Christian Civilization':[1] Missionaries and Colonialism at Home

Two master narratives have dominated the historical writing on missionization in Canada. One presents the missionary as a heroic figure who, through perseverance and extreme piety, performed almost superhuman feats of converting and utterly transforming the cultures of various First Nations peoples. The second is a story in which the missionary becomes an anti-hero wreaking utter destruction upon non-Christian societies, turning them into passive clients of an inexorable and monolithic imperial project. Both of these accounts dispense with the idea that Native peoples possessed agency. By uncritically accepting the success stories created by the missionaries themselves, they conceive of contact between European and non-Western societies in terms of a dualism between the 'civilized' and the 'Other,' with only one possible outcome, that of ultimate assimilation. Recently, a third perspective has emerged which presents a more complex interpretation of the cultural encounter between missionaries and non-Christian peoples. This view, while recognizing the unequal power relationship between the colonizing missionary and the colonized subjects, wishes to circumvent the notion of First Nations as simply the 'Other,' the polar opposite of Christian and white 'civilization.' It not only focuses upon the large role played by Native missionaries; it also emphasizes the degree to which aboriginal societies were able to select and reinvent the Christian message in order to fashion an indigenized but no less authentic expression of Christianity.

From this perspective, colonialism is not a coherent or monolithic process, but one characterized by many contradictions and tensions in which the settler, government officials, commercial interests (such as the fur traders, miners, and commercial fisheries), and missionaries sometimes reinforce each other insofar as they wish to establish European values and institutions, but more often, there are subtle but important differences in which the projects of these various representatives of empire were in conflict. The missionary enterprise was riddled with tension: at one level missionaries often critiqued colonialist exploitation, but they likewise participated in the broader political project of empire in that they were representatives of a culture which believed it was superior by virtue of its Christian faith. While missionaries must be recognized as colonizing forces which wrought tremendous long-term change to Native societies, it must likewise be acknowledged that missions were often a by-product of earlier phases of contact which were a feature of commercial interests, most notably the fur trade, which some historians have seen as more destructive of Native society than the arrival of the missions.

By contrast with other British settlement colonies such as South Africa, Australia, and New Zealand, overt coercion of Native societies by force and genocide was rarely employed on the Canadian frontier. Rather, colonial expansion occurred through an anti-conquest approach which preferred the extension of quasi-state surveillance in which the missionaries from the leading Protestant and Catholic churches were active participants. While missionaries may have shared the view of settlers and government officials that Native peoples were culturally inferior, their overall purpose was to convert rather than to merely 'civilize' them, and as a result missionaries were compelled to seek a greater understanding of and accommodation with Native cultures on a daily basis. Their intentions did not always conform to their discourse of heroism, success, and mastery over the benighted 'Indian' which formed the stuff of the vast missionary literature which was written in the main for white audiences in order to persuade churches at home to invest greater resources in the missionary enterprise. Missionaries were complicit with government in creating the destructive system of residential schools, whose signal aim was to eradicate aboriginal culture, but at the same time many individual missionaries fought against white alienation of Indian lands which occurred through the creation of Native reserves in the late nineteenth century. As we can see, the story of missionization both in the Canadian west and north, as well as overseas, was a process that was not monolithic, but was one in which the colonized peoples played an active role in determining the outcomes of the colonial project. The central question remains: did the missionaries actually have a goal of total cultural capitulation on the part of First Nations people, and if so, was this ever accomplished in terms of actual lived experience or was this simply a trope of missionary discourse?

All missionaries equated the acquisition of Christianity with a civilizing mission which envisioned the christianized aboriginal as a sedentary farmer. Some historians have argued that missionaries did not separate Western Christianity and Western civilization, and therefore they demanded a total transformation of First Nations converts. They thus aimed for the complete destruction of the traditional, integrated aboriginal way of life. However, this approach did not motivate all missionary activity. The Roman Catholic Oblates, who evangelized the Dene people in the northern regions of Athabaska, had little interest in limiting the traditional hunting economy because they wished to 'protect' Native peoples from what they saw as the negative features of European society. A good deal of the success of the Anglican Church can be attributed to the fact that many Native groups saw it as more elevated because it was the church of the British monarchy. The Anglicans and the Catholics were the dominant players in western and northern Canada, but their first inclination was not to convert Native peoples for they were invited to the northwest by the Hudson's Bay Company to serve the religious needs of its white employees. That they henceforth expanded their missionary enterprise was in large part at the behest of Native people themselves, who, through their own trading networks, had developed considerable interest in Christianity.

The period of missionary zeal reached its zenith after 1880 and was driven by a combination of rising imperial fervour and a self-image among Methodists and Presbyterians that they were now 'national' Canadian churches whose maturity was best demonstrated by the projection of Canadian religious power overseas. Although missions drew upon the most pious and evangelical segments within each denomination, the missionary enterprise manifested a great deal of internal diversity both in terms of funding and recruitment. The Anglican Church Missionary Society drew exclusively upon English evangelicals, most of whom were men drawn largely from the lower middle and working classes. The Methodist and Presbyterian missions were more directed to overseas endeavours in China, Japan, and India and tended to recruit more women, most of whom came from well-off rural families and were highly educated. By contrast, the Anglican missionaries were rarely ordained ministers but were typically pious lay workers. William Duncan, the celebrated Anglican missionary who, by his own account, turned the village of Metlakatla into a 'model' Christian community, was not atypical in terms of his iconoclastic individualism, autocratic methods, and conflictual relationships both with his Tsimshian converts and his own ecclesiastical superiors. The fact that he had to rely almost exclusively upon Native interpreters and catechists meant that, like other missionaries working on their own, he was ultimately compelled to alter his conviction that his European sense of superiority would allow him to dictate the religious direction of Tsimshian society. Many of the Anglican women missionaries continued to hold particularly negative and racialized views of Native women and children in British Columbia largely because, as schoolteachers and nurses, they experienced greater resistance to their attempts to alter traditional notions of nutrition, cleanliness, and the body. There was no one missionary enterprise, for the missionary impulse was fragmented by denominational loyalties, class and gender differences, as well as varying degrees of appreciation of Native mores and values.

Despite the fact that the Anglican and Catholic churches secured the initial advantage in the northwest, by the late nineteenth century this religious frontier began to exhibit the same high level of religious pluralism that characterized older, settled parts of Canada. Just as in the white-dominated areas of Canada, this environment contained greater potential for individual agency, and as a result Native peoples were just as adept as white settlers at exploiting interdenominational rivalry, which was even more apparent in frontier situations where clergy were few and financial support was precarious. If one accepts that Native peoples accepted Christianity on their own terms and selectively adapted only those aspects which conformed to their own cultural understandings, it follows that the shape of the missionary project was not simply imposed from above, but was constantly negotiated and renegotiated. The Tsimshian people of British Columbia welcomed Christian missions, especially those of the Methodists, because that church's evangelical ethos, with its emphasis on a distinct transformative experience, related directly to the notions of spiritual power within Tsimshian religion. More strikingly, no church made a significant impact upon the Blackfoot peoples of present-day Alberta between 1870 and 1900, and at best this group remained nominally Christian simply for the purpose of census enumeration. Since the missionary success was determined to a considerable degree by the attitudes of the host community, there could be no homogeneous missionary practice, even though there was a pattern of missionary involvement by which a particular church established a permanent mission and church buildings, to which were added an infrastructure of schools, hospitals, and lay societies. This process was not a linear one, nor was it necessarily hegemonic. More often than not, it was Native peoples rather than white missionaries who initiated local campaigns to build churches and found various religious societies as a means to reinforce and further empower community solidarities.

The establishment of British rule in post-revolutionary colonial Canada coincided with a revival of missionary enthusiasm attendant upon the rise of evangelicalism in the late eighteenth century. The aboriginal groups residing in the new colony of Upper Canada, established in 1791, were not strangers to white contact. In fact, for two centuries, they had both resisted and collaborated with French and British imperial interests. By the time that mainly Methodist missionaries were sent to evangelize Native communities, such as the Mississauga who resided along the Credit River and the Mohawk along the Grand River, the 'traditional' nature of their societies had already been significantly transformed. In addition there was already considerable knowledge and cultural incorporation of Christian teachings; indeed, a large proportion of Mohawk identified themselves as Anglicans, and even the Native prophet Handsome Lake's attempt to restore 'traditional' Native spirituality was greatly inspired by Christian doctrine. In 1823 there occurred a successful Methodist revival among the Mississauga which was celebrated in Methodist publications as evidence that if supposed 'uncivilized' peoples could convert, so too could white settlers. Although such Methodist propaganda was written for a largely white audience and underscored the dichotomous worlds of the Christian white and the non-Christian aboriginal 'Other,' the revival meeting in Ancaster had been orchestrated through the leadership of mixed-blood converts Mary and Peter Jones, the latter a chief of the Mississauga. The revival was thus the product of Native cultural movements rather than the imposition of white authority. Although Peter Jones would become one of the most celebrated missionaries of his day, the Native leadership in conversion movements began to wane with the succeeding generation. After the 1837 Rebellion, in which many Methodist clergymen were suspected of radicalism, the Methodist leadership wished to affirm their links with the colonial government in order to expunge the taint of republicanism. This had direct implications for their missionary endeavours, which became intertwined with a growing colonial 'humanitarian' intrusion into the lives of Native peoples. Influenced by the Aborigines Protection Society in England, the colonial government took up the policy of civilizing the Indian, which ensured that henceforth Christianity and civilization would become part of the moral agenda of the British state.

The implication for Upper Canada was that churches endorsed government-sponsored resettlement in more northerly areas for loyal aboriginal peoples and, under the urging of the Methodist leader Egerton Ryerson, undertook the management of a fledgling system of industrial or residential schools in which Native children were taught skills which were believed necessary to ensure their assimilation into the emerging liberal order. At the Orillia Conference of 1846 in which government officials, clergy of various denominations, and Native leaders met, all parties enthusiastically endorsed the concept of industrial schools. Aboriginal leaders welcomed residential schools as part of a strategy of selectively incorporating white knowledge into a process of cultural revitalization for their people. Initially, they believed that they could control both the personnel and curriculum of these institutions because the Orillia Conference encouraged the First Nations of Upper Canada to fund the schools out of their treaty revenues. However, in the space of a few years, such hopes were dashed as churches and missionary organizations tightened their control. The first of these new industrial schools opened in

1844 in Alderville and in 1849 in Mount Elgin. Thus began an era of removing Native children from their parents in order that they could become agents for diffusing Christian civilization among their people. This subtle shift by missionaries from voluntary conversion to a more coercive strategy culminated in the Gradual Civilization Act of 1857, which held out measures to induce Native people to adopt the values and habits of Euro-Canadians. Even though the missionaries had not acted as the primary catalysts of change in Upper Canada, they were, nevertheless, by 1850, complicit in the broader colonial impulse which saw assimilation as the only possible outcome for contact between European settlers and First Nations peoples.

Similar to Upper Canada, the missionary interest of the churches in the western and northern interior regions of British North America was accidental and hardly the product of a coherent strategy of cultural colonialism. Before these regions were incorporated into the Canadian Confederation in 1870, they had been governed by the Hudson's Bay Company (HBC). The Red River settlement, comprising the area around present-day Winnipeg, Manitoba, was the first contact zone in what was to be western Canada. Older accounts of the Christian encounter with Red River society have stressed the impositional nature of the churches' presence and the destructive character of missionary activity in this society that was delicately balanced between European, mixed-blood, and aboriginal elements. However, initially, the Anglican and Roman Catholic churches which were invited to Red River by the Hudson's Bay Company sought exclusively to minister to European settlers. Relations between the churches and the Company authorities were, however, always fraught with tension. Until 1846 the Company unofficially backed the Anglican Church and was forced to tolerate a significant Catholic presence because many HBC employees were either French-Canadian or Metis. More significantly, HBC officials actively discouraged evangelization of aboriginal peoples, as they viewed the churches' program of turning Native hunters into sedentary farmers as eco-nomically destructive of the fur trade. Indeed, what success the churches did enjoy in creating a network of Christian institutions at Red River depended largely on their culti-vation of links with both the English- and French-speak-ing mixed-blood communities. Many within the Red River mixed-blood society welcomed the presence of the clergy as a way of regularizing marriage, and some even adopted the pattern of sedentary farming promoted by Archdeacon Wil-liam Cockran. Once the churches established a firm organi-zational presence at Red River by the late 1840s, prominent Metis families like the Riels adopted religious values that closely approximated the clerical standard of conduct. By becoming active within the church, sending their sons and daughters to missionary educational institutions, and by exhibiting a fervent ultramontane Catholic piety, a number of mixed-blood families hoped to acquire greater power both vis-à-vis whites and their own community. However, for those mixed-bloods whose livelihood remained tied to the hunting economy, contact with missionaries was far more sporadic, and consequently the impact of missionaries was relatively slight prior to 1900.

However, the larger significance of the Red River contact zone lay in its role as the communications centre of the fur trade, with a large mixed-blood community to serve as cultural intermediaries for the transmission of Christianity to areas further west and north. Indeed, the period before 1860 was characterized by considerable Native initiative in the appropriation of Christianity, which entered many Na-tive societies without the apparatus of European clergy or in-stitutions. Indeed, groups as far west as the British Columbia interior were aware of Christianity as early as the 1830s, long before the establishment of an official missionary presence. The earliest promoters of Christianity in the areas beyond Red River were not the clergy themselves, but mixed-blood and Native leaders such as Spogan Garry, a young Kootenay of a family of chiefs who had travelled to Red River and brought back elements of Christian teaching to his own people. Moreover, the entire western interior in the 1840s witnessed a dramatic series of prophetic movements in First Nations societies, and while some of these were actively hostile to white culture, they all incorporated aspects of Christianity which could only have been derived from the cultural fluidity that so exemplified fur trade society.

Apart from the Methodists and Presbyerians, who drew their missionary personnel from central Canada, the Anglican and Roman Catholic churches staffed their missionary enterprise in western Canada with recruits from England and France, most of whom were of working-class or lower middle-class origins and who had at best a mediocre education. For example, the Anglican missionaries sent out by the Church Missionary Society had few ordained ministers among them; the least educated were sent to Canada, which was deemed a missionary field with much lower prestige than those in either India or South Africa, which attracted the best and the brightest Anglican evangelicals. In a similar vein, the Oblates, who were sent to the Canadian northwest from France, were from working-class origins and represented the most pious and evangelical elements of the church. Like all missionaries, they exhibited a strong individualism and resistance to ecclesiastical authority, which meant that these frontier regions of cultural contact became laboratories for some often unusual religious experiments in which the missionaries envisioned themselves as charismatic and heroic autocrats exerting minute control over communities of Native Christians. The educational attainments of Methodist missionaries also fell below the denominational standard: of the 133 missionaries in British Columbia, 45 per cent had not attended college and one-quarter had only attended for one year. This combination of working-class origins and lack of control by ecclesiastical superiors, coupled with inadequate training and a generally messianic self-perception that their own intense religious gifts could work a miraculous transformation among aboriginal peoples, frequently led to stridently racialist views of First Nations societies. However, some of the missionaries' evangelistic strategies – such as the Catholic Durieu system and the Anglican William Duncan's social experiment at Metlakatla in which intense surveillance methods were utilized to police the boundaries between converts and the unregenerated 'Indians' – were not necessarily racially motivated, but were merely the application of older disciplinary methods which had been the norm within all mainstream denominations prior to 1880.

There is no disputing the fact that missionaries believed that Christianity and European values were superior to the cultural attainments of First Nations societies, and they more often than not castigated Native peoples for their indolence, sexual promiscuity, greed, cruelty, superstition, general ignorance, and their inability to progress without the infusion of Christian values. It is true, too, that missionaries sought, along with Christianity, to introduce western liberal notions of family life and education, and championed the transformative nature of regular work, including the gendered notion of ideal womanhood, which equated female labour with backward societies. However, almost all missionaries subscribed to a monogenist view of evolution in which all human beings were seen as derived from a common origin, but in which certain societies were superior to others. This must be contrasted with late nineteenth-century scientific racism, which ascribed racial difference to varying human origins and thus relegated certain racial groups to permanent inferiority. Monogenists, on the other hand, believed that all cultures could be reformed or redeemed, although it was this perspective that gave missionaries the power to believe that their agenda to eradicate certain aspects of Native culture was in keeping with natural and moral laws. Just as monogenists might conceive of a hierarchy of cultures, they believed that each had an equal potential both for progress and decline; it was because they also feared that white society might revert to 'barbarism' that they were so intent on fashioning a missionary discourse that affirmed clear boundaries between 'savagery' and Christian 'civilization.' It likewise explains why the missionary texts were written largely for a white audience in which stirring tales of willing aboriginals who voluntarily converted once they encountered the intense piety of the heroic missionary were intended to so heighten the evangelical spirit of European society that they would continue to financially support and defend the missionary enterprise.

The missionary texts were themselves evangelistic tracts, and they must be read cautiously because they do not necessarily represent an accurate description of First Nations society or of the religious encounter between aboriginal peoples and the Christian message. Missionary discourse was intended for public consumption in the vast array of missionary publications, which included various Sunday school papers, accounts in the denominational press, religious novels, and immensely popular books such as W.H. Withrow's *The Native Races of North America* (1895) and John Maclean's *Canadian Savage Folk* (1896). These publications all highlighted the almost superhuman power of the missionary to utterly transform aboriginal culture. This published discourse contrasted with personal journals, which recorded missionaries' despair at making headway against the tenacity of a vibrant aboriginal culture. Missionary writings should not be taken at face value, because even Native catechists such as William Henry Pierce, a Tsimshian convert to Methodism who later became an ordained minister, likewise subscribed to the pervasive literary trope of the heroic and successful missionary. However, this does not detract from the fact that the missionary text did play a powerful role in structuring the misrepresentation and objectification of the Native 'other' juxtaposed against the dominant white colonizer. Pierce, the author of a personal memoir entitled *From Potlatch to Pulpit,* appeared to be a mere collaborator in the white colonial project by recommending that Native converts give up the wearing of blankets and the burning of dance regalia and abandon matrilineal social organization in favour of the Western nuclear family. But his account raises several questions: was he writing articles for the Methodist *Missionary Outlook* in order to elevate his status within the church? To what extent was Pierce actually instructing aboriginal congregations to adhere to these prescriptions? To what degree did his Native hearers actually conform to his beliefs? Some historians have argued that because Pierce was himself a mixed-blood and later married a white missionary teacher, he was more fully integrated into the white world than were many Native converts. While on many occasions he did merely parrot white missionary views, on other occasions he saw christianization as a means to empower Native people and worked to unionize the Native fishery and to defend Native land claims. As Pierce's experience demonstrates, missionization was not a wholly white affair, and the active and frequent participation of Native proselytizers in evangelization makes the colonialist project more ambiguous and undermines the easy polarity between white colonizer and indigenous colonized.

Moreover, if there were many degrees of response to Christianity among Native people, which ranged from outright indigenization to complete co-optation into white sensibilities, there were likewise many divergent attitudes to Native culture within what has generally been seen as a monolithic missionary ideology even though it was animated by a notion of cultural bias. For example, aboriginal peoples in Upper Canada were considered very advanced in terms of their technology and social organization; the Anglican William Duncan's first appraisal of the Tsimshian in British Columbia was that they were 'a fine, robust and intelligent race' characterized by superior industry.[2] Three major promoters of Methodist missions, Revs Egerton Ryerson Young, John Maclean, and George McDougall, shared a belief in the goal of redeeming Native people from their degraded culture, but their opinions as to the cause, character,

and solution to this inferiority diverged significantly. Young
was perhaps the most negative in his assessment, castigating
First Nations for their cruel and vicious nature, which he
traced to their idolatry. He was particularly disdainful of the
apparent freedom exercised by Native women, which did
not reflect the reality of women's roles in aboriginal society
as much as Young's own fears regarding the emergence
of a women's rights movement among middle-class Euro-
Canadian women. Maclean was far more positive regarding
Native religion and posited a number of parallels between
Christian doctrine and Native spirituality, although he still
ascribed aboriginal backwardness to the insufficiency of
their 'traditional' religion. Maclean, however, shared with
George McDougall the view that the Natives were doomed
because of the excesses and corruption of white contact
and indeed came closest to ascribing environmental causes
to Native inferiority due in part to the fact that he was married to an aboriginal woman. However, he did believe that
Native peoples must adopt the liberal values of a market
society as the precondition of their survival in a modern,
settler society.

There existed many silences within missionary propaganda, in which Native catechists, converted women, missionary wives, and female missionaries simply did not exist,
a situation that casts considerable doubt on the reliability of
their description of the complex process of cultural contact
and colonization. In constructing the missionary endeavour
as a largely male terrain, these narratives undermined the
extent to which women fully participated in the broader
process of cultural imperialism. Many historians interpreted the presence of women in the mission fields as one that
was more caring and thus less imbricated with colonialist
bias, but the fact that women largely staffed some of the
most repressive institutions, such as residential schools, im-
plicates them in the process of cultural assimilation. The
most significant silence in the missionary text surrounds
the agency of Native people themselves, because in the

missionary ideology the Native must necessarily be passive in order to better exalt the marvellous achievement of the missionary him/herself. This did not reflect actual social practice. Missionaries may have told their superiors that they were radically altering Native society in order to show that they were effectively serving the evangelistic goals of their respective churches, but even though Native people may have participated in Christian rituals this did not mean that Native peoples wholly conformed to the missionary standard.

Missionaries clearly had a vested interest in making it appear that they had effectively stamped out Native potlatching, feasting, and dancing, and the printed record obscures the depth of Native cultural tenacity. By analysing the cultural encounter between Native and European as one in which both sides influence each other, albeit unequally, it is possible to argue that there occurred a high degree of indigenization at the local level in which European religious practices were themselves altered or reinterpreted by Native groups. Even though the ideology of difference within the missionary outlook did provide the sense of cultural superiority which fuelled the missionary enterprise, the discourse of missionary propaganda did not in and of itself structure Native responses. These remained much more complex and served to limit the notion of Christian hegemony so idealized within the missionary text. Missionary discourse may not have wholly undermined Native self-definition, for they were not the primary consumers of this literature, but it did have a tremendous impact upon Euro-Canadians, who continued to give liberally to the missionary project both within Canada and overseas well into the twentieth century. More significantly, the power of missionary discourse was most evident at the level of shaping white Canadian attitudes to non-Western cultures, for the only perspective about aboriginal societies available to the vast majority of Protestant and Catholic Euro-Canadians was the story told by the missionary.

The standard treatment of missionization sees the process as one characterized by a vast disparity of power in which the white missionary easily imposed his or her values upon passive and culturally declining aboriginal groups. Some historians have upheld this interpretation by advancing the argument that so long as Native communities were able to preserve their 'traditional' way of life they had no reason to adopt the new value system of Christianity. They envisioned no basis for mutual understanding between the missionary and the aboriginal because Christian concepts such as sin, grace, and faith were incomprehensible in terms of the Native spiritual system. Thus, with few exceptions, Native people did not have the cultural capacity to become anything more than nominal Christians. However, once Native cultures were destabilized by white contact, they had little ability to resist or to formulate a creative response to the missionaries.

The consequence of this interpretation is that no conversion to Christianity is seen as legitimate or motivated for religious reasons because the only 'real Indian' is the non-Christian aboriginal. The dichotomy between white missionary and aboriginal proselyte, which has been adhered to by advocates of both the heroic narrative and that of the missionary as the quintessential colonialist, has been queried by other historians who have emphasized that Euro-Canadian clergy were always in a minority in all mission fields. The fact that the enterprise of missionization was not a wholly white experience, and that much of the expansion of missions occurred at the behest of mixed-blood or Native peoples and was not imposed from above by all-powerful Europeans, drastically alters the racial dynamic and forces historians to contemplate the fact that Christianity may have resonated deeply with individual converts. The significant presence of Natives as Christian evangelists prompts us to no longer view Christianity as merely a coercive and intrusive force acting against Native culture but as an integral part of First Nations history. Christianity was thus an authentic Native experience. Even though the longer-term impact of christianization was not always beneficial to Native peoples, the fact remains that the colonial act was itself a complex process in which Native peoples fully participated. Indeed, all across the missionary frontier, Native communities directly shaped the geographical and cultural expansion of missions. Just as Native peoples functioned in the role of middlemen within the fur trade, they acquired a similar status as intermediaries between their communities and Euro-Canadian missionaries. Indeed, between 1840 and 1890, it is not clear that the Europeans dominated the process, especially given the small numbers of missionaries, their inability to speak Native languages, and their isolation from white settlement and legal institutions. Given the limited presence of white missionaries, it is difficult to sustain the view that Europeans were so powerful that they could completely impose their culture on unwilling 'Others,' and so it has become necessary for historians to argue that Native peoples in the majority of cases willingly but selectively adopted Christian beliefs and values. Given that most of the actual evangelization occurred through the medium of a Native interpreter, it is not inconceivable that cultural change was a two-way process in which Christianity was re-interpreted and indigenized.

At no time during the entire period of missionization from the 1820s onward was evangelization simply a Euro-Canadian effort. In Upper Canada the key figures in Christianization were Native leaders themselves. For example, John Sunday, the chief of the Mississaugas at the Bay of Quinte was one of the foremost Methodist preachers of his day, while Peter Jones, chief of the Credit River Mississauga was renowned as a charismatic Christian leader. Two of the best-known evangelists in British Columbia were Spokan Garry and Kutenai Pelly, both of whom had been educated at Red River at the Anglican Church Missionary Society school. For many Native groups in the western interior the Christian message was not heard first from Europeans but was transmitted through already established trade networks. Even before the arrival of white missionaries, Native groups as far north as the Athabaska region had adopted many Christian practices including performing the sign of the cross, singing Christian hymns, and understanding the Christian concepts of heaven, hell, and resurrection. When the Methodist missionary Egerton Ryerson Young arrived at Norway House, the local Cree band already possessed Bibles written in their syllabic language, which they had acquired through trading connections. In British Columbia, prior to the acceleration of European missionary activity in the 1860s, Native Prophet Dance movements had become vehicles for the transmission of Native and Christian ideas, which had become combined into a syncretic religion. The teachings of the Prophet Bini, viewed by Native peoples as part and parcel of their own spiritual growth, incorporated many Christian precepts, such as the notion of dying and going to Heaven, the millennium, and the idea of conversion or a spiritual rebirth, as well as the concept of doing penance for one's sins.

The Hudson's Bay Company discouraged the expansion of missions for fear that they would render Native communities too sedentary, but they could do little to halt the constant invitations from mixed-blood and Native traders within their territory for priests and ministers to baptize their children. Indeed, Egerton Ryerson Young founded his mission at Norway House in northern Manitoba at the urging of the Saulteaux Indians from the Berens River and not at the behest of the Methodist leadership. Similarly, Catholic missions spread because of Native demand, and, indeed, as Bishop Taché of Red River reported in 1852, the Dene chose to stay at Fort Chipewyan all summer for the express purpose of seeing the Oblate missionary who performed 169 baptisms and 29 marriages. Aboriginal and mixed-blood catechists were key to the expansion of Christian missions: Jonathan Wood, an aboriginal Christian, proselytized from Red River to the Yukon, while Sara Riel, the sister of the famous Metis leader Louis Riel, became a Grey Nun and brought her intense ultramontane Catholic piety to the Dene, where she was particularly influential in converting Native women. She emerged as one of the most important intercultural brokers in the Canadian northwest because her language skills enabled her to establish relations between the male Oblate priests and their female Native converts. Like many other prominent Metis within the fur trade, Sara Riel used her conversion to Christianity as the means to enhance her social status within the Native community.

In the Tsimshian communities in coastal British Columbia many mission interpreters were Native women, who did not conceive this participation in the process of evangelization as assimilation into white society. Rather they saw it as a means to advance themselves and their families within the larger Tsimshian society. However, despite the large numbers of Native catechists, interpreters, and lay exhorters, many ordinary Natives preferred white missionaries because they saw this as a strategy to familiarize themselves with the rudiments of white modes of power. For example, the Haida people were at first reluctant to accept George Edgar, a mixed-blood Methodist missionary, largely because they wished to enhance their own spiritual power and social status through contact and identification with the European missionary. Again, it was the choice of Native peoples to hear European preachers and it was they who allowed a European religious presence into their communities on their own terms. However, while Christianity was less impositional, it is likewise true that in British Columbia only two Native missionaries were ever ordained within the Methodist Church, and only by the middle of the twentieth century were there any Native clergy within the Anglican and Roman Catholic churches. In this instance power to determine the structure of missionary leadership lay with the Europeans alone.

Generally speaking, historians no longer view the missionary process as an inevitable juggernaut that quickly and totally replaced Native culture with Christianity. Missionaries were not the sole agents of change although they were certainly catalysts in accelerating transformations that had begun with Native–white contact through the fur trade, waged labour, and permanent European settlement. In many instances, conversion to Christianity was genuine, largely because the process of missionization was one of negotiated identities in which Native and Christian beliefs were blended (syncretism), converged because of commonalities between Native and Christian world views and practices, or co-existed side by side but in separate compartments (dualism). In practice, individuals rarely experienced conversion as an absolute state because there was considerable give and take between the two cultural systems. Native and Christian identities were each altered through this encounter (dialogic).[3]

Three case studies of the cultural contact between the Oblate, Anglican, and Methodist missions to the Dene in the Athabaska region, the Shuswap in the interior of British Columbia, and the Tsimshian in coastal British Columbia will illustrate the way in which Native agency played a powerful role both in expanding and limiting the power of religious colonialism. The Dene were aboriginal caribou hunters who lived north of the Churchill and Saskatchewan rivers in the Athabaska region, a marginal environment of boreal forest and tundra. In 1847 Bishop Provencher of St Boniface (Red River) sent the first Oblate missionary, Father Alexandre Taché, to Fort Chipewyan, but the real impetus for the spread of Oblate missions in the north was provided by invitations to Catholic priests from mixed-blood hunters and traders after 1848. Despite limited contact with European missionaries such as the Oblates, the Dene had sufficient knowledge of Christianity from their trade networks that hundreds of them eagerly awaited the new priest. Typically, the missionaries represented the most zealous and uncompromising elements in any denomination, and the Oblates were no exception in that they considered it their duty to God to convert the Dene and lift them from a state of 'barbarism.' To read their official accounts it would appear that the Oblates, unlike the Jesuits, had no tradition of adapting Catholic doctrines to different cultures largely because they believed that all non-Catholic religions were unreasoned and superficial. Although they approached the Dene with this conception of their task, it soon became apparent that the reluctance of this Native society to view missionaries as significant figures obliged the Catholic missionaries to alter their initial suppositions.

At first, like so many other missionaries, the Oblates considered a sedentary way of life the most appropriate vehicle for rapid christianization. But because of the extreme dependence of the Dene upon the caribou they soon recognized that agricultural pursuits were not an option and that in order to reach the seasonal migrations of the Dene, priests themselves would have to itinerate, a decision that drastically modified the idealized model of the settled Euro-Canadian parish. Because of the dearth of missionary personnel in these northern regions, it became increasingly difficult for priests to travel, and eventually the creation of a mission station meant that Dene trade patterns were interrupted largely because of the Christmas and Easter feasts. This tendency towards gathering in large numbers at the mission station was not simply brought about because of Christianity; rather, the decline in the caribou population demanded greater reliance by the Dene upon fishing, which meant moving closer to the missions, which were usually strategically located near major lakes and rivers.

In other respects, the Oblates were very successful in deploying ceremonial and material elements of Catholicism. The singing of hymns, as well as the distribution of rosaries, medals, and holy pictures, were immensely popular, but most innovative was the production of tiny prayer books which the Dene could easily hang around their necks in the traditional medicine bundle so that they could transport these religious objects while they hunted. This material

representation of Catholicism was so effective that when
the evangelical Anglicans of the Church Missionary Society
(CMS) attempted to evangelize, the Dene ignored them
because they did not offer material tokens of their spiritual
power. However, the Dene condemned the representation
of evil and rejected popular Catholic images of the Virgin
Mary treading on the serpent. In addition, because the
Dene did not share the Catholic view that man was inher-
ently sinful and in need of redemption, they resisted learning prayers for forgiveness of sins. They were also reluctant
to accept Oblate prescriptions regarding Christian marriage and family life, refusing to give up polygamy, which
formed such a crucial part of their family economies. In
many aboriginal cultures, polygamy was a sign of higher
social status but also played a crucial household labour and
welfare function within these societies, with wives cared for
in extended kinship units.

For the most part, there was a large degree of convergence
between Dene beliefs and Catholic doctrines. For example,
the Dene followed a practice of public confession, had a
concept of the universal flood, believed in a monotheistic
God referred to as the 'Powerful One' or 'Yeddariya,' and,
most importantly, maintained, as did Catholics, that the
soul was immortal. As a result the Dene accepted the Oblate
demands for public confession and baptism, although they
interpreted these religious practices in ways quite different from Catholic teaching. For example, the Dene viewed
guilt and hence confession in communal rather than individual terms. In turn, because of the Dene's reliance upon
meat the Oblates refused to enforce the practice of Friday
abstinence, but even more significantly the sacrament of
baptism, especially of sick children, became a real source of
contention between the Dene and the Oblates because the
Dene began to connect baptism with the frequent death of
children.

Because priests saw the Dene only for short periods of
the year, it was difficult to impose religious conformity,

and the missionaries remained dependent upon the Dene's willingness to accept Catholicism, which was mediated on a day-to-day basis by Native lay leaders and interpreters (most of whom were Native women). It was only when the Oblates introduced medical assistance and the Grey Nuns began to educate Native children that official Catholicism had a greater impact upon Dene society. Because the Dene saw illness as integral with spirituality and the Catholic priests considered it a punishment for sin, medicine provided a terrain of mutual understanding. Indeed, after the devastating epidemics of 1865–7 in which sixty-seven people died, there was a groundswell of conversions among the Dene peoples. Disease could also create a backlash against Christianity, as occurred after scarlet fever ravaged the Dene community in 1864–5, resulting in a drastic decline in baptisms. It could, however, be argued that the greatest boon to Catholicism in the Canadian north was the repeated cycle of epidemic diseases, which so devastated the adult population that aboriginal kin groups had to send numerous orphans to the residential schools established by the Grey Nuns. Prior to the effects of disease, the Dene had only selectively sent their children for schooling, choosing to have the Catholic sisters care for children only when food was scarce, while on other occasions the Dene believed the church should reward them for leaving their children in educational institutions.

While the Oblate goal of enforcing religious conformity through intense catechizing within familial homes did not achieve the level of supervision which they had envisioned among the Dene, the Oblate missionaries were much more successful in establishing fixed and settled modes of Native life in the interior of British Columbia among the Shuswap, who had already experienced much higher levels of white contact through the fur trade. There the elaborate system of community surveillance known as the Durieu system, named for the Oblate Bishop Pierre Durieu, and modelled on the Jesuit mission villages of Paraguay, was a cultural survival from early modern times when community moral scrutiny was a common technique of both Catholic and Protestant churches. For example, the practice of making Shuswap moral delinquents stand at the front of the church while holding their hands above their heads was a form of shaming commonly used in Western churches, although it should be noted that this system of church discipline was falling into disuse in Euro-Canadian churches by the 1870s. Because this form of moral regulation was most effective in smaller, less urban centres, its promoters maintained that it was extremely useful in ensuring that new converts did not backslide. The Catholic Oblates were able to rapidly establish a dominant presence in a number of British Columbia villages not simply because of the coercive power of the Durieu system, but because of the willing cooperation of Shuswap chiefs, who saw in Catholicism a means to bolster their own authority and to secure better positions within the fur trade hierarchy. It should also be noted that as oppressive as the Durieu system appeared in that it prohibited drinking, dancing, gambling and sexual immorality – all of which featured within 'traditional' Shuswap culture – this process of regulation was administered not by missionaries but by Native collaborators, who were enticed with offices of chief, watchman, beadle, policeman, chanter, and bell ringer. As intrusive as this policing system was, these coercive aspects of Catholicism were balanced by more positive instruction such as daily catechism, frequent confession, and absolution, which ensured the constant indoctrination of the Native convert. Between the 1850s and the 1890s this system of authority was also endorsed by the colonial state, whose legal authority in the interior was quite insecure.

This Catholic system of intense scrutiny and moral discipline was, however, quite limited because it could only be enforced within closed villages, and for much of the year the Shuswap travelled far beyond the reach of the missionary as they participated in the fur trade or in waged labour. Catholic hegemony was thus fragile, all the more so because the process of missionization depended on the goodwill and acceptance by Native leaders. In the 1870s, Shuswap chiefs began to question their reliance upon Catholic missionaries to defend them against the incursions of white settlers, and they ejected the Oblates from their villages, reverting to Native forms of spirituality such as the Prophet Dance. Over the long term, despite decades of utilizing and reinterpreting Catholicism to create an indigenized Christianity that could stabilize their social order, the Shuswap and the Oblates were subject to the dominant colonial government, which deployed an increasingly effective legal authority to circumscribe both the power of Native chiefs and the authority of white missionaries. Particularly after the arrest of the Oblate Father Chirouse and a number of Native chiefs in 1892 for ordering the whipping of a young Shuswap woman accused of immorality, colonial legal authorities moved to curb the relative independence of missionaries and their converts. Thus, when the Durieu system was reintroduced by the Oblates in the 1890s, after a successful religious revival, it was recast under the more innocuous guise of the Indian Total Abstinence Society, a type of voluntary association familiar to white society.

The Anglican CMS missionary William Duncan attempted to implement a similar system of moral regulation among the coastal Tshimshian at Metlakatla in 1862. With the support of Native leaders such as Ligeekx, and with a plethora of offices for Native converts, Duncan hoped to completely christianize the Tsimshian through the exercise of a charismatic and authoritarian evangelism. Like many missionaries, Duncan chafed under the institutional constrains of both the parent missionary society and his local bishop, and later in his career he on several occasions came into conflict with the colonial government over its decision to place aboriginal peoples on reserves. As flamboyant and aggressive in his piety as Duncan was, his goal of completely transforming Tsimshian culture remained elusive and the continued power of the Native social order was made clear as soon as he arrived. When Duncan finally agreed to attend a Native spiritual ceremony, he interpreted their dancing, the emotional elements of their ritual, and their 'prayers' in Christian terms, and so began the process of negotiated contact in which both sides of the dialogue were shaped by previously held attitudes and expectations. In many cases, far from transforming Tsimshian culture, missionaries themselves were indigenized. Duncan's CMS colleague, Rev. Robert Tomlinson, was heartily welcomed into Nisga'a society because when tribal leaders saw the small dove that he had imprinted upon his clothing, they thought he was a member of the Raven Clan. Of course, Tomlinson was more than willing to play along because he saw it as advantageous to his cause.

Duncan's mission at Metlakatla relied completely on Tsimshian cooperation because he lacked expertise in the language. His preaching depended on Native interpreters and catechists, who became in practice the actual proselytizers within the Native community. Although Duncan did not himself envision giving power over to Native converts, the Anglican Bishop William Ridley quickly recognized that with a dearth of trained white missionaries, it was logical to involve Native leaders in the process of missionization. Indeed, Native catechists undertook much of the daily work of evangelization. David Leask, an Anglican convert, the son of a Tsimshian woman, and an Orkneyman employed by the HBC, was a prominent leader within Duncan's mission, serving as church elder and schoolteacher, and even worked in Duncan's store. While some historians would see him as a tool of the colonizers, Leask saw the conversion of the Tsimshian as an assertion of independence from white society. Interestingly, he later severely condemned Duncan for his authoritarian methods. By 1882, Duncan was forced to move on when he was abandoned by most of the hereditary chiefs and by his own bishop, who saw him as a loose cannon because he had overstepped his authority by not properly instituting Anglican sacraments such as communion.

Christianity was a key facet of post-contact Native history, but it was not the only force working upon Native societies. Prior to 1858 once British Columbia was opened up to American and British missions, there was no consistent mission presence in the area. Only by the 1860s was there a conscious effort to convert First Nations peoples, and this impetus towards evangelizing the empire's 'heathen' peoples was driven by international missionary societies. As a result the Anglicans dominated the field. Moreover, the colonial state remained fragile, the white population scattered, and the place of missionaries within the colonial order insecure. Perhaps the significant European impact upon aboriginal communities remained commercial activity both in the fur trade, the fisheries, the gold rush, and later factory work, all of which attracted willing Native workers. By 1885, fully 85 per cent of aboriginal people belonged to bands that earned incomes through paid labour.[4] Wages produced new levels of individual wealth such that older customs such as the potlatch were given a new lease on life. Whatever the impact of participation in the white labour force, the effect of the market economy was much more dramatic than the preaching of missionaries. Waged labour did however set the stage for missionary activity for it encouraged the formation of larger and more permanent Native villages, which became, in turn, the foundation for missionary endeavour.

However, the process of missionization cannot be read simply in terms of European cultural imposition and Native resistance, especially when the role of Native missionaries and catechists becomes part of the narrative of christianization. Despite missionary agendas, conversion rarely involved a replacement of pre-existing spiritual beliefs. In many ways, aboriginal and Christian religious frameworks were complementary rather than diametrically opposed to one another. The Tsimshian's willingness to enthusiastically embrace Christian doctrines and practices can be explained by the fact that these societies had long been accustomed to integrating new cultural practices into their culture, so that it was not unsurprising that they viewed Christianity as but another novelty to be added to the store of existing traditions. The Tsimshian were perhaps even more receptive to Christianity than other Native groups because the most prominent element in their spiritual system emphasized the individual's constant striving to become non-human, a person with other-worldly spiritual powers. From this perspective, all spiritual forces, including Christianity, were welcome as aids to individual spiritual power. Thus the emphasis of evangelical modes of Protestantism upon the primacy of the individual's direct spiritual contact with God was immensely appealing to the Tsimshian. From the standpoint of the Tsimshian, who saw life as a constant attempt to summon non-human spiritual powers, the Methodist notion of constantly seeking holiness did not seem alien, and Tsimshian peoples saw a direct affinity between missionary preaching and their own ceremonies, where the power of oratory was used to command the spirits. Both Christianity and Tsimshian religion shared a view of heaven or a concept of light as divinity while evangelicals and the Tsimshian saw their spiritual experience in terms of a decisive personal transformation or 'conversion.' Finally, Tsimshian spirituality was intensely emotive, which made the old-style evangelistic techniques of both the Anglican and Methodist missions extremely appealing. But most importantly of all, Native leaders hoped to associate themselves with white power by converting to Christianity either to preserve their social status in the hierarchy of Tsimshian society or to circumvent 'traditional' power alliances within their communities. Those who did convert did not see their choice as subjugation to a dominant European order but rather viewed Christianity as a mechanism to uphold and revitalize both individual spiritual power and the values of their own society.

Colonization became hegemonic only because of Native participation in the process, even though much of the

Christian message was brought by white male missionaries. Christianity did work a significant transformation in Tsimshian culture insofar as the lives of converts were no longer interpreted in terms of the potlatch or their own sacred histories, or practised in terms of Native performances, but rather were structured around the rituals of baptism, confession, Sabbath observance, and communion. Certainly the building of Christian churches gave the appearance of imposed colonialist structures, but the adoption of Christian values and practices did not immediately displace Tsimshian belief systems. For example, missionaries made much of the fact that through baptism they renamed Tsimshian families along patrilineal lines, but in reality, although the Tsimshian did adopt Christian names, they preserved their matrilineal clan identities. Tsimshian converts to Christianity did not accept it as a total package; rather they selectively integrated specific aspects of Protestantism into their own social codes, which they believed reinforced their own sense of cultural identity. Arthur Wellington Clah, another Tsimshian convert, appeared to have completely imbibed the missionary discourse in as much as he posited a dichotomy between the old Tsimshian ways and the new culture of the convert, but in reality his integration of Christian tenets to his own faith was much more complex. As a somewhat marginal character in his society, Clah saw in Christianity a means to attain higher social status through contact with the superhuman missionary figures. It is true that Clah imbibed a great deal of the missionary message: he absorbed the notion of backsliding, understood the moral codes of Methodism concerning drinking and wife abuse, and was well acquainted with the Bible, but in reality, as his daily journal reveals, his conversion experience was interpreted largely in terms of his own cultural perspective. Clah viewed the white missionaries as shamans or chiefs and he described tracking Jesus and encountering a physical presence of him much as 'traditional' Tsimshian spirituality emphasized the encounter with non-humans through a vision quest. However much white missionaries may have conceived of the world in black and white terms, of the wholly Christian or non-Christian, Native converts did not draw such absolute distinction. Arthur Wellington Clah professed himself a Christian, but he saw no conflict between his role as a Christian evangelist and his continued practice of Native medicine. Indeed, so effectively had Clah imbibed the evangelical message of the individual's unmediated access to scripture that Clah concluded that Native societies had no need of white missionaries in order to achieve spiritual power or salvation. Similarly, Nox Stabah, the female Nisga'a shaman, converted to Anglicanism but utilized her new-found Christian status as a means to elevate her role as a healer and, thereafter, became a leader of the White Cross women's group within the Anglican Church, whose special role was to nurse the sick.

The encounter between missionary and Native was a dialogic one in which Native converts reworked Christian forms and thus altered the process of missionization from one simply of racialist imposition. For example, white missionaries like William Duncan may have seen baptism as a Christian rite bestowing Christian names on Native converts, but the Native converts sought baptism because they believed it was a charm for bodily preservation or that adult baptism (they rejected the notion of infant baptism) awarded them a direct passage to heaven. Further, in keeping with Native belief in the physical manifestation of power, one Tsimshian convert placed the Bible on top of a stick, for although he could not read it, he nevertheless understood that it possessed great spiritual and symbolic power, saying that 'when my heart gets weak I just look up at the book, and say, Father that is your book ... then my heart gets stronger and the bad goes away.'[5] It is clear that white missionaries often had to alter their own modes of conduct: William Duncan was compelled by Native sensibilities to allow Native converts to relate their dreams at weekly prayer meetings, which then became a blend of Christian prayer and Native ceremony. The constant references in missionary literature to the high degree of backsliding within Native communities demonstrates the degree to which old ways of life persisted and co-existed alongside Christian practices. And indeed, white missionaries were even more alarmed when Native converts were too pious and initiated their own revivals, as occurred at Fort Simpson in 1876, largely because the white missionaries saw that the revivals, while ostensibly creating new Christian converts, were just as likely to be used as a front for initiation into 'traditional' Tsimshian secret societies.

What frustrated missionaries was that while they might present Christianity as not simply a belief system but as a means to 'civilize' aboriginal peoples, the impact upon daily life was often negligible, and indeed, missionaries were so ineffective at altering Native lifestyles that they needed the external sanction of the federal Indian Act of 1876 to make real inroads into halting potlatching and compelling the surrender of totem poles and sacred regalia. But even when white authorities appeared to have suppressed the potlatch, the practice took on a respectable guise when Tsimshian Christians raised money for the church through a system of feasting and public donations which all too closely resembled the prohibited potlatch! It is true that some Christian converts exhibited their new-found convictions by destroying 'traditional' symbols of Native culture such as the totem poles (a great number of which were collected by the white missionaries, who sold them to museums around the world), but the ridding of such important material symbols of Tsimshian society should not automatically be read as a decided declension. The story of missionization was not simply that of the advance of white Christian civilization, for despite the missionary attack upon Native marriage, ceremonies, and cultural artefacts, and their efforts to instil European work patterns, there existed a parallel process of an indigenization of Christianity. In the first few decades after contact, the impact of the missionary was slight, and some of the more decisive transformations in Native society were the result not of religious change, which as we have seen Native converts were able to negotiate and reinterpret, but of the integration of aboriginal individuals and communities into a commercial, capitalist order.

If, up until the 1890s, the missionary encounter remained a racially mixed one, in which white, mixed-blood, and Native proselytizers worked either cooperatively or singly to bring Christianity to Native communities, the balance of power between white and Native began to shift precipitously once larger missionary complexes of schools, both day and residential, and hospitals were constructed. An increasingly unequal balance of power characterized the missionary project in the twentieth century, when ever larger numbers of European and Euro-Canadian evangelists, school teachers, doctors, and nurses began to shift from a mode of christianization towards a policy described by one of its principal promoters, the Conservative MP Nicholas Flood Davin, as one of 'aggressive civilization.' These auxiliary workers within the larger missionary complex were much more likely than the pastor to encounter Native peoples in European settings such as hospitals and schools. Where the male missionary often met Natives in positions as interpreters and fellow evangelists, second-generation female missionaries were more likely to meet Native patients, pupils, or charges, and this in turn moulded a more hard-edged racialist conception of aboriginal society. Forty-three per cent of Methodist women placed at aboriginal mission stations resigned within three years, and 68 per cent worked for five years or less; it was these women who were the most disillusioned with their mission experience and who adopted the most derogatory attitudes to Native students and Native women. This is not to say that male clergy did not evince racialist attitudes. But in creating a self-image of themselves as the 'white mother,' missionary women were able to rationalize a much greater level of intrusion into the daily lives of aboriginal people, especially that of Native women and children. Involved as they were in literally transforming the bodies of Native people, missionary women such as Selina Bompas, the wife of the Anglican Bishop Bompas who worked among the Dene people, were particularly critical of the parenting skills of Native women, whom they described as wild, ugly, debased, dark, and barbarous. Even though Native women were much more likely to convert to Christianity than were aboriginal men, they nevertheless were constantly portrayed in missionary discourse as the weakest links in the chain of progress and thus were targeted, along with children, for even more aggressive intervention by the female mission worker. Female missionaries created an image of themselves as extraordinary women who, in order to make the heavy sacrifices involved in teaching such an undisciplined people, were bestowed with a particularly acute sense of Christian love. Given this attitude both of quasi-martyrdom and of racial supremacy, it was not surprising that missionary women who had the most consistent daily contact with aboriginal peoples regularly recorded tales of Native resistance at being remade into Europeans.

At first, white male missionaries did not demand that Native people learn English; rather, they either learned Native languages or relied upon male and female aboriginal and mixed-blood interpreters. In fact, it was the Native people themselves who expressed a desire to have their children learn English through study of the Bible, which the Tsimshian called the 'school-um-text.'[6] At first day schools were created within Native villages, which were largely confined to the teaching of religion. For the most part these were endorsed by Native converts and were particularly advantageous to low-ranking Tsimshian or those who had been former slaves and who saw in these European institutions a means to elevate themselves within their own communities. In aboriginal society as a whole, despite the prominent contemporary attention that has been given to residential schools, only one-third of Native children attended boarding or industrial schools away from their home communities. In 1889 the Report of Indian Affairs stated that boarding schools must become the chief vehicle for Native assimilation because only when separated from the supposedly deleterious effects of aboriginal tribal life could Native children be civilized. The churches became powerful agents of assimilation when they systematically entered into an educational partnership with the Canadian Department of Indian Affairs at the end of the 1870s whereby the churches agreed to build and staff the residential school in exchange for annual government grants. Where aboriginal groups previously had been able to play off one denomination against the other within the intensely pluralistic religious environment, they were now confronted with a religious monopoly in which every denomination collaborated in the state's policy of assimilation. In this way the inculcation of Christianity became wholly fused with a conscious policy of colonialism in which the aboriginal would be totally transformed into a Christian citizen. Under the imprint of this policy by 1931 there were 44 Roman Catholic schools (three-fifths of which were run by the Oblates), 21 Anglican, 13 United Church, and 2 Presbyterian. Rather than questioning the government policy of assimilation, all churches competed tooth and nail for the government handouts, which they thought would help bolster their larger aim of Christianizing Native peoples.

The schools were run on a half-day system, whereby after studying for part of the day, Native pupils, who had often been forcibly taken from their homes by Indian agents or the police, were compelled to labour for long hours either in the carpentry shop, the kitchens, or in the fields which supplied for the school. This was ostensibly designed to ensure that the pupils would acquire skills that would enable them to function in the white economy, but in reality they were being trained for unskilled occupations such as farm labour for boys and domestic service for girls. Some Native bands were able to negotiate the terms on which they sent their children to the residential schools. For example, the Shoal Lake Ojibway of northern Ontario stipulated to Presbyterian missionary authorities that their children should not be forced to work unduly long hours, proselytization of children would be limited, parents could take their children out of school to participate in tribal ceremonies, and most importantly, church authorities would not use the police to force runaways back to the school. This, however, was very exceptional, for most children were treated in highly repressive ways. They were regularly beaten and verbally abused if they failed to speak English, and a vast majority of Native pupils lived in near starvation and under conditions of appalling sanitation, a situation which was rife for diseases such as tuberculosis and influenza, which regularly carried off a high percentage of aboriginal children in these institutions. For example, at the Anglican Crowfoot School, out of thirty-nine children, twenty-two had contracted tuberculosis; across all Anglican schools 42 per cent of children had this respiratory disease.[7] Fear of church authorities often prevented abused children from speaking out, but the Canadian government had long been aware of the gross mismanagement and abuses endemic in the residential school system. In order to implement an assimilationist agenda laid down by the Canadian state, the churches continued to fund and build these industrial schools for Native children until the cultural changes of the 1960s, when religion was no longer deemed the critical foundation of Canadian citizenship. In the final analysis, the entire residential school partnership between church and state was an abject failure because, rather than assimilating Native peoples, it actually aroused intense resistance to the white social order.

4

'Canada Is Our Parish':[1]
Social Christianity and Its
Discontents, 1910–1940

During the 1890s, the concept of social Christianity, which placed personal conversion at the basis of Christian experience but insisted that its ultimate goal must be directed outwards towards the reformation and redemption of the entire society, remained very much contested within the mainline Protestant denominations. However, the success of male-centred Christian youth organizations, where the new ideals of practical Christianity and their connection to civic improvement were taught, meant that by the first decade of the twentieth century the tenets of the new social evangelism began to entrench themselves within the Methodist and Presbyterian churches. In 1902 the Methodist Church established the Department of Evangelism and Social Service and in 1906 the Presbyterians founded the Board of Social Service and Evangelism, bridgeheads from which progressive clergy eventually seized control of the denominational machinery. So successful were these two bodies that between 1920 and 1940, the leadership within these denominations all espoused the message that human religious experience must be demonstrated through an engagement with social reform. With the founding of the Social Service Council of Canada in 1914, the Protestant churches became the core element of a constellation of reform agencies, social policy research, and legislative lobbyists, which contributed in large measure to establishing the policy orientation of the modern liberal welfare state.

Before the creation of boards of evangelism and social service within the mainstream denominations, Christian women's organizations, such as the local chapters of the Woman's Christian Temperance Union (WCTU), local women's charitable institutions, and women's missionary societies, were the primary agents in fostering a new public consciousness within the churches and in pressing them to occupy the terrain of the social. Christian women were the first modernizers within the Protestant denominations insofar as they established the first pathways to social reform outside the local congregation. For example, the WCTU was not only committed to various moral reform projects such as temperance and anti-smoking campaigns, but it was also active in educational reform, erecting institutions for the care of orphans and the indigent aged, spearheading the social purity movement for the reform of prostitutes, establishing mother's meetings, and lobbying for reforms to the legal status of women. By 1914 the WCTU was a national association with over 16,000 members, but despite its Christian designation and commmitment to evangelical tenets, there was considerable tension with local ministers because it was interdenominational and did not focus on raising funds for local pastors. Women were also involved in the social settlement movement which, by 1920, had established thirteen settlement houses affiliated with interdenominational organizations. With their long-standing participation in social causes, it might well be argued that women were at the forefront in shifting Protestantism away from its nineteenth-century emphasis upon an other-worldly personal salvation concerned with the notion of the afterlife, to a more optimistic view that the purpose of religion was to establish the Kingdom of God on earth. This goal entailed reforming both the individual and the social ills of modern urban society.

Although it is true that women were drawn to reforming the deviant, the indigent, and the 'heathen' both at home and overseas because of their strong Christian faith, the discourse of gender complementarity, which stressed separate roles for men and women, meant that there was little space for women's activism or authority within the local parish, and consequently women were driven to express their religiosity beyond the confines of the local congregation. It is for this reason that women numerically dominated organizations such as the various overseas missionary societies sponsored both by specific denominations and by interdenominational bodies. By 1931 70 per cent of the 622 Protestant foreign missionaries in India were women who had deftly manipulated the notion of women's special moral qualities to create narratives of female heroism and sisterhood with Indian women. The typical missionary was single, female, middle-class, better educated than the Canadian average, and was largely drawn from rural families in which parents or relatives were highly evangelistic church members. In short, the female missionary abroad formed a highly exceptional and not representative cohort of women. In addition, they had to pass an exceedingly stringent selection process by their mission superiors, who privileged those with schoolteaching or medical experience and those who demonstrated a particularly acute sense of personal religiosity. Mission work was not for the lukewarm Christian. White Protestant women did achieve a remarkable degree of independence from male colleagues and authority over both male and female subject peoples. Consequently, some historians have concluded that women's missionary organizations contributed to the expansion of women's participation in the public sphere. However, this emphasis on the development of white women's feminist ideals must be tempered with the fact that female missionaries were at the forefront of colonial encounters in which the racialized imperatives of British imperialism were predominant.

As Protestant colleges for women expanded at a great rate at the end of the nineteenth century, and as long-established male church colleges such as Victoria College in Toronto became co-educational in the 1880s, an expanding number of women were taught that one's Christian duty lay in working for the redemption of the wider society. Finding few outlets at home, many of these well-educated women sought a career in the newly organized overseas missionary societies. A typical missionary candidate was Dr Florence J. Murray, a Presbyterian born in Pictou, Nova Scotia, in 1894, the eldest of six children and the daughter of a minister and a schoolteacher. After acquiring a medical degree at Dalhousie University, she found little opportunity for employment in her field other than missionary work. Thus while it might be argued that as a result of their missionary enterprise the most stellar were able to carve out influential professional careers, the majority of Christian women chose to be missionaries because of their intense evangelical piety, as a means to convert their 'heathen' sisters. As well, fully one-fourth of female missionaries married during their term of service. In the first decades of the missionary enterprise, religious conversion formed the principal goal of mission work, but over time, because one-third of the missionaries were medically trained, the emphasis upon personal evangelism declined and conversion became a consequence of, rather than the impetus for, social service.

By the early twentieth century the 'civilizing mission' was deemed more important than the Christianizing of foreign lands. This was particularly evident in China, where the long-term impact of the missionary project was not the conversion of large numbers of Chinese people (for in fact most missions were in cities and the vast majority of Chinese lived in rural areas), but the education of a Chinese elite and the establishment of a medical infrastructure in which, well into the twentieth century, for every Chinese hospital there were two mission hospitals. In terms of the work of conversion the missionary enterprise was a catastrophic failure in China, especially for the Protestant churches, which remained numerically inferior to the Catholic missions. By contrast with the Protestant churches, the Catholic effort focused on the conversion of ordinary Chinese, and orphanages, schools, and famine relief were instituted as inducements for conversion. Much of this effort backfired because of the concerted missionary attacks upon Chinese folk religion, which contributed in no small way to the emergence of various organized anti-Christian nationalist campaigns that touched off anti-imperialist demonstrations in 1919. The missionary outlook began to change quite dramatically during the interwar period because missionaries had turned away from overt expressions of cultural imperialism. This alteration in missionary goals was not always brought about quietly and was often forced upon missionaries by the host society, whose educated elites, themselves taught by missionaries, rejected Western leadership. Over time indigenous resistance created new circumstances in which the missionary could no longer complacently assume Western superiority and had to demonstrate cooperation with indigenous Christians and to understand non-Christian religious traditions.

While the phrase 'women's work for women'[2] characterized both the overseas, home mission, and settlement work in the pre-1914 period, the often-expressed belief that women were morally superior to men greatly troubled the Methodist and Presbyterian church leaders in the first decades of the twentieth century. At the University of Toronto, women far outnumbered men in social work, prompting the view that social reform must be linked to a concept of active Christian citizenship that was emphatically masculine. The discourse about moral motherhood may have been important for advancing the female college movement in the 1870s and 1880s, but there was in the same period a competing discourse articulated in the popular Epworth Leagues, which sought to promote a 'virile' Christianity firmly anchored in the reform of social ills. If the watchword of the 1880s was that by redeeming women the nation itself was saved, by the twentieth century the keynote of many a sermon was that both the home and the nation, the private and the public, must become centres of Christian manliness. This gender reversal was likewise linked to the reinterpretation of evangelism from an emphasis on personal conversion to one on individual redemption as the means to practical Christian endeavour in the world. Church leaders feared that the prominence of female activity in the sphere of the social was driving educated Christian men, such as the Presbyterians Mackenzie King and Adam Shortt (professor of political economy at Queen's University), into 'secular' careers.

If the church was to become a leader in the reform nexus, it had to reinvent moral and social reform as the 'natural' terrain of masculine endeavour. So successful were the Epworth Leagues in enjoining laymen to become active supporters of the new evangelism of practical Christian reform that almost the entire generation of Methodist progressive clergy had first encountered the link between male activism and social Christianity while they were youthful members of the Epworth movement. The WCTU was in decline by 1900, largely because the Methodist and Presbyterian boards of evangelism and social service had founded the interdenominational Social Service Council of Canada, which had actively sought to incorporate a wide range of female and labour organizations under its Christian male leadership. Significantly, when the Ontario government legislated temperance in 1916 this had been brought about not by female activism but by the lobbying of a now male-dominated reform network overseen by the Anglican, Methodist, and Presbyterian churches.

Advancing the cause of social Christianity involved not simply encouraging Protestant congregations to become involved in social reform work; it also required a shift in the purpose of preaching away from teaching a body of theological doctrine towards more optimistic narratives of everyday religious experience and Christian living. Many of the advocates of the new evangelism of practical Christianity were influenced by modernist thinkers such as the American philosopher William James, who assigned a priority to experience over the intellect in assessing the validity of one's religious convictions. Others were affected by the influential work by Albert Schweitzer, *The Quest for the*

Historical Jesus (1902), which stressed the human qualities of Jesus. The progressive movement within the Protestant churches discarded the traditional other-worldly sermons that focused upon death and the afterlife in favour of a more optimistic message of Christ's redemptive love and the possibility of achieving the 'city of God' on earth. Moreover, church reformers believed that people proved their devotion not simply through church attendance (although this focus was never abandoned entirely) but by participating in redeeming the wider civic order. This was achieved not simply through evangelizing individuals as had traditionally been the case, but through transforming institutions, social relationships, and government, which needed to be reformed in terms of Christian teachings. By contrast with American Protestantism, where the 'social gospel' – that is, the redemption of the social preceded the reformation of the individual – Canadian progressive leaders cannot be properly called social gospellers, as all but a handful believed that individual salvation must be the antecedent of the larger project of Christianizing the social.

Some historians have maintained that Canadian Protestant leaders' abandonment of a rigorous theology in favour of an experiential religion focused upon individual and social redemption meant preaching a watered-down concept of social ethics, which eventually faded to a vague humanism and thus constituted a capitulation of Christianity to modern thought. This, in their estimation, consequently led to the irrelevance of the Christian churches between 1880 and 1920. Others have seen in the implementation of the new social evangelism after 1900 a clear revitalization of religion in Canada. A vast number of changes did occur within the Protestant denominations in terms of how church rituals and practices were carried out, but theological training was never fully abandoned. The traditional study in biblical exegesis remained at the core of clerical training, but to this was added the study of sociology, psychology, social work, and economics, all of which were deemed to be criti-

cal to the new ideal of clerical professionalism. This ideal
involved the notion that the modern minister must also be
a civic leader and participate in improving the wider community. Far from losing its intellectual moorings, Canadian
Protestantism between 1900 and 1940 simply expanded the
notion of professional expertise to include shorter sermons,
the introduction of newer music, modern advertising techniques, and the use of current media, all of which aimed at
bringing the religion closer to the people.

However, traditionalists within the mainstream Protestant
denominations disliked the new innovations introduced by
the advocates of social Christianity. For example, in 1926,
Rev. David Howarth of Harding, Manitoba, complained
that although his church was always full on Sunday his congregation was imbued with religious indifference. In his
view they were not sufficiently religious as they did not practise family worship and did not engage in 'prayer in secret'
with sufficient frequency. Howarth's views on religion were
far removed from the newer ideas of defenders of the new
social Christianity such as the Rev. Ernest Thomas, an English Methodist who had worked among the labouring poor
in London, who believed that ministers should speak about
'the compelling personality of Jesus'[3] in order to elicit an
immediate response that would illustrate the incarnation of
God in human relations and institutions.

In some respects the litany of clergymen's complaints
about the increasing secularization of their society was a
common ploy, closely resembling the discourse of impiety
voiced by a host of clergymen during the nineteenth century. Discourses on the calamities of modern life were used by
clergymen to galvanize their congregations for a religious
revival. What was new was that critics saw in social Christianity the 'clutch of the material'[4] as the new social evangelism
had shifted the burden of religious expression away from
the inner life of prayer to the outward manifestation of
Christian action. The introduction of social Christianity in
the Protestant denominations created a sufficient backlash

among clergymen of a more conservative disposition that in 1924 a number of them founded *The Canadian Journal of Religious Thought*, which focused upon doctrinal issues and extolled the importance of inner faith. To combat the traditionalists, progressives like S.D. Chown, who was the superintendent of the Methodist church from 1914 to 1925, declared that the old theology was effeminate and that the new model of the manly activist minister learned in Christian sociology and ethics was the only means to adapt the church to the needs of industrial society and urban audiences. Far from viewing the world about them with alarm, the Protestant churches between 1900 and 1940 were imbued with a tremendous optimism and saw in the new social Christianity a great potential for strengthening the church within the modern world. If there was a harbinger of secularism it was to be found in what S.D. Chown called the 'clouds of intellectualism' which had characterized the doctrinal preaching of an earlier era. Those like J.S. Woodsworth, who saw a seamless interconnection between the sacred and the secular, blamed church conservatives for fostering an artificial distinction between the church and the world which he believed was the product of a 'withered ecclesiasticism' and which would inevitably lead to 'a more wretched secularism.'[5]

The turn towards the social within mainstream Protestantism and Catholicism was part of a broader international attempt to apply Christian social insights to solve modern social problems. This was an effort to reinterpret old-style liberalism and redirect it towards a more collectivist formulation in which the individual was seen as part of an interdependent society. In this respect, Canadian social Christianity was the counterpart of American Progressivism and British New Liberalism, but what made Canada unique was that the reform agenda was almost wholly directed by a Christian leadership, and its imperatives were directly informed by Christian values. The peculiar shape and slow development of Canadian welfare policies prior to the 1960s, their emphasis upon individual and familial self-sufficiency, and the large social role assigned to the voluntary sector with its corollary, a weak state structure, can be largely attributed to the continued dominance which the churches, both Protestant and Catholic, exerted over the direction of the larger reform agenda.

Prior to 1918, many individual clergymen flirted with Christian socialism. For example, Rev. C.S. Eby, a Methodist, believed that a reconstructed mankind must begin with labour unionism, and he founded a socialist church in Toronto in 1909. More typical, however, was Rev. C.W. Gordon, a Presbyterian progressive from Manitoba, author of a series of best-selling religious adventure novels under the pen-name 'Ralph Connor.' In his 1914 address to the founding convention of the Social Service Council of Canada, Gordon spoke on 'The New State and the New Church,' critiquing modern capitalism for its propensity to create warfare between employers and workers. As a remedy, he advanced a vision of the millennium in which church and state would cooperate in addressing modern social problems. Far from fearing that a larger government involvement in solving social ills would displace the churches, advocates of social Christianity both within the mainline churches and within the Social Service Council of Canada (which was sponsored by the churches) lobbied for a broad range of new government social policies. Under the rubric of 'the social question,' church leaders included child welfare reform, mothers' pensions, old age pensions, housing reform, protection for prostitutes, orphans, and the feeble-minded, as well as industrial legislation and a variety of social insurance schemes. Indeed, so pervasive was the influence of the church-led Social Service Council of Canada that prior to 1940 almost every facet of social investigation, social research, social surveys, and social reform legislation fell under the aegis of Christian leadership.

The first forays in lobbying for government legislation in 1907 focused upon moral reform issues such as temper-

ance and Sabbath observance, the latter cause representing the first cooperative alliance between the institutional
churches and organized labour. However, by 1918 this nar-
rower moral agenda had expanded into a wide range of social interests which included the reform of sweated labour
through minimum wages for children and women, government intervention to establish industrial democracy, and
the establishment of a living wage for workers, a broader
labour agenda intended to forestall more radical labour
protest from anarchists and syndicalists. Despite the many
individual clergymen who helped found Labour Churches,
more typical of the majority of Protestant ministers and
leading laymen was James (Jimmy) Simpson, a Methodist
lay preacher who worked as a printer before becoming a
leading figure in the Trades and Labour Congress. Simpson's labour activism was tempered by his strong devotion
to the individualistic tenets of Methodist social evangelism
and his leading position in the Epworth Leagues.

Some historians have interpreted the First World War
as a crisis of culture in Canada because social evangelism
was powerless to explain mass slaughter and the depths of
human evil which the ordinary soldier experienced in the
trenches. There were a few military chaplains, most notably
the Anglican Rev. Robert Shires, who, following the catas-
trophe of the Battle of the Somme, renounced his vocation,
unable to reconcile Christian teachings with the devastation
of the war. They believed that the traditional doctrines of
sin and hell held little meaning for the common soldier,
and they also reacted negatively to the conservatism and
perceived elitism of the church. This was less the expression of an anti-religious mentality than a reflection of the
fact that the chaplains were all of the officer class and part
of the military hierarchy. In terms of their religious faith,
soldiers were, not surprisingly, very interested in immortal-
ity and sermons about Christ's self-sacrifice, messages which
actually reawakened their faith. Above all, since many had
already been members of the popular YMCAs as adoles-

cents, they desired a more manly and robust religion that would be more socially inclusive by considering questions of industrial society, economics, and sociology. There was a large degree of conflict between the military chaplains and the largely working-class infantry. Chaplains constantly complained about how the soldiers did not conform to their notions of religiosity because they failed to regularly attend church parades or communion services. This was not a new rupture produced by the war, but the extension of a clerical critique of young men who were the least likely to be church members. However, the soldiers thought of themselves as religious, even though theirs was a less doctrinally sophisticated evangelical faith. The reaction of the military chaplains was as much a class-based phenomenon as it was a conflict between elite and popular forms of religion.

Although there were many within the churches who protested against the war, most prominently J.S. Woodsworth, who was forced to resign from the Methodist Church because of his pacifism, the iconography and literature of the war was cast in emphatically Christian terms and drew an explicit link between Christ's sacrificial death (the evangelical doctrine of the atonement) and the heroic sacrifice of the common soldier in the field. From the point of view of ministers back home, citizen soldiers were characterized as moral crusaders active in extending God's Kingdom on Earth. For the majority of clergy, the war simply reaffirmed their view that God was present in all history, but for the more conservative, the war had a destructive effect upon old-style evangelicalism. In the end, the war was a great success for the progressives because they saw a new and more Christian civilization emerging from the destruction. Indeed, a number of those veterans who had rebelled on the front against the older evangelical preaching of the chaplains were exceedingly active religiously and formed the backbone of the new Student Christian Movement, which became a rallying point for theological liberals who extolled the human Jesus.

If the war did have a negative effect, it was because, in setting the stage for a massive wave of labour protest between 1918 and 1920, it revealed the progressives to be much more conservative on issues of labour reform and socialism, prompting further defections among the more radical elements within social Christianity. Particularly in Winnipeg, which was convulsed by a massive General Strike in 1919, Christian activists like the Methodist ministers Revs A.E. Smith and William Ivens, and the prominent social purity lecturer Beatrice Brigden, were disappointed that the progressive leadership, which had endorsed a particularly radical labour platform in 1918, refused to support the strike. However, the lines of conflict in Winnipeg were not drawn between the churches and working people. Each church was divided not because the mainstream denominations were dominated by middle-class interests, but because congregations remained cross-class in character. Those who did defect, however, did not lose their religion: Smith, though later a Communist, never lost his faith that Jesus was the saviour of the working classes; Beatrice Brigden became a Quaker; and Ivens, though ejected by his working-class congregation because they disliked his sermons on social questions, remained committed to the ideal that the 'Brotherhood of Man' is based on the 'Fatherhood of God.'[6] Many of the defectors left the mainline churches because they chafed at the institutional constraints placed upon them, and thus many either went into politics or founded Labour Churches, which were never very popular among the working classes and quickly faded by the mid-1920s. The long-term effect of the Winnipeg General Strike upon social Christianity was not to destroy its impact but, rather, to shift it away from labour issues to a reform agenda that emphasized maternal feminist questions such as child welfare, mothers' allowances, maternity benefits for women, minimum wage legislation, prison reform, and public health issues, particularly those concerning women and children.

The progressive leadership within the Presbyterian and Methodist churches believed that social evangelism, with its discussion of the inequalities of modern capitalism, would democratize religion. In many respects, their hope that sermons on social questions would attract the working class, and especially working-class men, into the mainline churches was misplaced. It appears that the greatest successes of the new social evangelism occurred among urban audiences, especially among middle-class congregations. This is not particularly surprising for the links it espoused between the churches and reform appealed to a middle-class constituency, which had hitherto been the backbone of moral reform networks. Middle-class people, such as Beatrice Brigden's middle-class cousin Bertha, wholly imbibed the progressive rhetoric of biblical criticism, the view that social reform depended on individual salvation, that a redeemed democracy lay at the foundation of class harmony between employers and workers, and that well-placed sermons at Industrial Bureaus would quell working-class agitation.

The reality of working-class religious preferences was quite at odds with this middle-class portrayal. Certainly the Labour Churches with their sermons on industrial reform did find a constituency among the working classes, but for the most part working-class congregations wanted the old-style evangelism, a discovery which soon prompted the church progressives to revise the tenets of social evangelism to give a larger space to religious revivals and to stress once again the importance of personal conversion. During the 1920s, therefore, the respective boards of evangelism and social service within the Presbyterian and Methodist denominations hired British and American professional evangelists, whose expertise in the religious vernacular was meant to draw the working classes into mass religious venues where the message of social reform could be subtly introduced under the guise of emotional, old-style preaching. Immediately following the Winnipeg General Strike in 1920, the Protestant churches in Winnipeg invited the British evangelist Gypsy Smith to hold a series of mass meetings that they believed would create the requisite 'psychological atmosphere' and be followed up with discussions of labour politics and urban reform themes. With his theology of salvation Gypsy Smith attracted an audience of four thousand people per night at the Industrial Bureau and was especially popular among returned solders and working-class men.

Although mass revivalism had been largely discounted since the 1890s by mainstream church leaders because these meetings failed to create loyal denominational church members, by the 1920s, it was more palatable to church progressives because they no longer believed that religious experience was confined merely to the local congregation. The central message of social Christianity was that religion now occurred not simply in the institutional church but in the broader culture and social relationships. Religion could now be experienced in the industrial hall, in the factory, in reform associations, and in government. Moreover, by bringing their child welfare exhibits to the local fairgrounds, theatres, and other popular leisure venues, the church progressives were able to utilize modern marketing techniques and media (such as the lantern slide and radio) to bring religion to the masses. The conversion experience could even occur in areas remote from the institutional church. Ralph Connor's popular series of novels reached a Canadian and international audience numbering in the millions. As E. de B. Ramsay, an office clerk, wrote to Gordon in 1912, his novels had brought him into closer communion with God, and its message of 'glad Christianity' and social uplift not only relieved the tedium of office work but invigorated his faith in the power of 'spiritual intangible things' in an age dominated by the material.[7] The enduring appeal of personal evangelism among ordinary Canadians explains why individual piety rather than social regeneration formed the bedrock anchoring the modern principles of social service in the life of the churches between 1914 and 1940.

Despite Rev. Ernest Thomas's quip that 'we are all social reformers now,' the increasing dominance of social evangelism among the church leadership and the clergy within both Presbyterianism and Methodism throughout the 1920s aroused considerable backlash from adherents of old-style personal evangelism. Although mainstream denominations invited flamboyant American evangelists like Billy Sunday to employ traditional evangelism as a means to inculcate the values of social service, after the First World War revivalism occurred for the most part outside the machinery of the mainstream denominations. If the 1920s constituted the period in which liberal theology dominated the mainstream churches, it was also the decade that saw the greatest expansion of conservative Protestant movements. These, to a greater extent than the established denominations, worked within modern consumer society and instituted a commodified religion directed to a variety of religious tastes. Demographically the interwar years witnessed a proportional decline in the strength of the mainline churches, although their absolute numbers continued to grow. Between 1921 and 1931, the Anglican Church declined from 16.1 per cent of the Canadian population to 15.2 per cent; the Methodist and Presbyterian churches, which respectively in 1921 claimed 13.2 per cent and 16.1 per cent of the population, were not able to translate this total strength into the new United Church, which was formed in 1925. In 1931 the United Church claimed only 19.5 per cent of the Canadian population. The continuing Presbyterian church made up 8.4 per cent, but there had been a substantial bleeding from the Presbyterian and Methodist churches toward groups like Pentecostalism, which grew from a miniscule 0.1 per cent of the population in 1921 to 0.5 per cent in 1941 – a spectacular growth from only 515 Pentecostals in all of Canada in 1911 to 58,000 in 1941, a large number of whom were in British Columbia.[8]

Whether there was a direct causal link between the rise of social Christianity and the rapid development of Pentecostalism, faith healing, independent gospel churches, and fundamentalism has not been conclusively determined. However, the example of twenty-year-old immigrant Harold Davies, who worked as a plumber in Vancouver and who was converted in the 1923–4 Charles S. Price faith-healing campaigns is significant, for it is clear that he would have preferred to remain a Methodist. When Davies explained his religious views to his local minister, the clergyman tried to talk him out of the conversion experience. This encounter induced Davies to leave behind his family's Methodist roots in favour of Pentecostalism, a faith that extolled enthusiastic and emotional religion and privileged such spiritual manifestations as speaking in tongues, bodily agitations, extemporaneous prayer, and colourful preaching.

The religious character of British Columbia provides an excellent case study to evaluate the emergence in this period of conservative evangelicalism and to seek ways to understand why Protestantism in Canada was not dramatically split into fundamentalist and modernist theological camps as occurred in the United States. British Columbia formed an 'irreligious exceptionalism'[9] to the Canadian pattern of high levels of religious identity. The mainstream denominations were weak in that province. However, British Columbia was also exceptional because of the dynamism of conservative religious movements in that province, which were extremely effective in attracting those people who claimed no particular religious affiliation. Of course, the extremely high levels of single young men in the province at the turn of the century and the consequent gender imbalance also distinguished British Columbia from the other Canadian provinces and account for the higher-than-usual levels of non-affiliation with churches. Ethnically, British Columbia was also unique, for well into the twentieth century the province contained a large British-born element. Of particular note, the dominant Protestant groups in British Columbia were the Presbyterians and Anglicans with 23.5 per cent and 30.8 per cent respectively of the province's population. The relative weakness of Methodism (12.4 per cent),[10] which had traditionally emphasized experiential and enthusiastic evangelism, might well account for the rapid expansion of sects such as Pentecostalism, which rushed in to fill a religious vacuum. Lastly, because the period of rapid church expansion in British Columbia occurred just prior to the First World War, the period when social evangelism had asserted a firm grip upon the mainline denominations, most of the clergy were solidly within the camp of theological liberalism, making British Columbia one of the most theologically liberal areas of the country. There was little liberal–conservative theological conflict there before 1917.

One of the primary reasons why conservative evangelistic movements such as Plymouth Brethren and Pentecostalism flourished in British Columbia was that many of the British immigrants had been raised in these enthusiastic sects back home. And because these conservative evangelistic religious groups had been a minority in Britain, they had no sense of a lost religious authority when they came to British Columbia. This was one of the principal reasons why conservative evangelism was less combative than its American counterparts in this period. Another significant factor was that most conservative evangelicals prior to 1940 were located in mainstream denominations, such as Presbyterianism and Anglicanism. Rather than contesting the liberal orientation of these denominations, they simply established a parallel network of colleges, such as the Vancouver Bible Training School, designed primarily to train missionaries for the China Inland Mission and lay Sunday School leaders. Indeed, many of these conservatives maintained their moderate position because they rejected notions of miraculous healing and speaking in tongues, which often made conservative evangelicalism unrespectable in the eyes of some. Like Principal Walter Ellis of the Vancouver Bible Training School, they preserved a high level of scholarship upon which to ground their conservative orientation.

Pentecostalism also remained moderate and less separatist in inclination and less literalist in its interpretation
of the Bible. By contrast, in Ontario this movement was
much more aggressive in promoting the miraculous nature
of faith healing and speaking in tongues. This less militant
religious style was a strategy that made Pentecostalism more
socially inclusive. Most adherents were drawn from the upper working classes or the lower middle class but the primary determining factor in its success was that it appealed
greatly to youth (in the 10–19 age group); its emphasis
on small, tightly knit fellowship groups provided the very
sense of community that had been lost by transient male
workers who at first felt completely unconnected with formal religion. Small gospel churches such as Metropolitan
Tabernacle in Vancouver, although very separatist in its
orientation, were very successful in attracting new members because of the small, close-knit community life they
could promise their members. The immense success of
conservative evangelical groups, many of which differed
remarkably in their theology and religious practices, was
due to flexible institutional structures and their intent to
remain as inclusive as possible. These were spaces where
young people and the dislocated were given freedom to
pray or testify at church services, or even to participate in
leadership in church services and evangelistic street meetings. Pentecostalism grew exponentially, becoming in the
late 1920s the first explicitly evangelistic body to possess a
province-wide network of churches because of its extraordinary ability to integrate new immigrants within its fold – it
was overrepresented among German, Dutch, and Scandi-
navian immigrants. In turn, there was a very high birth rate
among these groups, which meant that Pentecostalism grew
not simply by converting outsiders through mass revival
techniques, but through social reproduction within the as-
semblies themselves. However, their growth was not simply
spontaneous but required an intense level of evangelistic
activity, much of which incorporated modern advertising

techniques, in order to sustain new congregations. So successful were these modernist conservatives that during the Depression when the mainline liberal denomations were forced to close many churches for 'financial' reasons, Pentecostalism thrived, growing by 130 per cent between 1931 and 1941. It successfully tapped into a popular evangelical ecumenism by downplaying rigid denominational differences or strict credentials of membership, and it welcomed all who believed in the ultimate authority of scripture, the priority on evangelism and missions, and who expressed an opposition to theological liberalism. This proclivity towards administrative and theological flexibility allowed conservative evangelicalism to constantly adapt to new geographical and social conditions so that by the end of the Second World War these groups were able to expand into the new suburbs in Vancouver and Victoria and, more significantly, were able to attract new immigrant groups, especially those from Asia.

The 1920s witnessed an explosion of Pentecostalism in Vancouver largely as a result of the Charles Price Mission (1923–4). Because Price explictly advocated faith healing, his popular mass meetings aroused a great deal of acrimony from progressive ministers in the mainline churches, thus giving rise to a public discourse which emphasized a polarization between liberal and conservative elements, even though at the social level conservative evangelicalism did not entirely view itself as functioning in response to liberal social evangelism. By contrast, in Ontario, social Christianity had to constantly battle against an entrenched conservative element, which could appeal to Methodist or Presbyterian 'traditions' to defend the importance of personal conversion. Thus there emerged higher levels of religious conflict in that province, with the Methodist and Presbyterian newspapers constantly sniping at the Pentecostals and other faith-healing revivals. The most celebrated modernist–fundamentalist split occurred among Ontario Baptists, many of whose clergy had been trained in the United States and had become acclimatized to the liberal–conservative clashes. The central issue was the allegation of Rev. T.T. Shields, who headed the denomination's most important congregation, Jarvis Baptist in Toronto, that modernist teaching had infected McMaster University. Shields was a rigid adherent of pre-millennialist dispensationalism, which meant that he believed that the second coming of Christ was imminent and that the Bible, as the literal record of truth, contained precise directives as to when this would occur. As an exponent of this miraculous return of Christ, he and many other Baptists adamantly rejected the idea so dear to social evangelists that human effort could bring about the Kingdom of God on earth. Significantly, Shields was an opponent of enthusiastic evangelism, faith healing, and Pentecostalism, which led not only to conflict with liberals but also to a further fracturing of conservative evangelism, a distinct contrast with the British Columbia pattern, where conservative evangelicals cooperated and so remained a significant cultural force. Social as well as theological motives lay behind Shields's charges, as it is clear that he spoke for a constituency of non-college-educated ministers who were aggrieved that McMaster graduates were obtaining the more prestigious pulpits and pastoral charges within the denomination. Unable in 1926–7 to oust his liberal opponents – most notably Chancellor H.P. Whidden, an unapologetic promoter of the inclusion of modern sociology and psychology in the theological curriculum – from control of McMaster University, Shields and his supporters split from the Baptist denomination to form the Union of Regular Baptists of Ontario and Quebec.

Despite the high levels of liberal–modernist conflict even within smaller evangelical churches in Ontario, the marketing of consumer culture created a truly mass audience for fundamentalism, decisively shaping urban evangelicalism and evident in the popular faith-healing campaigns during the 1920s which particularly appealed to women. Indeed, faith healing was so popular that it flourished within Pentecostalism and became a primary technique for conversion among independent evangelists like Oswald Smith. In 1928 Smith had founded the People's Church on Christie Street in Toronto. Like social evangelism, conservative evangelicalism prospered insofar as it was able to downplay its theological content and tap into a widely diffused popular desire for an unmediated faith that highlighted the immediate encounter – and in the case of faith-healing, a direct bodily encounter – between the individual and God. The message of salvation through individual choice characterized both liberals and conservatives, and both, in many respects, conformed to the ethos of liberal society. By the interwar years, public expressions of Protestantism claimed to transcend the specific and the local and in so doing largely eradicated older denominational and theological particularities. For both the exponents of social evangelism and conservative or fundamentalist Christianity, the aim of making religion more 'vitally related to the mass of the people'[11] ensured that the church as a local denominational entity was no longer critical to furthering the wider christianization of society. Mass culture or society, rather than the church proper, was the modern parish. Similarly, the important Catholic Action Movement within Roman Catholicism within both French- and English-speaking Canada similarly eroded the doctrinal authority of the clergy and the solidarities of the old parish community by establishing a mass organization whose touchstone of Christian engagement was the commitment of a new socially conscious lay elite acting in their daily lives to save the 'masses.' This new standard of what constituted a true Christian had a more tenuous connection with traditional, clerically defined religious practices such as regular church attendance or participation in the sacraments.

The response of the Catholic Church to the perceived social ills of the modern age followed a similar trajectory to Protestantism between 1900 and 1950. In 1901 Quebec Catholics lived in 650 parishes with over 100 missions in 9 dioceses; the clergy all held to a similar religious outlook, that of a conservative ultramontane orthodoxy which was promulgated by the Pope and the hierarchy of bishops. The Church was an enormous edifice with more human and financial resources than the existing provincial government. Between 1900 and the Second World War the church's political power expanded because it effectively inserted itself into both the educational and social welfare fields. By the 1920s it had established no fewer than fifty hospitals and asylums and dozens of specialized caregiving institutions for orphans, the aged, and the deviant, and entirely controlled the primary levels of public education, the francophone universities, and secondary education for the professional middle classes (the *collèges classiques*). For example, in 1929, the Catholic clergy and nuns made up 43 per cent of schoolteachers at all levels, and it also owned and operated 181 schools of household science and 31 normal schools to train lay teachers.[12] Like mainline Protestantism, the Catholic Church created a vastly expanded administrative machinery that included directors of Catholic social action, chaplains for the newly created Catholic trade unions, directors of mutual benefit and cooperative societies, and a director of Catholic publications, all of whom allowed the Church even greater control over the socialization of ordinary Catholics.

The conventional image of Quebec as 'a priest-ridden society' dates from the early twentieth century, but it did not make Quebec exceptional, because at the same time English-Canadian society was dominated by the Protestant churches. Where the penetration of the churches into the social order in English Canada was brought about largely by Christian laypeople, in Quebec this similar process of expanding the institutional church into the social was largely accomplished by the clergy. The traditional lay religious fraternities expanded markedly in this period, reaching a peak in 1935. In that year, the Franciscan orders alone reached 584 fraternities with 100,000 members.[13] These organizations remained one of the core centres of orthodox lay piety and only began to decline rapidly between 1962 and 1972. The key to the Church's power lay in the fact that between 1901 and 1931 the total Catholic population in Quebec increased by 72 per cent and the total numbers of clergy increased by 102 per cent, which meant that the institution was more than able not only to provide spiritual services to an expanding population, but also to engage in a massive program of educational and charitable institution building. More importantly, the religious orders that controlled much of the educational apparatus and most of the social assistance work of Quebec expanded by an impressive 146 per cent during these three decades.[14] To give a sense of the enormous spatial and visual presence of the Catholic Church in the twentieth century in Quebec, between 1870 and 1950 every medium-sized city in Quebec had a complement of convents, Catholic hospitals, colleges, and normal schools, as well as institutions to house the various religious orders.

In English Canada the Protestant churches achieved enormous public authority prior to the Second World War largely through their ability to control the 'secular' social reform networks and provide intellectual and political leadership for the foundation of university social services, through which they had a direct impact upon the direction of government policymaking on social welfare issues. By contrast in Quebec, the Catholic Church had a more remote relationship with government. However, the Church possessed a firmer hold on the day-to-day management of a vast number of social and educational institutions because of the huge human resources available to the Church. Although we tend to think of the Catholic Church as more monolithic and centralized than Protestantism, the constant jockeying between rival religious orders and between the clergy and various Catholic Action movements resulted in an apparently larger religious penetration in social life, but one that was less coordinated and hegemonic than was evident in Protestantism, where the boards of evangelism and social service exerted far more centralized control over the clergy prior to the Second World War. A telling illustration of the less-coordinated control of Catholicism over the response to social problems is that it never succeeded in establishing a National Catholic Welfare Conference. By contrast, the mainline Protestant churches and their reform allies did create the very powerful Social Service Council of Canada, which was, up until the Second World War, the leading sponsor of social research and social welfare legislation.

Where Protestant advocates of social Christianity believed that the emerging state would be firmly directed by religiously sponsored legislation, in Quebec the Catholic Church's relationship with the state remained much more ambiguous. The 1921 Public Charities Act set the tone of church–state relations in Quebec. While the Bishops welcomed permanent financial assistance from the state for their caregiving institutions, they remained suspicious that the state might use legislation in this field to extend its regulatory control over the churches. Where the mainline Protestant churches believed the whole society, including the state, was Protestant, the Catholic Church hierarchy saw a disjuncture between the church and the 'secular' government. Significantly, the two papal encyclicals that inspired the Catholic engagement with the social – *Rerum Novarum* (1891) and *Quadragesimo Anno* (1931) – both upheld the conventional liberal tenets of private property and individual rights against state expansion. While in 1891 the Pope gave a tepid endorsement of workers' associations as part of an international critique of the worst excesses of capitalism, this was coupled with a stern rebuke against the expansion of the state. By 1931 the Pope tolerated moderate forms of socialism with the caveat that these were ultimately anti-religious and that reform must occur through a corporatist approach. This meant that reform of the economy and society must be undertaken by civic voluntary institutions such as the family and associations of workers and employers, and not the state. What all the papal encyclicals issued between 1891 and 1961 shared in common was the belief that the reform of the social order must be based on the spiritual renewal of individuals.

Where the majority of clerics in Quebec were from rural areas, and thus somewhat insensitive to the challenges facing the urban working classes, among English-Canadian Catholics there was a greater degree of cohesiveness between the clergy and working people because the overwhelming majority of the hierarchy were from the ranks of worker families. While they were not necessarily opposed to the dominant economic system, a good many sensed the radical significance of the social encyclicals and their challenge to materialism. By contrast with the Quebec Catholic hierarchy, English-Canadian bishops were always more favourably disposed to labour unionism and moderate socialism. In the late nineteenth century Archbishop Lynch of Toronto endorsed the Knights of Labor, and in the 1930s there was a greater Catholic engagement with the Co-operative Commonwealth Federation (CCF). In English Canada one of the most enduring and successful manifestations of the emerging Catholic critique of modern industrial society was the Antigonish Movement led by Monsignor Moses Coady of St Francis Xavier University. Founded in 1921, the Movement taught fishermen and farmers in the Maritimes the techniques for forming cooperatives, and later assisted miners in Cape Breton in a form of economic rehabilitation that would at the same time forestall communism; a series of labour schools in Sudbury and Windsor in Ontario served a similar function. Although the English Catholic hierarchy endorsed the support of trade unions offered in the 1891 encyclical, in practice, they displayed little acceptance of unionism. It is this general atmosphere of opposition to industrial democracy that ultimately pushed many ordinary Catholic workers into secular trade unionism. In Quebec, the hierarchy's obstinate refusal to countenance secular trade unionism led to the creation between 1907 and 1930 of a structure of confessional trade unions which enlisted approximately one-third of Quebec's unionized workers and was particularly strong in smaller and medium-sized industrial centres outside of Montreal. Their strong anti-communist bias, however, led to a pattern of non-strike-based unionism. By the 1930s, the membership began to question the Catholic union philosophy of corporatism and its quietist approach to labour relations, and in the postwar period the union movement shifted towards a more social democratic and Christian humanist perspective, rejecting the stranglehold that the church hierarchy had exerted over union politics.

In English-Canadian Catholicism the church hierarchy was the principal forum for the introduction of modern techniques and philosophies for social action. It is striking that the two major Toronto Catholic newspapers – diocesan *The Catholic Register* and *Social Forum* – became vehicles for the dissemination of Catholic social teaching. In the 1920s much of this teaching focused on labour questions but eventually shifted towards a more overt promotion of corporatist values when the discourse began to concentrate on stabilizing marriage and the family, a conventional trope of liberalism. Given the Catholic hierarchy's positive engagement with modern social problems, lay-inspired movements such as Catholic Action only took off during the 1950s in English Canada. By contrast, in Quebec, where the bishops remained intransigently wedded to ultramontane conservatism, the Catholic Action movements were extremely vital for embedding modern social issues within Catholic culture in Quebec. The first phase of Catholic Action, which was adult-led, parish-based, and under the control of the local clergy, began in the first decade of the twentieth century and aimed at the rechristianization of Quebec society. With this goal in view, it generated a large number of charitable institutions and was best known for founding discussion groups such as the École Sociale Populaire, led by the Jesuit

Father Joseph-Papin Archambault and a number of associates. These groups produced an enormous number of tracts and pamphlets on moral and social questions ranging from alcoholism, family life, and Catholic trade unionism. In this phase the movement was conservative in terms of its social values, even though it did offer a temperate critique of unreformed capitalism.

Catholic Action entered a new phase in the 1930s when urban clergy began to fear the defection of working-class youth from religious observance. From these somewhat defensive beginnings, Catholic Action became a movement of laypeople that stressed class and age equality, thus telling working-class youth that they had a prominent role to play in moulding Catholic citizenship in Quebec. As part of its rejection of clerical leadership, the Catholic Action groups adopted a radical new principle of organizing Quebec youth, discarding the local parish structure in favour of mass-based class, gender, and workplace solidarities. Although many priests participated in the Catholic Action movements, especially in Montreal, these organizations met with considerable clerical resistance. For example, Archbishop Courchesne of Rimouski had initially endorsed Catholic Action in 1936, but by 1942 he concluded that the movement was too urban and too working-class and conflicted with his own nostalgic ruralism. Not only did he have disdain for lay Catholic youth, whom he believed had no place in the leadership of Catholicism, but he also believed that Catholic Action interfered within the clerical hierarchy because young clergy had imbibed the anti-authoritarian message of their lay associates in the movement. Courchesne recoiled at the age reversal of power relations expounded by Catholic Action, which he believed taught that 'those who are fifty or sixty don't understand anything.' Courchesne also disliked the more individualistic tenor of Catholic Action, retorting: 'Our milieu, in this diocese, is not class, but the parish. And in the parish, it is still the family that is the fundamental social group.'[15]

In the 1930s and 1940s these new movements promoted the interests of youth by establishing lodging for the homeless, legal protection for disadvantaged youth, savings banks, vacation camps, leisure activities, and local reading clubs. The most popular aspect of Catholic Action was the marriage preparation movement, which at its height in the 1950s attracted 50 per cent of all engaged Catholic couples in the Montreal diocese, who were attracted to the newer notions of companionate marriage and sexuality which it promulgated. Catholic Action successfully fused two types of organizations: one wing was devoted to leisure and popular education; another possessed a strong intellectual dimension, making it a political forum for the socialization of youth leaders in Quebec, whose vision was a christianized modern society. As a result of Catholic Action's efforts in Quebec the terrain of the social became synonymous with the category of youthful expertise. The defining element of Catholic Action was that modernity was to emerge within the non-clerical structures of the church, but significantly the discourse of the movements articulated a radical disjuncture between lay-inspired modernity and clerical obsolescence that enabled the Catholic laity to claim religious and spiritual superiority over the clergy. In Protestantism, the modernist–conservative debate generally occurred between the mainstream denominations and various evangelical sects, whereas in Quebec the more hegemonic, less pluralistic religious environment dictated that the 'culture wars' be fought out within Catholicism itself.

Aside from its vigorous promotion of youthful Catholic citizenship, the importance of Catholic Action lay in defining society not as an abstract entity, as traditional Catholic social philosophy had done, but as a concrete reality which was in need of practical social action. During the first phase of Catholic Action social thinkers like Leon Gérin, a lay Catholic, introduced European theories of sociology to a wider public through his studies of rural parishes. Between 1910 and 1940, a more doctrinally Catholic form of sociology emerged under the leadership of Esdras Minville, professor of political economy at the University of Montreal. This school interpreted modern social problems as the consequence of the ills of capitalism and of the situation of French Canadians as a colonized people, thus joining social ethics and French-Canadian nationalism under the banner of a religiously inspired remedy, the social philosophy of corporatism. To a greater degree than previous Catholic thinkers, Minville advocated state intervention. His fusion of nationalism, Catholic sociology, and corporatism inspired the *Programme de restauration sociale* of 1933, a document which, by envisioning a corporatist social and state structure, significantly reconfigured Quebec politics in the 1930s by splitting the dominant Liberal party into reformist and conservative wings. Indeed, the Church's corporatist program of the 1930s promulgated an officially Catholic state, a significant breach with both clerical ultramontanism and federalism, but advocates like Minville always feared that too much state centralization might imperil French-Canadian national survival.

After 1940, the dominant figure in Quebec sociology was Father Georges-Henri Lévesque, who was directly inspired by the second phase of Catholic Action. Lévesque founded the École des Sciences Sociales at Laval University; his guiding principles moved the discipline of sociology even further towards religious priorities, as he was committed to applying the concepts of Christian humanism and the philosophy of personalism, a tendency enormously influential in interwar and postwar Catholicism. Personalism stressed the absolute primacy of the human person and emphasized the centrality of the individual's engagement in society as an expression of spirituality. Thus, it played a key role in pushing Quebec Catholicism towards researching and reforming the problems of working-class life and urban social structures. Significantly all the major sociologists in Quebec from the 1920s to the 1960s had been influenced by Catholic Action and all of them remained wedded to the idea that modern sociology was the mechanism for establishing a truly Christian Quebec society. The introduction of sociology in Quebec was developed once the social question was publicized by Catholic lay movements and emerged out of reformist Catholic thinking that sought to use the social sciences as an instrument for the moral regeneration of society. Its aim was to train 'social apostles' who would be able to infuse Christian ethics into modern disciplines such as economics, industrial relations, social work, and sociology. So seamless was the intersection between Catholic social thought and Quebec sociology that as late as 1950, 80 per cent of the graduates of Father Lévesque's school of social science were members of the clergy; the number of priests and religious only began to decline rapidly after 1953.[16]

Catholic sociology closely resembled the general outlook and strategies of the Protestant progressives in its emphasis on the connection between scientific facts and moral reform, its belief in the use of sociology and social work to uplift individual character, and its general goal of revising and updating laissez-faire liberalism. In English Canada, the uniquely close connection between mainline Protestantism and the social sciences gave the churches a pre-eminence in defining the scope and method of the social sciences and thus gave a peculiar cast to the importation of specialized knowledge of social problems from Britain and the United States. The ultimate goal of the churches to create the Kingdom of God on earth meant that they consistently avoided the more objectivist forms of social science, such as behaviourist psychology and value-free sociology, in favour of social scientific investigation, which, although empirical in its method, was firmly anchored to the pursuit of an ethical standard and the advocacy of a type of reform explicitly animated by the concerns of social Christianity. The power the churches continued to wield over the character and agenda of the social sciences extended not only to the training and employment of social scientists, but more importantly to the identification of the problems and the very definition of a legitimate scope of activity for the social sciences in modern Canada. The authority of Protestant social Christianity over the social sciences persisted well into the 1930s and was responsible for delaying the introduction of objective and technocratic social engineering into the key disciplines of social work and sociology. By 1940 academic social science was only beginning to distance itself from its early relationship with social Christianity in favour of a new alliance with a growing federal state bureaucracy.

As in Quebec Catholicism, the major English-Canadian schools of social work at McGill University and the University of Toronto were built with the express aim of fostering a marriage between social research and social reform, both of which were believed to help bring about the social redemption of Canadian society. Indeed, the McGill Department of Social Service was largely funded by the theological colleges, and its goal of basing professional social work on Christian values was preserved under the leadership of Professor Carl Dawson, a Baptist minister. The majority of students trained in these schools were clergymen, female settlement house workers, and active Protestant laypeople employed in the various Protestant-funded charities and in the 'Protestant' state's industrial schools, juvenile courts, and homes for the aged, orphaned, and delinquent, thus fulfilling the schools' ideal that all social workers be professing Christians. Similarly, the Department of Social Service at the University of Toronto was founded in order to use social investigation as the means to establish 'a moral order which is Divine,' in the words of Sir Robert Falconer, the university's Presbyterian president.[17] Not only did the Presbyterian, Methodist, and Anglican churches take a leading role in establishing sociology and social work as university disciplines, they also in 1926 founded the Canadian Association of Social Workers, an organization that constructed a professional identity around the ideals of social Christianity. Moreover, the mainstream Protestant denominations controlled *Social Welfare*, virtually the only journal devoted specifically to social research and social reform in Canada prior to the Second World War. Because of the dominance that the Protestant progressives exerted over all social policy between 1914 and 1940, a large number of clergy undertook investigative work for governments, sat on government commissions, or directed provincial and federal social agencies.

By the latter stages of the Depression, however, the churches' control over social reform movements, social research, and welfare policymaking began to slowly erode. The first cracks in the link between social work and Christianity appeared in the mid-1930s when a number of prominent clergymen began to assert a dualism between the secular and the sacred, which would have appeared quite foreign to earlier progressives like J.S. Woodsworth. Rev. Claris Silcox, who became head of the Social Service Council of Canada, no longer believed in the engagement between the churches and wider society. Significantly he changed the name of the organization to the Christian Social Council of Canada, a recognition in part that some social workers did not necessarily work from overtly Christian motives. By the beginning of the Second World War, the previous institutional presence of the churches in the field of social welfare was replaced by a newer, more individualistic view of how religious principles should be embedded in the wider culture. As W.E. Taylor of Wycliffe College declared at the end of the 1930s, social reform should henceforth be brought about by having individual Christians, rather than the institutional church itself involved with social work and social reform.

Within Quebec Catholicism, the late 1930s marked a decisive movement away from direct institutional intervention under corporatist auspices in favour of a more individualistic assertion of personalism. The international Church hierarchy began to have doubts about the identification of corporatism with political doctrines of fascism. In Quebec itself, Catholic promoters of reform through corporatist principles were sorely disappointed by the Union Nationale

government of Maurice Duplessis, a traditional conservative. After 1937, both Catholic Action and socially conscious
clergy turned to the reform of the family and personal
relations in a more conservative desire to reinforce social
solidarity, identifying the nuclear family as the source of
personal spiritual fulfilment and emotional stability. New
social movements such as the Service de Préparation au
Mariage, founded in the early 1940s, and the populariza-
tion of child psychology by lay advocates such as Claudine
Vallerand, signalled this new turn to a personalist definition of family and social relations. However, this conservative turn had significant long-term implications. By shifting
the terrain of the 'social' from labour movements and the
structural reform of capitalism to the family, marriage, and
sexuality, the Catholic hierarchy tied the Church's social
action to a terrain where a celibate clergy could claim no
superior expertise over the laity. This led, in the postwar
period, to the emergence of family life, marriage, and re-
productive choice as terrains of contestation between clergy
and laity.

A similar pattern was emerging within the mainline Protestant denominations by the 1930s. By then the notion
that the institutional church should directly involve itself
in social reform and lobby for government legislation in
the field of economic and social reconstruction was increasingly viewed with discomfort by United Church clergymen,
even those who had been earnest champions of the ideal
of social Christianity before the Depression. What then
had changed to make social Christianity into such a con-
tentious issue within the churches themselves? First, the
agenda of the church progressives to awaken the nation
to the nature of modern social problems was all too successful. By the 1930s the various church-inspired social reform coalitions, university departments, and political lobby
groups had effectively generated government legislation in
the field, and new disciplines such as social work expanded
rapidly beyond immediate church control. Second, because

the economic crisis of the Depression resulted in the politicization of social and economic issues, many clergymen believed that supporting social Christianity implied making a distinct political choice between left-wing socialist or right-wing conservative alternatives. The emerging view that social Christianity could not remain non-partisan or under the control of the institutional church was not misplaced: younger radical clergy founded the Fellowship for a Christian Social Order, whose distinct left-wing bias articulated a direct equation between social Christianity and democratic socialism. This created a politicized atmosphere within the United Church itself, which compelled those not of a politically leftist persuasion to shift their allegiances away from an overt identification with social Christianity.

In the early stages of the Depression, J.R. Mutchmor, the head of the United Church's department of evangelism and social service, optimistically believed that the balance between social Christianity and personal evangelism could be preserved, and that this progresssive synthesis could adequately address what was still viewed as a temporary economic recession. However, as the economic and political crisis of the Depression deepened, and especially in the wake of the CCF's Regina Manifesto of 1933, which called for the eradication of capitalism and the nationalization of industry, the conventional progressive platform of blending voluntary and state reform now seemed obsolete and ineffective. In 1932, the United Church's Commission on the Church and Industry recommended the creation of a national economic research and planning board, comprehensive social insurance, and direct state intervention to 'humanize' economic conditions, a vision that largely restated the aims of the Social Service Council during the 1920s. In the political climate of the pre-Depression era, the Social Service Council had had few competitors in the field of social research; however, by the late 1930s, social science expertise had become far more secular. It was the cadre of young economists like Leonard Marsh, who was unconnect-

ed with church-based reform networks, to whom Mackenzie King and his cabinet turned to devise remedies for the
Depression and provide postwar social security planning. It
is of significance that not one Protestant or Catholic clergyman was invited to sit on King's Advisory Committee on
Reconstruction. All of these changes both within the wider
political climate and within the churches themselves meant
that many clergymen who had previously championed social Christianity as the primary demonstration of one's faith
now turned to individual piety as the non-political haven
and emotional salve of traditional evangelicalism.

The decisive shift away from the practical application
of Christian belief towards individual conversion as the
quintessential benchmark of the Christian experience was
driven by popular religious mores. As the Depression continued, an immense groundswell of popular piety accentuated not social endeavour but the 'sacredness of human
personality.'[18] Protestant clergy observed that ordinary Canadians weary of the Depression wished the churches to
officially withdraw from the acrimony of political controversy and sought in the churches an emotional appeal for
personal conversion, consolation, and solace that could be
best provided in the small fellowship meetings modelled
on the highly successful Oxford Group Movement that
toured Canada in 1933–4. At the Oxford Group meetings
people were encouraged to publicly unburden themselves,
a psychological release from the lengthy economic crisis.
Working-class people had always placed a great priority on
personal experience in religion, so the change from social
to personal evangelism, which was the focus of the clerical
discourse of this period, described a change in middle-
class religious temperament. By the beginning of the Second
World War the vast majority of clergymen now believed that
the best way to bring about the Kingdom of God on earth
was not through the direct management of the social by the
institutional church, but by the sending forth of christianized individuals into the secular world. The concept of the

institutional church in both Protestantism and Catholicism focused much more narrowly upon individual piety and the personal sphere of the family. Thus the parish was no longer viewed as co-extensive with the nation; rather the church had become privatized as it withdrew from the realm of the social. However, religion, as a cultural system carried by individuals, was still seen to inhabit the broader culture. Thus this institutional withdrawal did not entail a secularization of Canadian society, but it did represent an individualization of the project of Christianizing the social.

5

'The In-Group and the Rest':[1] The Churches and the Construction of a New Urban Lifestyle, 1940–1965

By the mid-1960s a group of university-educated professionals within the United Church, the Anglican Church, and Roman Catholicism were troubled by what they denounced as the unthinking conformity of the mass of Christian believers. A symposium held to debate Pierre Berton's immensely popular and controversial book *The Comfortable Pew* (1965) set forth the essential paradox of modern suburban society: religion as a cultural force was less dynamic, while the institutional churches were flourishing. What these public intellectuals outlined was a fundamental disjuncture between thoughtful religion, which they believed occurred both inside and outside the church, and the ritualistic practices of the faithful and regular churchgoer, which they considered devoid of religious values because they were merely conventional. At the heart of this ongoing critique of the mainstream churches was a more general anxiety about postwar affluence and an increasingly middle-class Canada, which they feared had become too materialistic, too conformist, and more interested in mass culture, than in offering through their religion a sustained critique of modern social forces. Berton and other intellectuals juxtaposed the ideal of the church as a university seminar in which faith was driven by constant discussion and social engagement against the notion of 'traditional institutional life,' which was conformist and unthinking. They declared that the issue now facing the churches was whether or not it was possible to break out of the present structures of middle-class religion and to face theological change in vigorous, open, and creative debate. Most importantly, they called upon the church to become more contemporary and authentic. Although Berton and his associates were highly critical of the institutional churches, they did not envision a secular Canada. Their aim was to reconstruct and modernize them so that religion continued to be the central animating force for the creation of a truly humanistic culture.

This portrayal of the churches as merely conservative, materialistic, and unthinking institutions (a perspective incorporated into many recent historical interpretations of the period) was simply a critique of the immense success enjoyed by all forms of Christian religion in the two decades following the Second World War. These were the views of a generation formed by the Depression. They fully imbibed the view of both Protestantism and Catholicism that true religious conviction could only be achieved through intense personal struggle. Even though many pessimists feared that the Second World War and its consequent migrations both from overseas and within Canada itself had emancipated individuals from the bonds of community, the statistics on churchgoing and church expansion during and after the war demonstrate that the majority of Canadians and recent immigrants continued to see the church as fundamental to their individual and collective identities. The United Church alone built 1500 new churches between 1945 and 1966, while church attendance remained buoyant: in 1946, 60 per cent of Protestants attended church on Sundays, and by 1956 this figure stood at 43 per cent, a level of attendance similar to that reported in 1896, the supposed heyday of evangelism. Only by 1965 had there been a further decline to 33 per cent. However, as late as 1961 the United Church Board of Evangelism and Social Service confidently reported that more people went to church than ever before and that suburban churches had had to create two morning services to accommodate everyone. Indeed the 1961 *Maclean's* magazine survey of Guelph, Ontario, stated that the majority of Protestant and Catholic respondents continued to see the church as a 'home' or 'refuge.'[2] And in British Columbia, known as the most secular province in Canada, Pentecostalism flourished into the 1960s and beyond and, more remarkably, was able to capture the allegiance of new immigrant groups through the utilization of mass media and an effective structure of Sunday schools. If identification with the institutional church, or at least with attendance at Sunday service, began to decline in 1965, religious belief remained intact. Sales of religious books and periodicals flourished in this period, with Protestant church papers surpassing the one million mark in circulation. In 1960, fully 42 per cent of Canadians read the Bible privately at least once a week. Despite this impressive evidence of popular identification with Christianity, many historians have recycled Berton's critique of mass culture and postwar consumerism by concluding that the expansion of church building and church attendance did not represent a real religious revival, and have assumed that material success in suburbia was synonymous with a superficial faith and a knee-jerk conservatism.

In part, the notion that Protestantism was in crisis and had become too middle-class and intellectually flaccid was promoted by lay intellectuals and clergy, who reacted to the tremendous success of Catholicism in both Quebec and English Canada. The Roman Catholic Church remained a vital community institution for the huge influx of European immigrants during the 1950s, and its activities transcended the purely spiritual and moral to encompass immigrant advocacy, language training, child care, leisure, and financial assistance. More tellingly, the Catholic parish served as a dynamic feature of modernity, providing opportunities for sociability and leadership that integrated immigrant individuals and families into the culture of English-speaking North America. So successful was Catholicism in urban

English Canada that Toronto, a city that in 1941 was solidly Protestant (80 per cent) had, by 1971, become 40 per cent Roman Catholic. Thus when Stewart Crysdale, a sociologist of religion, protested that the United Church was becoming too middle-class and suburban, what he was really exercised about was that the Catholic Church now dominated the inner-city population. In Quebec, between 1940 and 1968, the Catholic Church was highly effective in responding to the movement of people from rural to urban areas, and from the inner city to the suburbs. No less than 491 new parishes were created in this period, and three-quarters of these were subdivisions of older parishes, which allowed the church to improve the ratio of priests to people. The Catholic Church in Quebec was highly successful in reinvigorating the idea of the parish as an urban community centre, leading to a dramatic extension of activities that modernized the church but also allowed it to further control social change in an urban milieu. In addition, between 1930 and 1959, 74 new religious communities were established, thus allowing the church to become the largest employer in Quebec due to its management of education, social welfare, and cultural and charitable movements. Up until 1971, becoming a nun or a priest was still seen as socially prestigious, and only in that year did there occur the first decisive abandonment of clerical vocations.

Much of the criticism levelled at the postwar churches revolved around the issue of their material success. Influenced by the latest sociological theorists, Pierre Berton claimed that people were now going to church merely to become status seekers, and that a flourishing church was like a successful business, needing to show that its membership and budget were growing. Of course, the view that people were consumers of religious faith, shopping around for the right service, and that clergymen were obsessed with fund-raising and congregational growth, was hardly new, as this discourse had existed in one form or another since the Protestant Reformation in the sixteenth century.

It is true that the suburban churches did focus their attention on raising money, and the rapid expansion of church building also meant the incurring of enormous debt, a situation which replicated that of the 1880s. Indeed, the plea that the church become more interested in public affairs, in questions of socialized medicine, public housing, unemployment, and automation merely echoed the early twentieth-century campaign of the promoters of social Christianity. Similarly, the charge that the churches must become more relevant and 'manly' was a long-standing rhetorical trope within the mainstream Christian churches.

What was new about the postwar critique of the churches was not that the church had lost its appeal to working-class or immigrant groups – the success of Catholicism certainly belied this – but that as more Canadians became affluent, their values were becoming more 'middle-class,' a term which meant that they were no longer critical or questioning of prevailing social norms. In other words, the expression 'middle-class' became a synonym for social conformity and a lack of social engagement. As June Callwood remarked of the postwar churches, 'there is a dehumanizing pride in bigness, a preoccupation with prettiness and a viewpoint no taller than the steeple – but not including the Cross. Church work doesn't seem broadly enough defined to attract more than a minority of Christians.'[3] Rev. J.R. Mutchmor, the head of the United Church Board of Evangelism and Social Service, charged that the church was becoming too middle-class, which really meant that most people were simply interested in their personal religious faith and not in wider social questions.

Moreover, when Berton referred to the fact that people went to church not for theology but to find 'their own kind of people,' this did not necessarily mean that the churches were in fact becoming less socially inclusive. In postwar Canada, by contrast with earlier generations, fewer Canadians moved from church to church over their life course, and religious affiliation and identity were extremely stable.

Canadians were meeting their own kind at church, and this had distinct negative implications for the future potential of evangelizing outsiders. What most troubled Berton and young university-trained urban sophisticates was that they were unable to find people like themselves in positions of influence in church congregations. As Crysdale put it so well, the United Church had become 'with its clubs, societies, and circles, a cheap, lower middle-class country club.'[4]

The portrayal of the churches as quiescent middle-class country clubs was in fact part and parcel of a broader elitist backlash against mass civilization, popular culture, and growing state intervention that enlisted both liberal and conservative intellectuals. They feared mass culture because it seemed to create such a level of abundance that would lead to the eradication of a true social critique of modern society. Thus, along with their more left-leaning views that the church should become more relevant were exhortations of a more conservative nature. Berton and others hankered for a more community-centred local church, more doctrinal preaching, and greater church unity. Despite their recommendations for reformation of the divorce laws, more lenient treatment of homosexuals within the church, and support for birth control and even abortion, their belief that the churches must align themselves with the advance of personal freedom was designed to shore up the primacy of the family unit in a modern society characterized by the impersonal and the bureaucratic. To a large degree, the critique of the postwar church was merely a vehicle for expressing larger cultural anxieties about social conformity, a loss of the personal in modern society, and a withdrawal from political engagement in an affluent society. It also reflected a novel appreciation of what Crysdale called 'the urban frontier,' in which a 'conglomeration of people of diverse origins and backgrounds' was producing unprecedented levels of competition for mainstream Protestant denominations. Thus, even though in 1963 it was reported that 57 per cent of suburban congregations continued to increase their membership, this masked an underlying fear that unless the Anglican and United Churches 'got with it' they would eventually lose the numbers game to Roman Catholicism, sectarian evangelical, and non-Christian groups. The malaise that these intellectuals expressed marked a recognition that postwar Canada's 'pluralistic society'[5] was increasingly non-Protestant. The supposed spectre of 'secular humanism' expressed a fear not of secularization but of the displacement of the United and Anglican churches from the privileged public position they had enjoyed since the early twentieth century.

For many Protestant social commentators, true liberalism was identified with Christianity and, more specifically, with Protestant religion, which they believed was the only basis for individualism, democracy, and freedom in the modern world. The idea that the church remained one of the few established social institutions that protected and enhanced individual values was given greater currency in the postwar world largely as a reaction against the expansion of the modern social security state, which, in the estimation of both conservatives and liberals within the churches, eroded both spiritual and individual values. Although the progressive wing of the United Church continued to champion the ideal of a mixed welfare economy in which voluntary institutions like the church would maintain a key role in sponsoring social legislation, they shared with the traditionalists the fear that an expanded state would lead to secularism and materialism. Generally speaking, the greater intrusion of the state into economic and social life prompted a conservative backlash not only more generally within Canadian culture but also within the mainline Protestant denominations themselves. For example, the United Church Commission on the Church, Nation, and World Order (1944–5) articulated for the first time an absolute distinction between the church and the world, thus rupturing the equipoise that had sustained the earlier social evangelism. This commission was openly antagonistic to state expansion and more particularly to family allowances, not only because these were seen to uphold the Catholic tradition of large families, but because they believed that human (spiritual) values could be sustained only in the private sphere of the church and family.

A growing breach began to appear between those who desired an intellectualized high theology and those, like Joan Hollobon, who feared that the technical language of the church intelligentsia would drive out ordinary parishioners who might favour the simple themes of grace, salvation, and atonement, the verities which had formed the core of traditional evangelism. Although Hollobon and others favoured a more accessible faith, they also held pejorative views of those 'illiterates' who submissively accepted older dogmas of human sinfulness, which she believed had no place in modern society. Those ordinary parishioners who regularly attended Sunday service were viewed as part of the 'secret agnostic infection' because they were thought to be 'unbelievers'[6] who did not engage in the ferment of church reform. Where Hollobon and others like her endorsed the New Curriculum of the United Church which was introduced to Sunday Schools in 1964, because it represented a 'new theological stirring'[7] adapted to modern times, there was just as large a cohort of young people who preferred the inner personal religion over social questions, believing that theology and the modern social sciences were ultimately in conflict with each other.

The vast number of letters that Pierre Berton received from ordinary believers from a wide range of churches exposed the extreme bifurcation that had occurred across denominational lines between fundamentalists and modernists. Mrs Lyle Chappel of Dundas, Ontario, was distraught that Berton found fundamentalists personally repugnant, for while she too was dissatisfied with the hollowness of the preaching in the United Church, she had rediscovered vital 'Christian love' within a fundamentalist sect. By contrast,

Ida Galloway of the neighbouring city of Hamilton agreed with Berton's assessment of the church as outdated, but her remedy was a complete evisceration of formal religion and the institutional church, stating that Divinity lay only within each individual, which entirely removed the need for concepts of sin, grace, and atonement. All correspondents generally agreed that there was a religious stalemate within the mainstream denominations, that many apathetic 'vegetable Christians' inhabited the pews, that the clergy often appeared hypocritical or simply ineffective, and that people went to church merely for a 'sense of belonging.' However, the nostrums for what ailed the church ranged over a vast theological terrain upon which there was no consensus. Perhaps the most damning indictment of contemporary Christianity was stated by Jain Barnett, an eighteen-year-old student at Bishop Strachan School in Toronto, who concluded her letter by saying that 'I have come to the conclusion that agnostics and atheists care more about what happens to the church than complacent "pew-warmers" that merely accept and never question.'[8]

Although the split within the United Church was between proponents of evangelism and those who envisioned a social activism bereft of any attachment to old-style conversionism, contemporary observers like Crysdale attempted to apply the latest sociological theories to argue that this theological fragmentation was but the cultural expression of more fundamental socio-economic dichotomies between urban and rural lifestyles, between the university-educated and those who were not, between young and old, and between the social classes. Because he believed that differences in belief were the direct result of lifestyle and that there was a direct correlation between an urban perspective and a liberal theology, his remedy for these religious conflicts ultimately lay in the possibility of melding all Canadians into one coherent urban lifestyle. In short, he wished for the very conformity of culture he so adamantly accused middle-class church members of so slavishly following. Ultimately

Crysdale maintained that liberal theology could once again become hegemonic within the United Church. However, although the United Church remained ostensibly committed to the ongoing national revivalistic campaigns throughout the 1950s, this was not in fact supported by evangelical beliefs. In the end, an 'explosive split'[9] between liberals and conservatives in the United Church was not papered over by the mere manipulation of language; indeed, it continues to fester beneath the surface.

A similar pattern had emerged within the Catholic Church after the Second World War. The Quebec clergy was alarmed at a number of wartime social measures undertaken by the provincial Liberal government under Premier Godbout that had the effect of moving the state into areas traditionally defined as the purview of the church: education, family, and social services. The hierarchy's support for the conservative regime of Maurice Duplessis, who governed Quebec between 1944 and 1959, had less to do with anti-communism and more to do with the church's defence of a particular kind of liberalism that dictated the absolute separation of church and state, with the church functioning in an independent role in directly managing education and charitable assistance. In order to sustain this particular liberal vision, the Catholic clergy introduced several modern techniques of professional welfare management to forestall further state expansion. For example, Mgr Charles Bourgeois of Trois-Rivières pioneered the first francophone social agency in Quebec and was one of the leading advocates in elaborating youth social policy prior to 1960. This illustrates that an invigorated Roman Catholicism, together with a charismatic leader, could effectively head off new child protection legislation. In the long run, although the church did take considerable initiative in the field of social welfare and health up until the mid-1960s, it was ultimately dependent upon government for financing this expanding system. Although clergy and religious orders were reluctant to give up their Catholic orphanages, by the 1950s the new orientations in social work were clearly moving in the direction of foster care. The special relationship that developed between the church and the Duplessis regime created a polarization within both the clergy and the laity over state expansion, labour relations, and the clergy's direct management of orphanages, hospitals, classical colleges, and universities. These deep-seated divisions between the political left and right within the Catholic Church, representing those who supported a more independent Catholic Action and those (largely clergy) who wished to incorporate the movement into the traditional parish structure, came to a head in 1949 with the particularly bitter Asbestos Strike. In 1950 the Quebec Bishops issued a Pastoral Letter which seemingly aligned the church with the labour movement's demands for co-management, but under the pressure of more conservative elements, advocacy of worker democracy was watered down to support for a fair wage. This dashed the hopes of the religious left and resulted, by 1956, in the public assertion by André Laurendeau, editor of the influential Montreal Catholic newspaper *Le Devoir,* that parties of 'left' and 'right' existed within the church.

Commentators on the left, including Pierre Trudeau, Gérard Pelletier, André Laurendeau, Claude Ryan, and Fernand Dumont, offered a critique remarkably similar to that of their English-Canadian counterparts like Pierre Berton. They wished to reinforce the power of Catholicism as a force outside the state by calling for its engagement with modernity, which they maintained could only be accomplished by reducing the clergy's control over the day-to-day institutional life of Quebec. Claude Ryan, national secretary of Catholic Action, complained that although the institutional church had succeeded in preserving orthodox piety among ordinary believers over the course of three centuries, Catholic religious life in Quebec lacked a solid intellectual foundation. Worse, he charged that the clergy were too closely linked to the 'traditional' Quebec elites of lawyers, politicians, and businessmen and, in consequence, had not developed ties with those 'vital elites' of modern Quebec – by which he meant university professors, journalists, intellectuals, and artists – so critical to the articulation of public opinion and the foundation of authority in an age of democracy. Trudeau and other writers for the left-leaning magazine *Cité libre* expounded a clear distinction between true faith, by which they meant an intellectually driven and thoughtful consideration of theology, and superficial piety, which they derided as conformist because ordinary parishioners (largely women) unquestioningly followed the traditional rituals of the church. What so exercised these reformist intellectuals was that although this popular Catholicism was very vital in the postwar period – as exemplified by the outpouring of devotion at the 1947 Marian Congress in Ottawa, which attracted over 500,000 believers – they feared that because it was conformist in nature and not innovative or responsive to social change, it might very well become the vehicle for secular values, especially a derivative, American-style materialism.

By the end of the 1950s Catholic Church leaders in Quebec were beginning to recognize a worrying pattern of declining religious practice: in 1948 it was estimated that 30–50 per cent of Montrealers did not regularly attend Sunday mass, and in a 1958 survey of the working-class parish of Saint-Simon-de-Drummond, 75 per cent of parishioners followed the prescriptive rituals outlined by the clergy, with 25 per cent of families responding that they were lukewarm in their public worship. Most troublingly, it appeared to observers that young people aged 17–25 were 'losing their faith.'[10] To counteract this apparent drift away from the parish, the church devised a new collective pastoral plan called the 'Grande Mission,' which sought to awaken individuals so that they would become committed to a more communitarian piety through a systematic plan of preaching, lay activity, charitable works, and the application of modern sociological principles. This new trajectory marked the church's validation of the work of Catholic Action, which had operated since the 1930s as a parallel religious structure outside the immediate control of the local parish. This desire among church leaders to move Catholicism further into the public sphere came too late. The polarization over labour issues that had split the church along political lines since the late 1940s, induced many influential Catholics, both lay and clerical, to favour disengagement from forms of direct institutional management that might involve them in political controversy. For example, in 1965 church officials withdrew their support for Catholic Action because they feared that organizations such as the Jeunesse ouvrière catholique and the Jeunesse étudiante catholique were developing into avenues for youth participation in politics and that these 'Christian' youth groups might become a conduit for socialist and even Marxist ideas.

The significant development within social Catholicism in the 1950s was a concentration on more personal and private issues. For example, by 1952 Catholic schools began to introduce courses on dating, marriage, and birth control, particularly geared to working-class youth. This move towards family values and private life meant that the church began to shift its emphasis from orphanages, hospitals, and social assistance programs from the late 1950s onwards to stress Catholic schooling as the most crucial means to further Catholic values within Quebec society. By the early 1960s church leaders had come to the conclusion that the religious values of families and youth were in crisis and that a new partnership between church and state, in which the church would continue to control religious education, would have to be created in order to ensure the continued authority of Catholic values in Quebec. Between 1963 and 1965, the Catholic bishops employed the language of democratic pluralism and the new imperative of the Second Vatican Council, which enjoined a refurbished public partnership between the Catholic Church and modern democratic states to forge a compromise with the reformist Liberal provincial government. Under its terms, church authorities, convinced that Catholicism would continue to form the basis of social cohesion in modern Quebec, agreed to a thoroughgoing reform of public education in Quebec, conceding to the government the power to directly manage primary, secondary, and university education. The institutional church retained a significant presence within a confessional structure, which would allow it to more effectively preach a modernized Christian message to students.

In the ensuing decades the church ultimately lost control over the direction of both school administration and curriculum even though this secular trend in education had not been foreseen in the 1960s. In addition, with the expansion of the state during the Quiet Revolution under the Liberal government of Jean Lesage, the idea of the parish as a community centre lost its purpose as the government began to take over activities such as leisure, savings banks, and local cooperatives; after 1965 civil registration meant that marriage was no longer the exclusive domain of the Catholic Church. By contrast, in Toronto, Catholics in this period created a proliferating structure of leisure activities, banks, social clubs, and language schools for immigrants, thus further enhancing the importance of the parish for recent immigrant communities and continuing the dynamic linkage between ethnicity and the institutional church.

Within the United Church there was similar evidence of an unbridgeable split between those clergy and laity who wished to maintain evangelical traditions and those, such as the contributors to *The Sea Is Boiling Hot*, who proposed a socially activist theology they termed 'an evangelism oriented to the future not the past.'[11] Pierre Berton's charge that humanistic agnostics had a more elevated social conscience than actual churchgoing Christians and that the mainstream Protestant denominations had become quiescent and too linked to the social establishment was a criticism taken seriously by the United Church, which had always seen social engagement as part of its mission. However, much of what Berton wrote was directed at the Anglican Church, which was more conservative on a range of political, social, and moral questions. From the end of the Second World War onwards, the United Church Board of Evangelism and Social Service was actively engaged in a wide range of social questions from problems of unemployment, housing for the poor, the status of refugees, the condition and rights of aboriginal peoples, nuclear disarmament, the Vietnam War, liberalization of abortion and birth control, and reforms of divorce laws, all of which indicated that it was still a church militant and not, as many critics believed, a church devoted merely to social complacency. In 1965 the Board addressed issues such as sex and the new morality, poverty, and the negative effects of automation, and defended the concept of universal health care; in 1966 they urged decriminalization of marijuana, campaigned for state support for unwed mothers, and introduced topics such as 'Bob Dylan as Theologian' and 'The Holy in Coffee Houses,' which were explicitly designed to make the church relevant for modern youth. By 1970 the Board's publications openly quoted from Joan Baez's anti–Vietnam War songs, but by that time there was little reference to personal conversion and its importance for social reform.[12]

While United Church leaders never openly repudiated evangelistic practices, they quietly set about abandoning the church's evangelical tenets. By the 1950s the United Church rescinded its endorsement of mass revival campaigns such as those held by Billy Graham, even though the attendance at Charles Templeton's popular evangelistic missions, managed in the 1950s by the Board of Evangelism and Social Service, indicated that widespread support for evangelism among ordinary Canadians persisted. By the 1960s, there was a clear separation between evangelicalism and social service, in part because evangelicalism had come to be seen as just another Americanism (in an era of intense anti-Americanism particularly in the intellectual community) and liable therefore to 'turn people off.'[13] The United Church dissolved the Board of Evangelism and Social Service in 1971, and large numbers of people began to defect from the United Church.

It might well be argued that the mainstream Protestant churches simply failed to cope with the vast cultural and social changes that occurred during the 1960s and, as Berton claimed, had simply become irrelevant institutions more interested in maintaining external conformity than in providing a Christian perspective on modern social problems. It could be alternatively argued that the United Church in particular remained fragmented and divided not simply between liberals and conservatives, but within the liberal ranks themselves. Throughout the 1960s liberals agreed on the need to reform theology, church rituals, Sunday school curriculum, and the social and political issues to be addressed. Ultimately, there was no agreement on whether the United Church as an institution should interface with other collective institutions, such as labour unions, government, business, and social movements, or whether social reform should be accomplished by the action of Christian individuals in the workplace, the shop, the social club, and the classroom. Crysdale had hoped that the United Church could move beyond older Protestant notions of personal responsibility towards a 'modern' notion of 'corporate responsibility,'[14] but in the midst of a social climate dominated during the postwar period by an extreme individualism, both in terms of rights and obligations, the United Church was driven back to its individualistic roots. This occurred not because of a compromise with conservatives who championed personal evangelism, but because of the pressure from female reformers within the church who desired a greater degree of personal satisfaction within marriage and family life.

Despite the United Church's abandonment of the concept of personal conversion by the mid-1960s, the notion of the individual conscience and the importance of the individual within society became more prominent during this period, within both Protestant and Catholic traditions.

Since the 1930s Catholic Action had attempted to establish an uneasy compromise between a theology of personalism, which elevated the human person above institutional constraints, and older doctrines of social corporatism founded upon notions of hierarchy and authority. By the 1950s, however, the personalist element was clearly becoming dominant and was, as in the United Church, largely driven by women's desire to enter the workforce, which necessitated compromises by the church hierarchy on issues of birth control and sexuality. The impetus for modern views of family and gender relations, which included the ethic of personal fulfilment rather than procreation as the core value of marriage, came from the laity, especially laywomen, rather than from the institutional hierarchy. The campaigns of Catholic Action, however, resulted in a more reformist attitude among the clergy, even though most remained reluctant to endorse even the most tepid liberalization of birth control. During the 1950s a majority of Quebec men and women seemed to follow church regulations regarding the use of the rhythm method, which allowed both a modicum of sexual pleasure but upheld older doctrines of sexual abstinence, to the point where social observers described these practices among ordinary Catholics as a 'baptized Neo-Malthusianism.'[15] However, by the 1960s, as the Pill provided an almost foolproof alternative, combined with a greater cultural priority for personal fulfilment, there was a massive defection by ordinary Catholics from church moral teachings. In Quebec, this translated into a complete abandonment of the church as a whole, as many Catholics tended to equate access to Catholic ritual and practice with adherence to moral teachings regarding sexual ethics and birth control. The vicious circle that was created by offering only a temperate support for birth control was best described by a Quebec woman who wrote in 1964 to the Catholic organization founded to promote the rhythm method. This woman explained why she reluctantly but finally left the church. In her words, the rhythm method failed to prevent her pregnancies, and so she turned towards methods of birth control that were condemned by the church. As a result, she felt guilty when praying to God, and in fact the clergy consistently refused the sacraments to her, and so her only recourse was to choose either unwanted pregnancy or the church. She ultimately chose personal freedom. Most Quebeckers, like this woman, continued to believe in God, but as the church's position on sexual issues hardened after a papal encyclical condemned the Pill in 1968, they could no longer participate in good conscience in the sacrament of confession, the church's remaining regulatory authority over the individual.

By the late 1950s the United Church had moved from an emphasis on the 'social witness'[16] to an accent on the 'conscience of the sincere individual,'[17] which clearly indicated that human values did not reside in the corporate or public spheres, but that the private sphere of the family and, most crucially, the realm of personal fulfilment, were the only authentic buttresses of the spiritual when the 'world' was increasingly defined as secular. In many respects, the United Church also experienced difficulties because of the women's movement. Between 1945 and 1966 the United Church's perception of sex changed radically from an emphasis on original sin to a view of sex as the highroad to the Kingdom of God. Prior to the 1957 Commission on Marriage and Divorce, many clergymen had already turned towards family issues, seeing in this private realm a bulwark of the human personality and an antidote to the mass cultural conformity brought about in their view by the modern technocratic state. By the late 1950s the family was no longer seen merely as a protection for democratic freedom, but was viewed as the most important focal point for religiosity in which commentators equated the home with the divine. After the commission recognized the dramatic upsurge in married women in the workforce and realized the need to keep divorced people within the United Church, they jettisoned the concept of original sin and enunciated a new concept of sexual morality in which sexual fulfilment was seen as the principal means of preserving the individual personality. In fact, some church liberals began to define sex within marriage as sacramental. Although the goal of making sex more fulfiling for women was to keep married women at home and the family intact, it had fewer conservative long-term implications for the United Church. In abandoning the concept of sex as sinful, and by thus leaving sexual morality to individual choice, the church eviscerated much of its evangelical heritage, which, in the final analysis, rested upon universal moral principles and the individual need for redemption. Once sexual morality became relativistic, so too, by implication, did all other social codes and conventions. In the final analysis, the United Church was unable to uphold a notion of Christian Canada when it had itself abandoned an explicit distinction between sin and salvation. Thus, it can be argued that evangelicalism in the United Church foundered upon the rock of modern gender identities and human sexuality. Although both the Protestant and Catholic denominations did address the problem of the sexual revolution, the churches' attempts to provide leadership in the realm of sexual morality did not lead to a reinvigorated religion. Rather, it led to mass defection in the case of Catholicism and, in the case of the United Church, to even deeper theological divisions surrounding issues of the politics of the body.

By 1965, both Protestant and Catholic institutional churches had been weakened in terms of their ability to frame consensual positions on public issues, either because the churches chose to focus upon private issues of the family, sexuality, and leisure, or because the emergence of an expanded state in the postwar era led to a narrowing of the church's role from the terrain of the social to the confines of the rituals of individual religious practice. There was no more potent symbol of the fact that Christianity no longer automatically defined citizenship than the fact that the new Canadian flag, introduced in 1965, did not feature a cross, as had the old Union Jack. The flag symbolized the emergence of a new civic nationalism that made no reference to religious identities, and, significantly, its unveiling coincided with the divisions within organized Christianity brought to the surface with *The Comfortable Pew*, the United Church's New Curriculum, and the liturgical reforms of Vatican II. The new nationalism marked an emphatic secularization of the public sphere, a questioning and dismissal, in the name of cultural and religious pluralism, and of the ability of the Christian religion and of the mainline Christian churches alone to legitimize and sacralize the state. In short, the mainline religious denominations were reduced to one among many interests who sought a claim upon the multicultural liberal state, and, consequently, the Canadian churches could no longer sustain the project of a Christian society.

More detrimental for the preservation of their public authority, the mainline religious denominations also experienced a rapid decline in terms of church attendance and participation in the sacraments. Between 1965 and 1975, for example, weekly attendance at mass for Roman Catholics fell from 83 per cent to 61 per cent, with a further steep drop to 43 per cent by 1986. Among Protestants, the decline was less steep, but nonetheless palpable: in 1956, 43 per cent of Protestants attended weekly services, 32 per cent in 1965, and 25 per cent in 1975. But if the churches had declined in terms of their wider cultural authority, religious belief itself continued to have a firm hold in terms of individual choices and values, which indicated a general decline within the society of associational life and the notion of joining an organization as the vehicle of either class and ethnic identity or as a benchmark of civic belonging. The idea that one could believe without belonging to a particular religious organization had been promoted by many church leaders within the United Church who believed that organizations of any type constituted a threat to privacy and so promoted the idea of the concept of the 'hidden Jesus,'[18] in which spirituality might pervade society (in this case industry) without any visible institutional manifestation. The long-standing tradition of popular religiosity in which individuals were free to choose their affiliation had always been resisted by the clergy, who saw the institutional church as an important locus of social regulation. However, the notion of freedom of religious choice was now the institution's official policy.

Ultimately individuals did not think they needed the churches. In 1965, Stewart Crysdale found that fully 84 per cent of Protestants believed in a personal God, 81 per cent in the divinity of Christ, 74 per cent considered private prayer indispensable in their personal lives, 85 per cent had experienced salvation, and 76 per cent believed the Bible to be God's truth. Interestingly, fully 65 per cent of the United Church members surveyed regularly took communion. When Crysdale's survey of the United Church is compared with the popular religious surveys of Reginald Bibby undertaken in the 1980s, there are a number of key similarities: similarly high levels of belief in the divinity of God (83 per cent) and Christ (79 per cent), and, most surprisingly for a supposedly secular society, a continuing high value placed upon private prayer (53 per cent). Most surprisingly of all, fully 89 per cent of both men and women continued to keep some sort of church affiliation if only for the purposes of baptism, marriage and funerals. Although the church as a public institution experienced a cyclical rhythm of growth and decline over the century between 1840 and 1960, religion as a system of private practices and personal values remained remarkably unchanged despite the vast social, economic, and political alterations in the fabric of Canadian life. What had changed, however, was that institutional churches, which until the 1960s had been widely regarded as both fundamental and necessary to the expression of private and public identities, were rejected by many ordinary Canadians as conformist and constraining to individual freedom, to the 'sovereign individual conscience,'[19] which was now the measure of all things. The story to be told is not one of long-term religious decline into irrelevance in the face of modernity, but one in which the fit between church and its clergy and religion and the people was always uneasy, ambiguous, and fraught with tension.

Notes

1. The Religious Cultures of Discipline and Dissidence in Colonial Society

1 United Church Archives [UCA], Records of the Glasgow Colonial Society [GCS], Vol. 1, Reel 1, Rev. John Sprott, Musquodoboit, N.S. to Rev. Dr Burns, May 1827.

2 Elias Elliot to his Brother, Richard Elliot, 24 Sept. 1832, in Wendy Cameron, Sheila Haines, Mary McDougall Maude, eds, *English Immigrant Voices: Labourers' Letters from Upper Canada in the 1830s* (Montreal and Kingston: McGill-Queen's University Press, 2000), 87, quoted in Nancy Christie, '"Proper Government and Discipline": The Epistolary Discourse of Family Religion,' paper delivered to conference on 'Churches and Social Order,' Université de Montréal, 2002.

3 T.W. Acheson, 'Methodism and the Problem of Methodist Identity in Nineteenth-Century New Brunswick,' in C.H.H. Scobie and John Webster Grant, eds, *The Contribution of Methodism to Atlantic Canada* (Montreal and Kingston: McGill-Queen's University Press, 1992).

4 Library and Archives of Canada [LAC], William Gibson Papers, David Gibson to Uncle, 6 March 1843.

5 Acheson, 'Methodism and the Problem of Methodist Identity.'

6 Hannah Lane, 'Tribalism, Proselytism, and Pluralism: Protestants, Family, and Denominational Identity in Mid-

Nineteenth-Century St Stephen, New Brunswick,' in Nancy
Christie, ed., *Households of Faith: Family, Gender, and Community in Canada, 1760–1969* (Montreal and Kingston: McGill-Queen's University Press, 2002), 103–37.

7 William Westfall, *Two Worlds: The Protestant Culture of Nineteenth-Century Ontario* (Montreal and Kingston: McGill-Queen's University Press, 1989).

8 Paul Romney, 'On the Eve of Rebellion: Nationality, Religion, and Class in the Toronto Election of 1836,' in David Keane and Colin Read, eds, *Old Ontario: Essays in Honour of J.M.S. Careless* (Toronto: Dundurn Press, 1990).

9 'Advice to a Young Clergyman,' *The Christian Guardian*, 31 May 1843.

10 Christine Hudon, *Prêtres et fidèles dans le diocèse de Saint-Hyacinthe, 1820–1875* (Quebec: Septentrion, 1996); Ollivier Hubert, *Sur la terre comme au ciel: la gestion des rites par l'Église catholique du Québec (fin XVIIe siècle – mi-XIXe siècle* (Sainte-Foy: Les Presses de l'Université Laval, 2000).

11 Baptist Archives, McMaster University, Joseph Clutton Diary, 3 May 1846.

12 *Canadian Independent Magazine* (Congregationalist), 12 June 1859.

13 Allan Greer, *The Patriots and the People: The Rebellion of 1837 in Rural Lower Canada* (Toronto: University of Toronto Press, 1993); Hudon, *Prêtres et fidèles*; Hannah Lane, 'Evangelicals, Church Finance, and Wealth-Holding in Mid-Nineteenth-Century St Stephen, New Brunswick, and Calais, Maine,' in Michael Gauvreau and Ollivier Hubert, eds, *The Churches and Social Order in Nineteenth- and Twentieth-Century Canada* (Montreal and Kingston: McGill-Queen's University Press, 2006), 109–50.

14 United Church Archives, Gould Street Presbyterian, Minutes, 19 Mar. 1875.

15 Westfall, *Two Worlds*.

16 Hubert, *Sur la terre comme au ciel*.

17 Bettina Bradbury, 'Mourir chrétiennement: la vie et la mort dans les établissements catholiques pour personnes âgées

à Montréal au XIXe siècle,' *Revue d'histoire de l'Amérique française* 46, no. 1 (été 1992): 143–75; Brigitte Caulier, 'Les confréries de dévotion traditionnelles et le réveil religieux à Montréal au XIXe siècle,' *Études d'histoire religieuse* 53 (1986): 23–40.

18 United Church Archives, Bath Wesleyan Church Minutes, 28 November 1840.

19 Lynne Marks, 'No Double Standard? Leisure, Sex and Sin in Upper Canadian Church Discipline Records, 1800–1860,' in K. McPherson, Cecilia Morgan, and Nancy M. Forestell, eds, *Gendered Pasts: Historical Essays in Femininity and Masculinity in Canada* (Toronto: Oxford University Press, 1999); Nancy Christie, 'Carnal Connection and Other Misdemeanours: Continuity and Change in Presbyterian Church Courts, 1830–1890,' in Gauvreau and Hubert, eds, *The Churches and Social Order*, 66–108.

20 United Church Archives, Gould St Presbyterian Church, Minutes, 14 February 1870.

21 Canadian Baptist Archives, Murray St Baptist Church, Peterborough, Minutes, 1868.

2. Machinery of Salvation: The Making of a Civic Christianity

1 Louise A. Mussio, 'Communities Apart: Dissenting Traditions in Nineteenth-Century Central Canada,' PhD thesis, McMaster University, 2000.

2 Brian Fraser, *The Social Uplifters: Presbyterian Progressives and the Social Gospel in Canada, 1875–1915* (Waterloo: Wilfrid Laurier University Press, 1988), 68.

3 David Marshall, *Secularizing the Faith: Canadian Protestant Clergy and the Crisis of Belief, 1850–1940* (Toronto: University of Toronto Press, 1992), 52.

4 Quoted in Neil Semple, *The Lord's Dominion: The History of Canadian Methodism* (Montreal and Kingston: McGill-Queen's University Press, 1996), 224.

5 Quoted in Patricia Dirks, 'Reinventing Christian Masculinity and Fatherhood: The Canadian Protestant Experience,

1900–1920,' in Nancy Christie, ed., *Households of Faith: Family, Gender, and Community in Canada, 1760–1969* (Montreal and Kingston: McGill-Queen's University Press, 2002), 291.

6 Michael Gauvreau, *The Evangelical Century: College and Creed in English Canada from the Great Revival to the Great Depression* (Montreal and Kingston: McGill-Queen's University Press, 1991), 125.

7 Hamilton Public Library, Special Collections, 'Knox Presbyterian Church,' clipping, *Hamilton Herald*, 25 January 1902.

8 Quoted in Kenneth L. Draper, 'A People's Religion: P.W. Philpott and the Hamilton Christian Workers' Church,' *Histoire sociale/Social History* 35, no. 71 (May 2003): 109.

9 'Three Prominent City Pastors,' *Hamilton Herald*, 28 November 1903.

10 Quoted in Mark G. McGowan, *The Waning of the Green: Catholics, the Irish, and Identity in Toronto, 1887–1922* (Montreal and Kingston: McGill-Queen's University Press, 1999), 52.

11 Quoted in Phyllis D. Airhart, *Serving the Present Age: Revivalism, Progressivism and the Methodist Tradition in Canada* (Montreal and Kingston: McGill-Queen's University Press, 1992), 25.

3. 'Their Advance in Christian Civilization': Missionaries and Colonialism at Home

1 Rev. Thomas Crosby, quoted in Susan Neylan, *The Heavens Are Changing: Nineteenth-Century Protestant Missions and Tsimshian Christianity* (Montreal and Kingston: McGill-Queen's University Press, 2003), 236.

2 Quoted in ibid., 71.

3 For a detailed discussion of these definitions of cultural contact, see ibid., 15.

4 John Lutz, 'After the Fur Trade: The Aboriginal Labouring Class of British Columbia, 1849–1890,' *Journal of the Canadian Historical Association*, new series, 3 (1992): 81.

5 Quoted in Neylan, *The Heavens Are Changing*, 229.

6 Ibid., 228.

7 Ibid., 91.

4. 'Canada Is Our Parish': Social Christianity and Its Discontents, 1910–1940

1 C.E. Silcox, *Church Union in Canada* (1933), quoted in Robert A. Wright, 'The Canadian Protestant Tradition, 1914–1945,' in G.A. Rawlyk, ed., *The Canadian Protestant Experience, 1760–1990* (Burlington: Welch, 1990), 151.

2 Ruth Compton Brower, *Modern Women Modernizing Men: The Changing Missions of Three Professional Women in Asia and Africa, 1902–69* (Vancouver: University of British Columbia Press, 2002), 3.

3 Richard Allen, *The Social Passion: Religion and Social Reform in Canada, 1914–1928* (Toronto: University of Toronto Press, 1973), 224.

4 David Marshall, *Secularizing the Faith: Canadian Protestant Clergy and the Crisis of Belief, 1850–1940* (Toronto: University of Toronto Press, 1992), 189.

5 Nancy Christie and Michael Gauvreau, *A Full-Orbed Christianity: The Protestant Churches and Social Welfare in Canada* (Montreal and Kingston: McGill-Queen's University Press, 1996), 1.

6 Ibid., 19–20.

7 Ibid., 37.

8 Wright, 'The Canadian Protestant Tradition,' 140–1.

9 Lynne Marks, '"Leaving God Behind When They Crossed the Rocky Mountains": Exploring Unbelief in Turn-of-the-Century British Columbia,' in Eric W. Sager and Peter Baskerville, eds, *Household Counts: Canadian Households and Families in 1901* (Toronto: University of Toronto Press, 2007), 372.

10 Robert K. Burkinshaw, *Pilgrims in Lotus Land: Conservative Protestantism in British Columbia, 1917–1981* (Montreal and Kingston: McGill-Queen's University Press, 1995), 27–8.

11 Christie and Gauvreau, *A Full-Orbed Christianity*, 10.

12 Jean Hamelin and Nicole Gagnon, *Histoire du catholicisme québécois: Le XXe siècle, tome 1, 1898–1940* (Montreal: Boréal Express, 1984), 251.

13 Brigitte Caulier, 'L'ordre franciscain séculier (Tiers-Ordre),' in Jean Hamelin, ed., *Les Franciscains au Canada, 1890–1990* (Sillery: Septentrion, 1990), 103.

14 Hamelin and Gagnon, *Histoire du catholicisme québécois*, 129.

15 Lucie Piché, *Femmes et changement social au Quebec: L'apport de la jeunesse ouvrière catholique féminine, 1931–1966* (Quebec: Les Presses de L'Université Laval, 2003), 80.

16 Jean-Philippe Warren, *L'engagement sociologique: La tradition sociologique du Québec francophone (1886–1955)* (Montreal: Boréal, 2003), 97, 100.

17 Christie and Gauvreau, *A Full-Orbed Christianity*, 144.

18 Ibid., 225.

5. 'The In-Group and the Rest': The Churches and the Construction of a New Urban Lifestyle, 1940–1965

1 June Callwood, '"The In-Group" and the Rest: A Commentary on the Local Congregation,' in United Church of Canada, Board of Evangelism and Social Service, *Why the Sea Is Boiling Hot: A Symposium on the Church and the World* (Toronto: Ryerson Press, 1965), 19.

2 Pierre Berton, *The Comfortable Pew* (Toronto: McClelland and Stewart, 1965), 69.

3 Callwood, '"The In-Group" and the Rest,' 22.

4 Stewart Crysdale, *The Changing Church in Canada* (Toronto: United Church Evangelism Resource Committee, 1965), 16.

5 United Church Archives, Department of Christian Social Action, 81.001C, 250/15, Board of Evangelism and Social Service, Report, 1963.

6 Joan Hollobon, 'Digging the Lingo,' in *Why the Sea Is Boiling Hot*, 25–8.

7 United Church Archives, Department of Christian Social Action, 501/7, 'New Curriculum, 1955-65.'

8 Pierre Berton Papers, Box 266, file 1, letters from Mrs Lyle Chappel, 17 February 1965, Ida Galloway, 17 February 1965, A Christian, 1 February 1965, Linda Brooks, 22 February

1965, Yvette Manigan, 3 January 1965, Margaret Sellers, 4 February 1965, Jain Barnett, 25 January 1965.

9 Crysdale, *The Changing Church in Canada*, 24.

10 Jean Hamelin, *Histoire du catholicisme québécois: le XXe siècle, Tome 2* (Montreal: Boréal Express, 1984), 134.

11 United Church of Canada, *The Sea Is Boiling Hot*, vi.

12 United Church Archives, Board of Evangelism and Social Service, 'Minutes', 1965, 1966, 1970.

13 David Plaxton, 'We Will Evangelize,' in George Rawlyk, ed., *Aspects of the Canadian Evangelical Experience* (Montreal and Kingston: McGill-Queen's University Press, 1997), 121.

14 Crysdale, *The Changing Church in Canada*, 87.

15 Quoted in Michael Gauvreau, *The Catholic Origins of Quebec's Quiet Revolution, 1931–1970* (Montreal and Kingston: McGill-Queen's University Press, 2005), 186.

16 United Church Archives, National Evangelistic Mission, 82.078, 'Report,' 1956.

17 Quoted in Nancy Christie, '"Look out for Leviathan": The Search for a Conservative Modernist Consensus,' in Nancy Christie and Michael Gauvreau, eds, *Cultures of Citizenship in Post-War Canada, 1940–1955* (Montreal and Kingston: McGill-Queen's University Press, 2003), 76.

18 United Church Archives, Board of Evangelism and Social Service, 'Hamilton – A Ministry in Industry', 1970.

19 Quoted in Claude Ryan, *A Stable Society* (Montreal: Éditions Heritage, 1978), 323.

Bibliography

Books

Abel, Kerry. *Drum Songs: Glimpses of Dene History.* Montreal and Kingston: McGill-Queen's University Press, 1993.

Acheson, T.W. *Saint John: The Making of a Colonial Urban Community.* Toronto: University of Toronto Press, 1985.

Airhart, Phyllis D. *Serving the Present Age: Revivalism, Progressivism and the Methodist Tradition in Canada.* Montreal and Kingston: McGill-Queen's University Press, 1992.

Allen, Richard. *The Social Passion: Religion and Social Reform in Canada, 1914–28.* Toronto: University of Toronto Press, 1973.

Austin, Alvyn. *Saving China: Canadian Missionaries in the Middle Kingdom, 1888–1959.* Toronto: University of Toronto Press, 1986.

Austin, Alvyn, and Jamie S. Scott, eds. *Canadian Missionaries, Indigenous Peoples: Representing Religion at Home and Abroad.* Toronto: University of Toronto Press, 2005.

Berton, Pierre. *The Comfortable Pew: A Critical Look at Christianity and the Religious Establishment in the New Age.* Toronto: McClelland and Stewart, 1965.

Bibby, Reginald W. *Fragmented Gods: The Poverty and Potential of Religion in Canada.* Toronto: Stoddart, 1987.

– *Religionless Christianity.* N.p., n.d.

Bienvenue, Louise. *Quand la jeunesse entre en scène: L'Action catholique avant la Révolution tranquille.* Montreal: Boréal, 2003.

Blumhofer, Edith L. *Aimee Semple McPherson: Everybody's Sister.* Grand Rapids: William B. Eerdmans, 1993.

Brouwer, Ruth Compton. *New Women for God: Canadian Presbyterian Women and India Missions, 1876–1914.* Toronto: University of Toronto Press, 1990.

– *Modern Women Modernizing Men: The Changing Missions of Three Professional Women in Asia and Africa, 1902–69.* Vancouver: UBC Press, 2002.

Burke, Sara Z. *Seeking the Highest Good: Social Service and Gender at the University of Toronto, 1888–1937.* Toronto: University of Toronto Press, 1996.

Burkinshaw, Robert K. *Pilgrims in Lotus Land: Conservative Protestantism in British Columbia, 1917–1981.* Montreal and Kingston: McGill-Queen's University Press, 1995.

Carter, Sara, Lesley Erickson, Patricia Roome, and Char Smith, eds. *Unsettled Pasts: Reconceiving the West through Women's History.* Calgary: University of Calgary Press, 2005.

Chaline, Nadine-Josette, René Hardy, and Jean Roy, eds. *La Normandie et le Québec vus du presbytère.* Rouen: Publications de l'Université de Rouen, 1987.

Ch'en, Jerome. *China and the West: Society and Culture, 1815–1937.* Bloomington and London: Indiana University Press, 1979.

Choquette, Robert. *Language and Religion: A History of English-French Conflict in Ontario.* Ottawa: University of Ottawa Press, 1975.

Christie, Nancy. *Engendering the State: Family, Work, and Welfare in Canada.* Toronto: University of Toronto Press, 2000.

– ed. *Households of Faith: Family, Gender, and Community in Canada, 1760–1969.* Montreal and Kingston: McGill-Queen's University Press, 2002.

Christie, Nancy, and Michael Gauvreau. *A Full-Orbed Christianity: The Protestant Churches and Social Welfare in Canada, 1900–1940.* Montreal and Kingston: McGill-Queen's University Press, 1996.

Clarke, Brian P. *Piety and Nationalism: Lay Voluntary Associations and the Creation of an Irish-Catholic Community in Toronto, 1850–1895.* Montreal and Kingston: McGill-Queen's University Press, 1993.

Cook, Sharon Anne. *'Through Sunshine and Shadow': The Women's Christian Temperance Union, Evangelicalism, and Reform in Ontario, 1874–1930*. Montreal and Kingston: McGill-Queen's University Press, 1995.

Courville, Serge and Normand Séguin, eds, *La paroisse. Atlas historique du Québec*. Sainte-Foy: Les Presses de l'Université Laval, le Fonds Gérard-Dion, 2001.

Cox, Jeffrey. *Imperial Fault Lines: Christianity and Colonial Power in India, 1818–1940*. Oxford: Oxford University Press, 2002.

Crouse, Eric. *Revival in the City: The Impact of American Revivalists in Canada, 1884–1914*. Montreal and Kingston: McGill-Queen's University Press, 2005.

Crysdale, Stewart. *The Changing Church in Canada: Beliefs and Social Attitude of United Church People*. Toronto: Evangelism Resource Committee, United Church of Canada, 1965.

Curtis, Bruce. *The Politics of Population: State Formation, Statistics, and the Census of Canada, 1840–1875*. Toronto: University of Toronto Press, 2001.

Danylewycz, Marta. *Taking the Veil: An Alternative to Marriage, Motherhood and Spinsterhood in Quebec, 1840–1920*. Toronto: McClelland and Stewart, 1987.

Emery, George. *The Methodist Church on the Prairies, 1896–1914*. Montreal and Kingston: McGill-Queen's University Press, 2001.

Ferretti, Lucia. *Entre voisins: La société paroissiale en milieu urbain: Saint-Pierre-Apôtre de Montréal, 1848–1930*. Montreal: Boréal, 1992.

Fisher, Robin. *Contact and Conflict: Indian-European Relations in British Columbia, 1774–1890*, 2nd ed. Vancouver: UBC Press, 1992 (originally published 1977).

Fraser, Brian J. *The Social Uplifters: Presbyterian Progressives and the Social Gospel in Canada, 1875–1915*. Waterloo: Wilfrid Laurier University Press, 1988.

– *Church, College, and Clergy: A History of Theological Education at Knox College, Toronto, 1844–1994*. Montreal and Kingston: McGill-Queen's University Press, 1995.

Gagan, Rosemary R. *A Sensitive Independence: Canadian Methodist*

Women Missionaries in Canada and the Orient, 1881–1925. Montreal and Kingston: McGill-Queen's University Press, 1992.

Gagnon, Serge. *Plaisir d'amour et crainte de Dieu: sexualité et confession au Bas-Canada.* Sainte-Foy: Les Presses de l'Université Laval, 1990.

– *Mariage et famille au temps de Papineau.* Sainte-Foy: Les Presses de l'Université Laval, 1993.

Gagnon, Serge, and René Hardy, eds. *L'église et le village au Québec, 1850–1930: l'enseignement des Cahiers de prônes.* Ottawa: Leméac, 1979.

Gauvreau, Michael. *The Evangelical Century: College and Creed in English Canada from the Great Revival to the Great Depression.* Montreal and Kingston: McGill-Queen's University Press, 1991.

– *The Catholic Origins of Quebec's Quiet Revolution, 1931–1970.* Montreal and Kingston: McGill-Queen's University Press, 2005.

Gauvreau, Michael, and Ollivier Hubert, eds. *The Churches and Social Order in Nineteenth- and Twentieth-Century Canada.* Montreal and Kingston: McGill-Queen's University Press, 2006.

Grant, John Webster. *Moon of Wintertime: Missionaries and the Indians of Canada in Encounter since 1534.* Toronto: University of Toronto Press, 1984.

– *A Profusion of Spires: Religion in Nineteenth-Century Ontario.* Toronto: University of Toronto Press, 1988.

Greer, Allan. *The Patriots and the People: The Rebellion of 1837 in Rural Lower Canada.* Toronto: University of Toronto Press, 1993.

Hamelin, Jean. *Histoire du catholicisme québécois: le XXe siècle, Tome 2, de 1940 à nos jours.* Montreal: Boréal Express, 1984.

Hamelin, Jean, and Nicole Gagnon. *Histoire du catholicisme québécois: le XXe siècle, tome 1, 1898–1940.* Montréal: Boréal Express, 1984.

Hardy, René. *Contrôle social et mutation de la culture religieuse au Québec, 1830–1930.* Montreal: Boréal, 1999.

Hubert, Ollivier. *Sur la terre comme au ciel: la gestion des rites par l'Église catholique du Québec (fin XVIIe – mi-XIXe siècle).* Sainte-Foy: Les Presses de l'Université Laval, 2000.

Hudon, Christine. *Prêtres et fidèles dans le diocèse de Saint-Hyacinthe, 1820–1875*. Quebec: Septentrion, 1996.

Kee, Kevin. *Revivalists: Marketing the Gospel in English Canada, 1884–1957*. Montreal and Kingston: McGill-Queen's University Press, 2006.

Little, J.I. *Borderland Religion: The Emergence of an English-Canadian Identity, 1792–1852*. Toronto: University of Toronto Press, 2004.

– *The Other Quebec: Microhistorical Essays on Nineteenth-Century Religion and Society*. Toronto: University of Toronto Press, 2006.

Marks, Lynne. *Revivals and Roller Rinks: Religion, Leisure, and Identity in Late-Nineteenth-Century Small-Town Ontario*. Toronto: University of Toronto Press, 1996.

Marshall, David B. *Secularizing the Faith: Canadian Protestant Clergy and the Crisis of Belief, 1850–1940*. Toronto: University of Toronto Press, 1992.

McCarthy, Martha. *From the Great River to the Ends of the Earth: Oblate Missions to the Dene, 1847–1921*. Edmonton: University of Alberta Press, 1995.

McGowan, Mark G. *The Waning of the Green: Catholics, the Irish, and Identity in Toronto, 1887–1922*. Montreal and Kingston: McGill-Queen's University Press, 1999.

Miedema, Gary. *For Canada's Sake: Public Religion, Centennial Celebrations, and the Re-making of Canada in the 1960s*. Montreal and Kingston: McGill-Queen's University Press, 2005.

Miller, J.R. *Equal Rights: The Jesuits' Estates Act Controversy*. Montreal and Kingston: McGill-Queen's University Press, 1979.

Milloy, John S. *A National Crime: The Canadian Government and the Residential School System, 1879 to 1986*. Winnipeg: University of Manitoba Press, 1999.

Neylan, Susan. *The Heavens Are Changing: Nineteenth-Century Protestant Missions and Tsimshian Christianity*. Montreal and Kingston: McGill-Queen's University Press, 2003.

Opp, James. *The Lord for the Body: Religion, Medicine, and Protestant Faith Healing in Canada, 1880–1930*. Montreal and Kingston: McGill-Queen's University Press, 2005.

Owram, Doug. *The Government Generation: Canadian Intellectuals and the State, 1900–1945.* Toronto: University of Toronto Press, 1986.

Piché, Lucie. *Femmes et changement social au Québec: l'apport de la jeunesse ouvrière catholique féminine, 1931–1966.* Quebec: Les Presses de l'Université Laval, 2003.

Pickles, Katie, and Myra Rutherdale, eds. *Contact Zones: Aboriginal and Settler Women in Canada's Colonial Past.* Vancouver and Toronto: UBC Press, 2005.

Rawlyk, George A. and Mark A. Noll, eds. *Amazing Grace: Evangelicalism in Australia, Britain, Canada, and the United States.* Montreal and Kingston: McGill-Queen's University Press, 1994.

Rousseau, Louis and Frank Remiggi, eds. *Atlas historique des pratiques religieuses: le sud-ouest du Quebec au XIXe siècle.* Ottawa: Les Presses de l'Universite d'Ottawa, 1998.

Roy, Jean, and Christine Hudon, eds. *Le journal de Majorique Marchand, curé de Drummondville, 1865–1889.* Sillery: Septentrion, 1994.

Rutherdale, Myra. *Women and the White Man's God: Gender and Race in the Canadian Mission Field.* Vancouver and Toronto: University of British Columbia Press, 2002.

Ryan, Claude. *A Stable Society.* Montreal: Éditions Héritage, 1978.

See, Scott. *Riots in New Brunswick: Orange Nativism and Social Violence in the 1840s.* Toronto: University of Toronto Press, 1993.

Selles, Johanna M. *Methodists and Women's Education in Ontario, 1836–1925.* Montreal and Kingston: McGill-Queen's University Press, 1996.

Semple, Neil. *The Lord's Dominion: The History of Canadian Methodism.* Montreal and Kingston: McGill-Queen's University Press, 1996.

Struthers, James. *No Fault of Their Own: Unemployment and the Canadian Welfare State, 1914–1941.* Toronto: University of Toronto Press, 1983.

United Church of Canada, Board of Evangelism and Social Service. *Why the Sea Is Boiling Hot: A Symposium on the Church and the World.* Toronto: Ryerson Press, 1965.

Valverde, Mariana. *The Age of Light, Soap, and Water: Moral Reform in English Canada, 1885–1925.* Toronto: McClelland and Stewart, 1991.

Vance, Jonathan F. *Death So Noble: Memory, Meaning, and the First World War.* Vancouver: UBC Press, 1997.

Van Die, Marguerite. *Religion, Family, and Community in Victorian Canada: The Colbys of Carrollcroft.* Montreal and Kingston: McGill-Queen's University Press, 2005.

Warren, Jean-Philippe. *L'engagement sociologique: la tradition sociologique du Québec francophone (1886–1955).* Montreal: Boréal, 2003.

Westfall, William. *Two Worlds: The Protestant Culture of Nineteenth-Century Ontario.* Montreal and Kingston: McGill-Queen's University Press, 1989.

Articles

Acheson, T.W. 'Methodism and the Problem of Methodist Identity in Nineteenth-Century New Brunswick.' In C.H.H. Scobie and John Webster Grant, eds, *The Contribution of Methodism to Atlantic Canada.* Montreal and Kingston: McGill-Queen's University Press, 1992.

– 'Evangelicals and Public Life in Southern New Brunswick, 1830–1880.' In Marguerite Van Die, ed., *Religion and Public Life in Canada: Historical and Comparative Perspectives,* 50–68. Toronto: University of Toronto Press, 2001.

Airhart, Phyllis. 'Condensation and Heart Religion: Canadian Methodists as Evangelicals, 1884–1925.' In Rawlyk, ed., *Aspects of the Canadian Evangelical Experience,* 90–105. Montreal and Kingston: McGill-Queen's University Press, 1997.

Baillargeon, Denyse. '"We admire modern parents": The École des Parents du Québec and the Post-war Quebec Family, 1940–1959.' In Nancy Christie and Michael Gauvreau, eds, *Cultures of Citizenship in Post-war Canada, 1940–1955,* 239–76. Montreal and Kingston: McGill-Queen's University Press, 2003.

Bradbury, Bettina. 'Mourir chrétiennement: La vie et la mort dans les établissements catholiques pour personnes âgées à

Montréal au XIXe siècle.' *Revue d'histoire de l'Amérique française*, 46, no. 1 (été 1992): 143–75.

Brouwer, Ruth Compton. 'Shifts in the Salience of Gender in the International Missionary Enterprise during the Interwar Years.' In Austin and Scott, *Canadian Missionaries, Indigenous Peoples*, 152–76.

Brown, Jennifer S.H., in collaboration with Maureen Matthews. 'Fair Wind: Medicine and Consolation on the Berens River.' *Journal of the Canadian Historical Association*, n.s., 4 (1993): 55–74.

Brownlie, Robin, and Mary-Ellen Kelm. 'Desperately Seeking Absolution: Native Agency as Colonialist Alibi?' *Canadian Historical Review* 75, no. 4 (Dec. 1994): 543–66.

Brunoni, Hugues. 'La culture religieuse des Beaucerons: permanences et formes nouvelles, 1852–1940.' *Études d'histoire religieuse* 67 (2001): 69–79.

Burnett, Kristin. 'Aboriginal and White Women in the Publications of John Maclean, Egerton Ryerson Young, and John McDougall.' In Sara Carter, Lesley Erickson, Patricia Roome, and Char Smith, eds, *Unsettled Pasts: Reconceiving the West through Women's History*, 101–22. Calgary: University of Calgary Press, 2005.

Carter, Sara. 'The Missionaries' Indian: The Publications of John McDougall, John Maclean and Egerton Ryerson Young.' *Prairie Forum* 9, no. 1 (spring 1984): 27–44.

– 'Creating "Semi-Widows" and "Supernumerary Wives": Prohibiting Polygamy in Prairie Canada's Aboriginal Communities to 1900.' In Pickles and Rutherdale, *Contact Zones*, 131–55.

Caulier, Brigitte. 'Les confréries de dévotion traditionnelles et le réveil religieux à Montréal au XIXe siecle.' *Études d'histoire religieuse* 53 (1986): 23-40.

– 'Les confréries de dévotion et l'éducation de la foi.' *Études d'histoire religieuse* 56 (1989): 97–112.

– 'L'ordre franciscain séculier (Tiers-Ordre).' In Jean Hamelin, ed., *Les Franciscains au Canada, 1890–1990*, 99–121. Sillery: Septentrion, 1990.

– 'Developing Christians, Catholics, and Citizens: Quebec

Churches and School Religion from the Turn of the Twentieth Century to 1960.' In Gauvreau and Hubert, *The Churches
and Social Order*, 175–94.

Christie, Nancy. 'Sacred Sex: The United Church and the Pri-
vatization of the Family in Post-War Canada.' In Nancy Christie, ed., *Households of Faith: Family, Gender, and Community in*
Canada, 1760–1969, 348–76. Montreal and Kingston: McGill-
Queen's University Press, 2002.

– '"Look out for Leviathan": The Search for a Conservative Modernist Consensus.' In Nancy Christie and Michael
Gauvreau, eds, *Cultures of Citizenship in Post-War Canada,*
1940–1955, 61–94. Montreal and Kingston: McGill-Queen's
University Press, 2003.

– '"A Witness against Vice": Religious Dissent, Political Radicalism, and the Moral Regulation of Aristocratic Culture in
Upper Canada.' In Jean-Marie Fecteau and Janice Harvey,
La régulation sociale entre l'acteur et l'institution/Agency and In-
stitutions in Social Regulation, 420–34. Sainte-Foy: Presses de
l'Universite du Quebec, 2005.

– 'Young Men and the Creation of Civic Christianity in Urban
Methodist Churches, 1880–1914.' *Journal of the Canadian His-*
torical Association, n.s., 17, no. 1 (2006): 79–106.

– 'Carnal Connection and Other Misdemeanours: Continuity and Change in Presbyterian Church Courts, 1830–1890.'
In Gauvreau and Hubert, eds, *The Churches and Social Order*,
66–108.

Christie, Nancy, and Michael Gauvreau, 'Modalities of Social
Authority: Suggesting an Interface for Religious and Social
History.' *Histoire sociale/Social History* 35, no. 71 (May 2003):
1–30.

– '"The World of the Common Man Is Filled with Religious Fervour": The Labouring People of Winnipeg and the Persistence
of Revivalism, 1914–1925.' In G.A. Rawlyk, ed., *Aspects of the Ca-*
nadian Evangelical Experience, 339–50. Montreal and Kingston:
McGill-Queen's University Press, 1997.

Cole-Arnal, Oscar. 'The Prairie Labour Churches: The Methodist Impact.' *Studies in Religion* 34, no. 1 (2005): 3–26.

Coops, P. Lorraine. 'That Still Small Voice: The Allinite Legacy and Maritime Baptist Women.' In Daniel C. Goodwin, ed., *Revivals, Baptists, and George Rawlyk: A Memorial Volume*, 113–31. Wolfville, NS: Acadia Divinity College, 2000.

Cumbo, Enrico Carlson. 'Salvation in Indifference: Gendered Expressions of Italian-Canadian Immigrant Catholicity, 1900–1940.' In Christie, ed., *Households of Faith*, 205–33.

Dessureault, Christian and Christine Hudon. 'Conflits sociaux et élites locales au Bas-Canada: le clergé, les notables, la paysannerie et le contrôle de la fabrique.' *Canadian Historical Review* 80, no. 3 (Sept. 1999): 413–39.

Dirks, Patricia. 'Reinventing Christian Masculinity and Fatherhood: The Canadian Protestant Experience, 1900–1920.' In Christie, ed., *Households of Faith*, 290–316.

Draper, Kenneth L. 'Redemptive Homes – Redeeming Choices: Saving the Social in Late-Victorian London, Ontario.' In Christie, ed., *Households of Faith*, 264–89.

– 'A People's Religion: P.W. Philpott and the Hamilton Christian Workers' Church.' *Histoire sociale/Social History* 35, no. 71 (May 2003): 99–122.

Edwards, Gail. '"The Picturesqueness of His Accent and Speech": Methodist Missionary Narratives and William Henry Pierce's Autobiography.' In Austin and Scott, eds, *Canadian Missionaries, Indigenous Peoples*, 67–87.

Erickson, Lesley A. '"Bury Our Sorrows in the Sacred Heart": Gender and the Metis Response to Colonialism – The Case of Sara and Louis Riel, 1848–83.' In Carter et al., eds, *Unsettled Pasts*, 17–46.

Ferretti, Lucia. 'L'Église, l'État et la formation professionnelle des adolescents sans soutien: le Patronage Saint-Charles de Trois-Rivières, 1937–1970.' *Revue d'histoire de l'Amérique française* 56, no. 3 (hiver 2003): 303-27.

– 'Caritas-Trois-Rivières (1954–1966), ou les difficultés de la charité catholique à l'époque de l'État-providence.' *Revue d'histoire de l'Amérique française* 58, no. 2 (automne 2004): 187–215.

Furniss, Elizabeth. 'Resistance, Coercion, and Revitalization: The

Shuswap Encounter with Roman Catholic Missionaries, 1860–1900.' *Ethnohistory* 42, no. 2 (spring 1995): 231–63.

Fyson, Donald. 'La paroisse et l'administration étatique sous le Régime britannique (1764–1840).' In Courville and Séguin, eds, *La paroisse*, 25–39.

Gauvreau, Danielle. 'La transition de la fécondité au Québec: un exemple de transgression de la morale catholique?' *Études d'histoire religieuse* 70 (2004): 7–22.

Gauvreau, Michael. 'Protestantism Transformed: Personal Piety and the Evangelical Social Vision, 1815–1867.' In G.A. Rawlyk, ed., *The Canadian Protestant Experience, 1760–1990*, 48–97. Burlington, ON: Welch, 1990.

– 'Covenanter Democracy: Scottish Popular Religion, Ethnicity, and the Varieties of Politico-religious Dissent in Upper Canada, 1815–1841.' *Histoire sociale/Social History* 36, no. 71 (May 2003): 55–84. (Special journal issue, 'Intersections of Religious and Social History,' edited by Nancy Christie and Michael Gauvreau.)

– 'Factories and Foreigners: Church Life in Working-Class Neighbourhoods in Hamilton and Montreal, 1890–1930.' In Gauvreau and Hubert, *The Churches and Social Order*, 225–73.

– 'The Emergence of Personalist Feminism: Catholicism and the Marriage-Preparation Movement in Quebec, 1940–1966.' In Christie, ed., *Households of Faith*, 319–47.

Gervais, Diane. 'Morale catholique et détresse conjugale au Québec. La réponse du service de régulation des naissances Seréna, 1955–1970.' *Revue d'histoire de l'Amérique française* 55, no. 2 (automne 2001): 185–215.

– 'Les couples au marges du *permis-défendu*. Morale conjugale et compromis pastorale à Montréal dans les années 1960.' *Études d'histoire religieuse* 70 (2004): 23–38.

Gewurtz, Margo. '"Their Names May Not Shine": Narrating Chinese Christian Converts.' In Austin and Scott, *Canadian Missionaries, Indigenous Peoples*, 134–51.

Gidney, R.D., and W.P.J. Millar. 'The Christian Recessional in Ontario's Public Schools.' In Marguerite Van Die, ed., *Religion* and *Public Life in Canada: Historical and Comparative Perspectives*, 275–93. Toronto: University of Toronto Press, 2001.

Gould, Jean. 'La genèse d'une modernisation bureaucratique.' In Stéphane Kelly et al., eds, *Les idées mènent le Québec: essais sur une sensibilté historique*, 145–174. Quebec: Les Presses de l'Université Laval, 2003.

Graham, John R. 'The Haven, 1878–1930: A Toronto Charity's Transition from a Religious to a Professional Ethos.' *Histoire sociale/Social History* 35, no. 50 (1992): 283–306.

Graham, John R., and Alean Al-Krenawi. 'Contested Terrain: Two Competing Visions of Social Work at the University of Toronto, 1914–1945.' *Canadian Social Work Review* 17, no. 2 (2000): 245–61.

Greenlaw, Jane. 'Choix pratiques et choix des pratiques: le non-conformisme protestant à Montréal (1825–1842).' *Revue d'histoire de l'Amérique française* 46, no. 1 (été 1992): 91–113.

Harkin, Michael, and Sergei Kan. 'Introduction.' *Ethnohistory* 43, no. 4 (autumn 1996): 563–71. (Special issue on Native American Women's Responses to Christianity.)

Hubert, Ollivier. 'Ritual Performance and Parish Sociability: French-Canadian Catholic Families at Mass from the Seventeenth to the Nineteenth Century.' In Christie, ed., *Households of Faith*, 37–76.

– 'La religion populaire est-elle une legende du XIXe siecle?' *Histoire sociale/Social History* 36, no. 71 (May 2003): 85–98. (Special journal issue, 'Intersections of Religious and Social History, edited by Nancy Christie and Michael Gauvreau.)

– 'Ritualite ultramontaine et pouvoir pastoral clerical dans le Québec de la seconde moitie du XIXe siecle.' In Jean-Marie Fecteau and Janice Harvey, eds, *La regulation sociale entre l'acteur et l'institution/Agency and Institutions in Social Regulation*, 435–47. Sainte-Foy: Presses de l'Universite du Quebec, 2005.

Hudon, Christine. 'Beaucoup de bruits pour rien? Rumeurs, plaints et scandals autour du clerge dans les paroisses gaspésiennes, 1766–1900.' *Revue d'histoire de l'Amérique française* 55, no. 2 (automne 2001): 217–40.

Hudon, Christine, and Ollivier Hubert. 'The Emergence of a

Statistical Approach to Social Issues in Administrative Practices of the Catholic Church in the Province of Quebec.' In Gauvreau and Hubert, eds, *The Churches and Social Order*, 46–65.

Klassen, Pamela E. 'Textual Healing: Mainstream Protestantism and the Therapeutic Text, 1900–1925.' *Church History: Studies in Christianity and Culture* 75, no. 4 (Dec. 2006): 809–48.

Lane, Hannah. 'Tribalism, Proselytism, and Pluralism: Protestants, Family, and Denominational Identity in Mid-Nineteenth-Century St Stephen, New Brunswick.' In Christie, ed., *Households of Faith*, 103–37.

– 'Evangelicals, Church Finance, and Wealth-Holding in Mid-Nineteenth-Century St Stephen, New Brunswick, and Calais, Maine.' In Gauvreau and Hubert, eds, *The Churches and Social Order*, 109–50.

Lanthier, Pierre. 'La paroisse dans les villes moyennes de 1900 à 1960.' In Courville and Séguin, eds, *La paroisse*, 106–13.

Little, J.I. 'The Fireside Kingdom: A Mid-Nineteenth-Century Anglican Perspective on Marriage and Parenthood.' In Christie, *Households of Faith*, 77–100.

– 'The Mental World of Ralph Merry, Tinware Peddler and Religious Ecstatic, 1798–1863.' In Little, *The Other Quebec*, 17–44.

Lutz, John. 'After the Fur Trade: The Aboriginal Labouring Class of British Columbia, 1849–1890.' *Journal of the Canadian Historical Association*, n.s., 3 (1992): 69–94.

– '"Relating to the Country": The Lekwammen and the Extension of European Settlement, 1843–1911.' In R.W. Sandwell, ed., *Beyond the City Limits: Rural History in British Columbia*. Vancouver and Toronto: UBC Press, 1999.

Macleod, David. 'A Live Vaccine: The YMCA and Male Adolescence in the U.S. and Canada, 1870–1920.' *Histoire sociale/Social History* 11 (May 1978): 5–25.

Marks, Lynne. 'No Double Standard? Leisure, Sex, and Sin in Upper Canadian Church Discipline Records, 1800–1860.' In Kathryn McPherson, Cecilia Morgan, and Nancy M. Forestell, eds, *Gendered Pasts: Historical Essays in Femininity and Masculinity in Canada*. Toronto: Oxford University Press, 1999.

– 'Railing, Tattling, and General Rumour: Gossip, Gender, and Church Regulation in Upper Canada.' *Canadian Historical Review* 81, no. 3 (Sept. 2000): 380–402.
– '"Leaving God Behind When They Crossed the Rocky Mountains": Exploring Unbelief in Turn-of-the-Century British Columbia.' In Eric W. Sager and Peter Baskerville, eds, *Household Counts: Canadian Households and Families in 1901*, 371–404. Toronto: University of Toronto Press, 2007.
Morgan, Cecilia. 'Turning Strangers into Sisters? Missionaries and Colonization in Upper Canada.' In Marlene Epp, Franca Iacovetta, and Frances Swyripa, eds, *Sisters or Strangers? Immigrant, Ethnic, and Racialized Women in Canadian History*, 23–48. Toronto: University of Toronto Press, 2004.
Neylan, Susan. 'Longhouses, Schoolhouses, and Workers' Cottages: Nineteenth-Century Protestant Missions to the Tsimshian and the Transformation of Class through Religion.' *Journal of the Canadian Historical Association*, n.s., 11 (2000): 51–86.
– '"Eating the Angels' Food": Arthur Wellington Clah – An Aboriginal Perspective on Being Christian, 1857–1909.' In Austin and Scott, eds, *Canadian Missionaries, Indigenous Peoples*, 88–108.
Noll, Mark. 'What Happened to Christian Canada?' *Church History: Studies in Christianity and Culture* 75 (2006): 245–73.
Pannekoek, Frits. 'The Anglican Church and the Disintegration of Red River Society, 1818–1870.' In Carl Berger and Ramsay Cook, eds, *The West and the Nation: Essays in Honour of W.L. Morton*, 72–90. Toronto: McClelland and Stewart, 1976.
Perin, Roberto. 'The Churches and Immigrant Integration in Toronto, 1947–1965.' In Gauvreau and Hubert, eds, *The Churches and Social Order*, 274–291.
Perry, Adele. 'Metropolitan Knowledge, Colonial Practice, and Indigenous Womanhood: Missions in Nineteenth-Century British Columbia.' In Pickles and Rutherdale, eds, *Contact Zones*, 109–30.
Plaxton, David. '"We Will Evangelize with a Whole Gospel or None": Evangelicalism and the United Church of Canada.' In

G.A. Rawlyk, ed., *Aspects of the Canadian Evangelical Experience*, 106–22. Montreal and Kingston: McGill-Queen's University Press, 1997.

Prang, Margaret. '"The Girl God Would Have Me Be": The Canadian Girls in Training, 1915–39.' *Canadian Historical Review* 66, no. 2 (1985).

Romney, Paul. 'On the Eve of Rebellion: Nationality, Religion and Class in the Toronto Election of 1836.' In David Keane and Colin Read, eds, *Old Ontario: Essays in Honour of J.M.S. Careless.* Toronto: Dundurn Press, 1990.

Routhier, Gilles. 'Governance of the Catholic Church in Quebec: An Expression of the Distinct Society?' In Gauvreau and Hubert, eds, *The Churches and Social Order*, 292–314.

– 'La paroisse québécoise: évolutions récentes et révisions actuelles.' In Courville and Séguin, eds, *La paroisse*, 46–59.

Roy, Jean. 'Le prélèvement écclesiastique dans le diocèse de Nicolet, à la fin du XIXe siècle: la fabrique.' *Études d'histoire religieuse* 67 (2001): 57–68.

Rutherdale, Myra. 'Mothers of the Empire: Maternal Metaphors in the Northern Canadian Mission Field.' In Austin and Scott, eds, *Canadian Missionaries, Indigenous Peoples*, 46–66.

– '"She Was a Ragged Little Thing": Missionaries, Embodiment, and Refashioning Aboriginal Womanhood in Northern Canada.' In Pickles and Rutherdale, eds, *Contact Zones*, 228–45.

Scott, Jamie. 'Cultivating Christians in Colonial Canadian Missions.' In Austin and Scott, eds, *Canadian Missionaries, Indigenous Peoples*, 21–45.

Semple, Neil. 'Ontario's Religious Hegemony: The Creation of the National Methodist Church.' *Ontario History* 77, no. 1 (March 1985): 19–42.

Smith, Edward. 'Working-Class Anglicans: Religion and Identity in Victorian and Edwardian Hamilton, Ontario.' *Histoire sociale/Social History* 35, no. 71 (May 2003): 123–44.

Stackhouse, John G. 'The Protestant Experience in Canada since 1945.' In G.A. Rawlyk, ed., *The Canadian Protestant Experience, 1760–1990*, 198–252. Burlington, ON: Welch, 1990.

Stanger-Ross, Jordan. 'An Inviting Parish: Community without
    Locality in Postwar Italian Toronto.' *Canadian Historical Review*
    87, no. 3 (Sept. 2006): 381–407.
Stanley-Blackwell, Laurie. '"Tabernacles in the Wilderness":
    The Open-Air Communion Tradition in Nineteenth- and
    Twentieth-Century Cape Breton.' In Charles H.H. Scobie and
    George Rawlyk, eds, *The Contribution of Presbyterianism to the
    Maritime Provinces of Canada*, 93–117. Montreal and Kingston:
    McGill-Queen's University Press.
Trigger, Rosalyn. 'Protestant Restructuring in the Canadian City:
    Church and Mission in the Industrial Working-Class District
    of Griffintown, Montreal.' *Urban History Review* 31, no. 1 (fall
    2002): 5–18.
– 'Irish Politics on Parade: The Clergy, National Societies, and
    St Patrick's Day Processions in Nineteenth-Century Montreal
    and Toronto.' *Histoire sociale/Social History* 37 (2004): 159–99.
Vallières, Catherine. '"Apprendre à bien mourir: les écoliers et
    la mort au Quebec, 1853–1963." *Études d'histoire religieuse* 65
    (1999): 29–51.
Van Die, Marguerite. 'Revisiting "Separate Spheres": Women,
    Religion, and the Family in Mid-Victorian Brantford, Ontario.'
    In Christie, ed., *Households of Faith*, 234–63.
Warren, Jean-Philippe. 'La découverte de la "question sociale":
    Sociologie et mouvements d'action jeunesse canadiens-
    français.' *Revue d'histoire de l'Amérique française* 55, no. 4
    (printemps 2002): 539–72.
– 'Sciences sociales et religions chrétiennes au Canada (1890–
    1960).' *Revue d'histoire de l'Amérique française* 57, no. 3 (hiver
    2004): 407–24.
Wright, Robert A. 'The Canadian Protestant Tradition, 1914–
    1945.' In G.A. Rawlyk, ed., *The Canadian Protestant Experience,
    1760–1990*, 139–97. Burlington, ON: Welch, 1990.

Unpublished Material

Christie, Nancy. '"Proper Government and Discipline": The
    Epistolary Discourse of Family Religion.' Paper delivered to

conference on 'Churches and Social Order,' Université de Montréal, 2002.

Draper, Kenneth L. '"Religion Worthy of a Free People": Religious Practices and Discourses in London, Ontario, 1870–1890.' PhD thesis, McMaster University, 2000.

Flatt, Kevin N. 'Loud Orthopraxy, Quiet Heterodoxy: The Survival and Decline of Evangelicalism in the United Church of Canada, 1932–1966.' Paper delivered to the American Society of Church History, annual meeting, 7 January 2007.

Hanlon, Peter. 'Moral Order and the Influence of Social Christianity in an Industrial City, 1890–1899: A Local Profile of the Protestant Lay Leaders of Three Hamilton Churches: Centenary Methodist, Central Presbyterian and Christ's Church Cathedral.' MA thesis, McMaster University, 1984.

Hogan, Brian Francis. 'Salted with Fire: Studies in Catholic Social Thought and Action in Ontario, 1931–1961.' PhD thesis, University of Toronto, 1986.

Lane, Hannah M. 'Re-numbering Souls: Methodism and Church Growth in St Stephen, New Brunswick, 1861–1881.' MA thesis, University of New Brunswick, 1993.

– 'Methodist Church Members, Lay Leaders, and Socio-economic Position in Mid-Nineteenth-Century St Stephen, New Brunswick.' PhD thesis, University of New Brunswick, 2004.

Mussio, Louise A. 'Communities Apart: Dissenting Traditions in Nineteenth-Century Central Canada.' PhD thesis, McMaster University, 2000.

Index

abortion, 184, 193
Acheson, T.W., 58
age, 53, 80–5
Anglican Church Missionary
Society, 110, 123, 131
Anglicanism, 39, 184; background of clergy, 26–7,
88–9; and Pierre Berton (*see*
Berton, Pierre); and charity,
56; conflicts within, 12; and
William Duncan, 110, 131,
136; and evangelicalism (*see*
evangelicalism); and missions, 109–10, 123, 131–3

Baptist: background of clergy;
88–9; concept of covenant,
29–30; conflicts within, 12,
161–2 (*see also* McMaster
University; Shields, T.T.); on
temperance, 54
Berton, Pierre, 179–89, 192–4.
See also Anglicanism; middle
class
Bibby, Reginald, 7, 199

biblical criticism, 93–4, 155. *See
also* evangelicalism

church and state, 22–4, 184–6;
and Catholic Church, 22,
25–6, 188–91; and Clergy
Reserves, 23–5; and missionaries, 112–14, 138–41; in
social Christianity, 62, 150–2,
173–4, 178. *See also* social
Christianity; United Church;
welfare state
Cité Libre, 190. *See also* Trudeau,
Pierre; Ryan, Claude
Clarke, Brian, 36
Connor, Ralph. *See* Gordon,
C.W.
contraception, 175, 184, 191–3,
195–6; and rhythm method,
195. *See also* Roman Catholicism; United Church;
women
Co-operative Commonwealth
Federation (CCF), 167, 176.
See also social Christianity

THEMES IN CANADIAN HISTORY

Editors:
Colin Coates 2003–
Craig Heron 1997–
Franca Iacovetta 1997–1999